D0844804

A DRIFTLESS CONNECTICUT SERIES BOOK

This book is a 2012 selection in the Driftless Connecticut
Series, for an outstanding book in any field on a
Connecticut topic or written by a Connecticut author.

ELLA GRASSO

Connecticut's Pioneering Governor

Jon E. Purmont

WESLEYAN UNIVERSITY PRESS

Middletown, Connecticut

*The Driftless Connecticut Series is funded by the
Beatrice Fox Auerbach Foundation Fund
at the Hartford Foundation for Public Giving.*

Wesleyan University Press
Middletown CT 06459
www.wesleyan.edu/wespress
© 2012 Jon E. Purmont
All rights reserved
Manufactured in the United States of America

Wesleyan University Press is a member of the Green Press Initiative. The paper
used in this book meets their minimum requirement for recycled paper.

Library of Congress Cataloging-in-Publication Data
Purmont, Jon E.
Ella Grasso : Connecticut's pioneering governor / Jon E. Purmont.
p. cm. — (A driftless Connecticut series book) (Garnet books)
Includes bibliographical references and index.
ISBN 978-0-8195-7343-8 (cloth : alk. paper) —
ISBN 978-0-8195-7344-5 (ebook)
1. Grasso, Ella. 2. Governors — Connecticut — Biography.
3. Women governors — Connecticut — Biography. I. Title.
F101.3.G73P87   2012
974.6′043092 — dc23   2012022001
[B]

5 4 3 2 1

To
Helen and Howard Purmont
who were
the best of Parents

CONTENTS

Illustrations follow page 140

ACKNOWLEDGMENTS

I had long hoped to write a book about my experiences as assistant to Governor Ella Grasso. The idea gained momentum as a result of dinner conversation years ago at Judge Anna Conn Forder's home in St. Louis, Missouri. Numerous questions were asked about Ella Grasso that evening, demonstrating that there was real interest in learning about her unique career. As a result, I began the research and writing about Connecticut's Pioneering Governor, the first American woman governor elected in her own right who did not succeed her husband in office.

Ella's husband, the late Dr. Thomas A. Grasso, encouraged me and agreed to several interviews spending many hours discussing his beloved Ella and her political career. The Grasso children, Susane and James, were always helpful to me throughout this long journey and shared numerous interesting observations about their mother and particularly their childhood in Windsor Locks.

Members of the Governor's office staff, political associates, Grasso administration Commissioners, state legislators, Grasso family friends, especially Yvonne Goldstein, reporters, and journalists provided insight and opinions that were forthright, thoughtful, and respectful of Ella Grasso. My gratitude is extended to each and every person who agreed to answer a multitude of questions about this pioneering woman politician.

State Senator Linda Malconian (D-Mass.) was especially helpful regarding Ella's years in Congress. Commissioner of Economic Development

Acknowledgments

Edward Stockton spent a great deal of time with me recalling his close association with Ella Grasso during the gubernatorial years. I am indebted to him and Anthony Milano for their cooperation and insight into this engaging public figure.

Dr. Nancy Lewinsohn, Chief of Staff during Ella Grasso's Congressional years and who served in the same capacity in Hartford during the Governor's first term, deserves special acknowledgement and appreciation for sharing her perspective on Ella Grasso—the person and politician. Her perceptive observations, recollections, and knowledge of government and politics provided interesting, often fascinating material about Governor Grasso, John Bailey, and other political figures. Nancy spent many long hours in conversations with me, and she also graciously read, reviewed, and critiqued the manuscript at every stage of its development. I benefitted enormously from her expertise and personal encouragement.

Many individuals responded to my requests for interviews regarding Ella Grasso. Their names appear frequently throughout the book and in the chapter endnotes. They represent a wide circle of friends, political associates, staff colleagues, and public officials. All represent different phases of Governor Grasso's life. Special gratitude is extended to her Mount Holyoke College classmates who gave generously of their time and recollections, helping me to understand Ella's formative years at the college.

Washington Post columnist David Broder was especially helpful with his observations about Ella Grasso as Secretary of the State and Governor of Connecticut. His masterful columns about John Bailey and Ella Grasso proved indispensable, and our personal discussion at the *Post*, a distinct pleasure.

A very special word of appreciation is extended to the archives staff at Mount Holyoke College Library, especially archives librarian Patricia Albright, whose knowledge of the archival resources was boundless and matched by her extensive understanding of Mt. Holyoke's institutional history. Her unfailing kindness and professional courtesies added to the pleasure of my visits to the campus in South Hadley, Massachusetts. Ella Grasso's Congressional papers are located there, as well as material about her undergraduate and graduate years. The Mount Holyoke College Archives abound with helpful material on Ella's beloved mentor Professor Amy Hewes, whose influence on Ella Grasso and other Mount Holyoke students was profound.

The outstanding staff at the Connecticut State Library Archives is commended for their many courtesies, patience, and assistance extended over many years. The extensive collection of Ella Grasso's gubernatorial papers, photographs, and letters in the State Library Archives is vital to understanding her years as Governor of Connecticut.

Information on the Hudson Shore Labor School is located at the Franklin D. Roosevelt Library in Hyde Park, New York. Professor Amy Hewes' study of women munitions workers at the Remington Firearms Plant was found at the Bridgeport, Connecticut Public Library. I appreciate the assistance that staff provided at both institutions.

Several Southern Connecticut State University History Department colleagues, Richard Gerber, Lewis House, and Troy Rondinone, read various chapters of the manuscript, and they were always encouraging as this project wound its way through various stages of completion. Their advice is gratefully acknowledged.

I thank the editorial staff at Wesleyan University Press, especially Parker Smathers and Leslie Starr, who worked closely with me on this book. Their helpful suggestions along with their inevitable deadlines kept me focused and determined to see this biography through to the end.

Family members, especially my sisters Helen Beebe, Mary Ardith Nowak, and the late Virginia Donovan, were constant in their support as I worked on this biography over time. They know my gratitude to them is abundant.

Acknowledgments

I remain profoundly grateful to Ella Grasso for the opportunity she offered to join her staff in May 1979. She advised me to "observe the pageantry." I followed her advice. She was the inspiration for writing this book, and she continues to inspire many "to go where no one else has been and do what no one else has done."

INTRODUCTION

Several years ago, on a visit to St. Louis, Missouri, a Commissioner for the County of St. Louis queried me about Ella Grasso. She asked, "How did she do it? I want to know all about her." Momentarily startled, I replied, "she labored in the political vineyards for a very long time."[1]

The commissioner sat quietly listening to my response. Then she mentioned that, in Missouri, women political candidates traditionally have had a difficult time gaining political leverage on a statewide basis. At that time, despite electing two able women, Harriet Woods as Lieutenant Governor and Leonor Sullivan a long serving member of Congress, women candidates in the Show Me state exerted minimum clout in the high echelons of both the Republican and Democratic Parties in that large mid-western state. In November 2006, however, women's political standing was expanded with the election of Claire McCaskill (D) to the United States Senate from Missouri.

This brief exchange with the commissioner triggered in my mind memories of the journey I shared with Ella Grasso. It was then I realized how important it would be to write about the life and career of this widely known and respected Connecticut governor.

Election of women to high political office still remains a difficult and tough challenge in the United States. In 2008, Senator Hillary Rodham Clinton (D-N.Y.) came close to becoming the first woman nominated for President by a major national political party. While the Presidency remains elusive for women, the statehouse has become a reachable political goal — witness the election of numerous women governors in several states of the union.

The first American woman elected governor in her own right, not succeeding her husband, was Ella Tambussi Grasso. Her remarkable journey to reach that political goal in Connecticut is one that broke through seemingly insurmountable barriers and set an admirable example for others to follow.

One day in March 1979, I was invited to travel to Hartford, Connecticut, to talk with the Governor in her second-floor office in the Executive Chambers of the State Capitol. I had met Mrs. Grasso on several occasions in my capacity as Assistant to the Mayor of West Haven, Connecticut. I was taken aback, however, by her request. "I want you to consider taking the position (Executive Assistant) and observe the pageantry of the next four years," explained the Governor.[2] Her offer, which I accepted, provided a most unusual opportunity to observe, with special interest, the pageantry of which she spoke.

While my association with the Governor would last a mere twenty-one months, it would be time enough to observe the central figure of that memorable period. It was Ella Grasso around whom the panoply of events revolved.[3] Her remarkable political career, unusual in its steady upward ascent, was unprecedented in the annals of American political history, and it was never marred by electoral defeat. She placed herself before the voters ten times and survived the scrutiny of the electorate in each of those elections. In fact, in two of those contests, she received more votes than any other candidate including the men who ran for governor.

Her life reflects much that is good about America. Like so many other Americans, Ella Tambussi Grasso was a child of immigrants who lived frugally and who achieved a better life for themselves and their daughter in this country. As a first generation Italian-American her remarkable ascent to political distinction represents the emergence of the first woman of that ethnic background elected Governor in the history of the United States.

She was encouraged by her parents, particularly her mother, to pursue her academic endeavors, first at Saint Mary's School in Windsor Locks, Connecticut, then the Chaffee School in Windsor, Connecticut, and eventually Mount Holyoke College, in South Hadley, Massachusetts. Fortunately, Ella was endowed with superb intelligence and driving ambition, which enabled her to excel at her studies and eventually in public life.

This notable American woman's story is an unusual one not characterized by the usual uphill struggle most women endured to gain a place at the table of political power. Rather, Ella Grasso reached the pinnacle of political success by the sheer force of her will, by disciplined work habits and determined ambition. Also, her close working relationship with John M. Bailey, Connecticut's powerful Democratic leader, combined with the extensive network of women achievers in her life who served as significant role models, impacted her determination and drive to pursue a public career.

Blessed with considerable political talents and writing skills, she also possessed a keen understanding of people, combined with an intellectual brilliance that was matched by an uncanny ability to articulate and communicate opinions and views on issues with consummate adroitness. Unquestionably a great deal of luck, staying power, and endurance helped her rise steadily in that bastion of male dominance — the world of politics.

That world, where Ella Grasso achieved remarkable success, must be seen within a wider context of historical developments in the fascinating kaleidoscope of the twentieth century. Interwoven within those events are several overriding themes that have dramatically affected and changed Connecticut and the nation over many decades. Whether it was political reform efforts, constitutional changes, fundamental shifts in Connecticut's economy or wrenching social and political issues, Ella Grasso was usually in the forefront of the political whirlwind and public discourse, which has been so much a part of both the nation's history and Connecticut's recent past.

This account of Governor Grasso's life, endeavors to be narrative biography, which historian Barbara Tuchman has called the "spine of history."[4] Contemporary biographer Richard Brookheiser suggests that biographies should include "vivid details," of the subject's life.[5] One way in which that objective can be achieved is through oral history.

Interviews with Ella's late husband, Dr. Thomas A. Grasso, with her children Susane and James, and with numerous friends, colleagues, and political associates became vital components of this story. Oral interviews provided valuable insight, and personal remembrances and recollections offered unique perspectives about this woman whose impact on Connecticut was profound and long lasting. Those elements helped to substantially reconstruct various aspects of Ella Grasso's character and personality and aided in developing major themes of the Governor's life and achievements.

The author brings an unusual perspective to the Governor's story. It is not often a biographer has an opportunity to work alongside his subject. In this instance, I was privileged to work with Governor Ella T. Grasso for nearly two years. During that period of observation, I realized how special was the opportunity I had to observe this first lady Governor who was not first a Governor's First Lady.

Encouraged by Frederick Kershner, professor of history at Teachers College, Columbia University, to keep a diary of the time spent working with the Governor, I followed his sage advice and have referred to those recollections while writing this biography. Professor Kershner emphasized that, while engaged in working as the Governor's aide, keeping a diary would be essential because one's memory of events, conversations, and activities fades rapidly over time. His advice was appropriate and extremely valuable, and I am indebted to him for his wise counsel.

Historian Arnold Toynbee wrote that, "the only good reason for writing a book is because one's wish to write it is a master passion."[6] Writing

Introduction

Ella Grasso's story has been a master passion of this writer for a very long time. Chronicling her life provided an opportunity to write of Ella Grasso's journey amidst important and significant events and developments in Connecticut and American history, encompassing many decades of the twentieth century. In that respect her life and achievements must be seen within the context of momentous events, including the Great Depression, World War II, the Vietnam War, the Women's Rights Movement of the 1960s, and the Watergate controversy.

Governor Ella Grasso remains an inspiration to many people. She was a woman who succeeded in a political world where women often feared to tread. Many opportunities came her way, and she benefited from the solid groundwork laid down by women activists and social reformers who preceded her. Women activists like Jane Addams, Secretary of Labor Frances Perkins (a Mount Holyoke graduate like Ella Grasso), and First Lady Eleanor Roosevelt were leaders whose political and social activism, achievements, and advocacy for social justice helped pave the way for women to find fulfillment in American public life. And like those who preceded her, Ella Grasso's success made the way easier for women who have followed her in elective public office.

Ella Tambussi Grasso's achievements in the political world were path breaking, and they developed as a result of many factors, one of which was the famed tradition of service and commitment instilled in students at Mount Holyoke College, her Alma Mater. The Mount Holyoke woman, Ella proudly noted, was an "uncommon woman" a pioneer always "mindful of our responsibilities."[7] And she exemplified that ideal by achieving what no woman had ever accomplished in her own right: the governorship of one of the fifty states of the Union. Her remarkable career in public service, sustained over nearly three decades, is an outstanding example of a life filled with tenacity, zeal, drive, and ambition. It was a notable journey, one that reminds us how important education, individual dedication, and commitment to public service can be to develop leaders who endure the multiple challenges that political life presents.

ELLA GRASSO

❧ 1 ❧

CHILD OF TWENTIETH-CENTURY PILGRIMS

Ella Grasso's remarkable journey commenced on May 10, 1919, in Windsor Locks, Connecticut, at a time when America and Europe were recovering from the turbulence of military conflict accompanied by uncommon human mortality on the battlefields of Europe.

As the first and only child of Maria (Natalina) and James (Giacomo) Tambussi, Ella Rosa Giovanna Oliva Tambussi was born into a world described as one where the "future of women, like the future of peace, could be influenced by individual decisions in a way that had never seemed possible."[1] It was a world tired of conflict, which sought respite from the terror of destructive weapons, and it was a world that would never again be quite the same.

In one small corner of the United States the joy of holding a healthy young, baby girl helped erase the recollection of war from the minds of Maria and James Tambussi. As emigrants from the Old World, they had escaped the cauldron of war that had swept through all of Europe, including their Italian homeland. As twentieth-century pilgrims, they sought and found a better life in America, and they could not imagine the remarkable journey that lay ahead for their newborn daughter.

Ironically, a few weeks after her birth, the United States Senate, on June 4, 1919, passed the Nineteenth Amendment, granting women the voting franchise. It was passed without the affirmative support of Connecticut's two Republican Senators, George McLean and Frank Brandegee. In fact, Senator Brandegee emphasized his strong opposition to the Amendment when he advised women to "go home and knit bandages and pick lint" instead of "bleating about their saving democracy."[2] Despite such diatribes the requisite number of thirty-six states ratified the Nineteenth Amendment in 1920. Sadly, Connecticut was not among them. Connecticut became the thirty-seventh to approve. Yet no one could have foretold how the ratification decision would deeply affect the future opportunities for this young child from Windsor Locks, or the political history of Connecticut, or that of the nation.

Ella Tambussi's childhood was a happy period in her life. Her affectionate parents doted on her, and the neighborhood on Olive Street in Windsor Locks, Connecticut, was filled with relatives and friends whom her parents had known in Italy. In that neighborhood among a "very close clutch of friends,"[3] Ella grew up, and it was there her sense of community was developed and nurtured.[4]

Census data for the first decade of the twentieth century (1900–1910) indicates a wave of 56,954 immigrants arrived in Connecticut from many foreign lands. The statistics also reveal that Italian immigrants made up nearly 16 percent of the people who journeyed to the state during those first ten years of the new century.[5] A number of Italian new arrivals settled in a small town north of Hartford called Windsor Locks, Connecticut. The town's population included a sizeable number of people from the Tortona region of northern Italy, located between Milan and Genoa, where Maria Oliva and James Tambussi were born. Ella's mother was born in 1892 in Voghera, Italy, and her father James Tambussi, born in 1887, came from Perleto, Italy. While they hailed from neighboring towns, they did not meet until they immigrated to America. "They were two people who came over on steerage," Ella would recall.[6] "My father told me he had a great big sign pinned on him," she explained, "to get him to his final destination. He arrived in Hartford by boat from New York and then by train to Windsor Locks."[7] Both parents settled in Windsor Locks where various family members and friends resided. James Tambussi, at the age of seventeen, along with his parents, a brother Elisio, and a sister settled there in 1904. James' older brother Natale and a sister Claudina joined them in 1909. Ella's mother, Maria Oliva, together with her sister-in-law arrived in Windsor Locks in 1906 to join Maria's two brothers.[8] Maria Oliva and James Tambussi were married five years later in their adopted hometown.

Windsor Locks, in 1904, was a small town with a population of slightly more than three thousand citizens. The locale has been described as a "milieu of scant means and status, but rich with striving and pervading tradition."[9] Located alongside the Connecticut River, it was predominantly an industrial town where immigrants found work in factories, mills, and nearby industrial plants. It was a small community where families knew one another, where children "baked potatoes in autumn leaf fires"[10] and where one child remembered a happy childhood digging up wild violets and playing "neighborhood games—hide and seek, croquet."[11]

It is important to understand Windsor Locks' indelible imprint on Ella Tambussi's life, not only because it helped nourish and strengthen her in her youth, but also because it remained one constant in her life, no matter what honor or adulation she received. She resided there all her life, stayed deeply rooted in the community, close to its people, moving there at the time of her marriage, and later served as a State Representative from her hometown. She maintained a home there until her death in 1981.

Windsor Locks was the place her father worked first as a machine operator at the Anchor Mill for a dollar a day and later at General Electric in Windsor, Connecticut, and also at the Horton Chuck Company in Windsor Locks. In 1920, he opened the Windsor Locks Bakery with his brother Natale, "working twelve-hour nights, six days a week."[12] Ella recalled that, "He'd come home from work about 10 o'clock in the morning, and I would rush out to meet him so we could walk back home together. I would tell him all my secrets and he would listen patiently and kindly."[13]

The Tambussi brothers would eventually sell the bakery in 1938 and open a tavern in Windsor Locks. Ten years later, after selling the tavern, James became a partner in a machine shop called the Windsor Locks Machine Company from which he retired.[14]

Many years later Ella described her father as "a doer,"[15] and noted that she was so "proud of his achievements as a baker and machinist, as an officer in the Credit Union—and he was proud of me. We were a mutual admiration society."[16] Her father's life provided an example of how success could be achieved: hard work, determination, coupled with aggressive ambition. It was a lesson she learned early in life, and it provides evidence that James Tambussi's presence, influence, and enter-prising endeavors loomed large in his daughter's life, and that much of her strength and spirit was drawn from him.

She was closest to her father whom, she revealed, "indulged and spoiled me." "My father called me 'my boy' and was delighted when I sneaked off and had my hair cut into a 'boyish bob.' He took me to ball games and once to New Haven on the train to a Yale-Army game, and to Hartford when the Yankees and Brooklyn Dodgers played exhibition games."[17]

The close father-daughter relationship continued well into Ella's adulthood. She "absolutely adored him," noted James Grasso, Ella's son, and she felt a "greater tie to him rather than her mother."[18] James Tambussi died in 1971 at the age of eighty-four. "I got the shock of my life when he died," she said. "I became a pathetic fifty-year-old orphan."[19] In a poignant remembrance of her father, Ella wrote, "He worked long hours, six days a week but he always had time for me and he took me seriously. From him I learned respect for others and persistence. By his example, I learned that one does not abandon a task. Quit? We didn't quit anything." And then she added, "When I think of my father, I think of him in a golden glow. I loved him dearly, and I respected him. He was one of the great people in my life."[20]

James Tambussi's rise from impoverished immigrant to successful small businessman and later a member and officer of a local credit union sustained the family's needs. His success enabled his wife to remain at home to oversee the domestic household, and she became "the disciplinarian." While Ella grew up under a "rigid code of conduct," years later she described her domineering mother as "less happy" than her father and "frustrated because there was no effective outlet for her talents."[21]

Maria Tambussi, who arrived in America at age fourteen, worked first in a cotton mill and as an assembler in an electric motor shop prior to Ella's birth. She did not achieve "her real potential" said her daughter, because "there were few opportunities for leadership — except organizational — and she was too shy to project herself in these areas."[22] James Grasso, Ella's son, characterized his grandmother as "not the warmest of people," who often "dwelt on petty issues."[23] He credited his grandmother, however, for pushing his mother to excel at her educational studies.

Maria Tambussi's focus on "petty issues" reflects a decidedly less pleasant demeanor: more authoritative and critical, combined with a feisty, quick-tempered personality, it contrasted sharply with that of her husband. Some of those maternal traits Ella acquired and displayed in her often-fiery personal relationships with others. Those traits blended, however, with the outgoing "warm and friendly"[24] personality of Ella's father.

In many ways, the Tambussi household resembled a traditional, "most conventional" Italian family. However, it was unusual in one way. Ella's parents encouraged their only child to aspire to an education.[25] While many Italian immigrant families aspired to take advantage of educational opportunities in America, formal education was generally felt to be of less value for girls than boys.[26]

Her parents had limited schooling: her father went as far as the second grade and her mother to the sixth grade.[27] Both were "very intelligent and generous people,"[28] and they made "many sacrifices . . . with limited income" to provide educational opportunities for Ella that were not generally available to children of immigrants.[29] They provided well for their daughter, including piano lessons along with private school elementary education at St. Mary's in Windsor Locks and later at the fashionable, private Chaffee School in Windsor, Connecticut. Pursuit of an education, however, became the goal for this child of immigrants. It was a goal, Ella later recalled, that her parents—particularly her mother who had a passionate love for education—"could dare to dream."[30]

The quest for an education, a vital theme in the future Connecticut governor's life, was first demonstrated in her youth. She noted that she "liked to study" and "was an avid reader" and "read all the books in a neighbor's library" and "did a job on the public library as well."[31] In a weekly "forage from the Town Library,"[32] young Ella Tambussi gained an appreciation for reading. Many years later, she said she realized as early as the fourth grade that she could strive for and achieve academic success.[33] Thereafter, she pursued her education and learning with eagerness and determination that would characterize her later political career. Her favorite childhood reading included Louisa May Alcott's *Little Women* and William Makepeace Thackery's *Vanity Fair*, which she read in the seventh grade.[34] However, she noted that she did not think about a career as a woman in public service since "maybe there were no books in the Windsor Locks Library on the subject."[35]

Ella's mother is the key to where her love of books and reading emanated. Maria Tambussi nurtured Ella's interest in reading and bought her books including "department store markdowns and books in the five and ten cents store."[36] Though largely unschooled, Mrs. Tambussi, according to Ella's future husband, Thomas Grasso, was "very bright." She read books that Ella "had to read . . . and she would sit down and discuss the books with Ella."[37] "My mother," Ella explained, "gave me two special gifts a love of people and a love of learning." Ella also commented that her mother believed learning "was a special key to living . . . and . . . books were my 'open sesame' to a whole new world."[38] "My mother," Ella wrote, "was self-taught. She had a quick wit and charm. She had great respect for learning and encouraged me in my studies."[39]

Fortunately, Ella's reading offered endless possibilities for daydreams about what her future career path might be. Those thoughts ranged from being a great scientist like Madame Curie, a woman lawyer like Shakespeare's Portia, or a great actress like Katherine Cornell. Yet, she noted, while "Florence Nightingale might be a nurse, I would be a surgeon."[40] A young girl's dreams are not in themselves unusual or unique. They do provide, however, an early glimpse at what would become a defining characteristic of this daughter of immigrants. It is a vision of a future life and career that would extend beyond the conventional career expectations to which many females aspired. In later years, she confided that she was not concerned, in her youth, about the "limitations of my sex . . . the quest was only for the unreachable star."[41]

Her youthful ambitions and determination to seek the seemingly unreachable became part of young Ella's character. Fortunately, her youthful path crossed with that of an exceptional teacher who became Ella Tambussi's life-long friend and confidante. Ella attended elementary school at St. Mary's School (1925–1932) in Windsor Locks where she met Sister DeChantal who taught her in the eighth grade. This nun, whom Ella later described as being a "truly modern woman," emerges in Ella's young life as a larger than life figure—a true role model who advised and counseled her until the nun's death during Ella's third term as Connecticut's Secretary of the State.[42]

Sister DeChantal's strong religious faith and devotion to the Catholic Church greatly influenced Ella and helped to solidify the young girl's lifelong faithfulness to her Church and its teachings. Always dutiful and conscientious about attending Sunday Mass, years later when asked to name heroines whom she admired, she listed two "from my church—Mary, St. Theresa."[43] That strong religious faith remained a vital part of Ella Tambussi's character and it defined her moral outlook throughout her life.

Ella frequently mentioned Sister DeChantal's influence. It was she who "encouraged me to 'do my thing' whatever it might be," she explained. And it was another teacher, Professor Amy Hewes, who "opened the windows of my mind to a new and exciting world."[44] It was Sister DeChantal, however, Ella said, who "conveyed to us the idea that each of us was special; there was something we could do better whether it was woodworking or working with machinery. You had to develop your potential. I loved that theory. And I've always tried to do my best."[45]

Besides noting that the nun was the "most remarkable woman I've ever met," many years later Ella named her as one of five women she most admired.[46] (The others were her own mother, Madame Curie, Mother Teresa, and Margaret Mead). This inspiring classroom teacher, along with other teachers and politicians whose paths would cross with Ella's, became nurturing mentors and cherished role models in her life. Sister DeChantal emerges as the first of several women of achievement and the first in a female support network to whom Ella would turn for counsel, advice, and guidance throughout her life.

Sister DeChantal's friendship, mentoring, and encouragement was for Ella Tambussi the beginning of a network of women mentors similar to that which sustained and encouraged women like Eleanor Roosevelt: women who worked "for changes and equality in a world they were not supposed to inhabit, a world that continually erected barriers to their presence and all their contributions."[47] And that would be the world Ella encountered as she grew into adulthood.

While Ella's youth was a pleasant time for her, she had "few close friends" nor was she close to any girl with whom she shared her personal thoughts.[48] Her own recollection of her childhood mentions that she "played alone with my dolls and . . . remember wonderful celluloid doll dishes and kitchen things neighbors gave me for Christmas." She recalled she "usually played with girls when we had neighborhood games . . . hide and seek." Her closest childhood friend was a "little boy neighbor" Robert Carroll, who eventually became a priest of the Archdiocese of Hartford.[49] He was someone Ella knew well and she recalled fondly in later years that one of her happiest childhood memories was "playing hide and seek with my friend, Robert, in his father's warehouse."[50] Reverend Carroll, many years later, reminisced about his youthful days in Windsor Locks and remembered how Ella's father would make homemade wine and call it "black coffee," and how he and Ella used to "fashion Christmas wreaths from evergreen branches, and pick berries in the summer."[51] That childhood playmate, whose mother gave Ella a book of poems by William Butler Yeats, "a gift she never forgot," would remain a lifelong friend and, ultimately, Reverend Robert Carroll became Ella's religious confessor.[52]

What is striking is how often Ella mentions being happiest around her parents and their friends and relatives, not among her own peers. "You are part of all that you've been," she noted in an interview. "My parents were very hard working, devoted people, and they had a warm circle of family and friends, so that I always felt very cherished and part of something."[53] She went on to say that she had the "kind of upbringing and schooling that breathed a sense of responsibility into you for your country and your time . . . ours was a warm household where I was . . . encouraged to achieve."[54]

The centrality of her closeness to her parents, relatives, and family friends was at the matrix of her early childhood and is vital to understanding Ella's formative years. While most young people focus their attention not only on their parent's friends and relatives but also on friends they develop, she did not. Ella's friends were her mother and father's friends to the exclusion of friends her own age (Robert Carroll being the exception). Her later admission that, "I loved spending time with adults and listening to talk of my parent's friends," is recognition of this factor in her youth and it reveals the absence of her own friends with whom she might have confided her hopes, dreams, and ambitions.[55]

As an only child, Ella did not experience the interplay and mutual sharing that underscores sibling relationships within the parameters of family life. She was often alone, and her contacts and interactions with other neighborhood children were limited. Introspective, bookish, and shy, this child found satisfaction in activities that were more self-directed. "I liked to study and read," she emphasized, and "played alone with my dolls" rather than interact with other neighborhood children.[56]

Ella's reticence is not unusual in light of the struggle for acceptance and assimilation European immigrants and their children confronted in American society, particularly in the era after World War I. It was a time of resurgent anti-European, anti-immigrant attitudes, which surfaced in the aftermath of the devastating military turmoil, characterized by thousands of casualties and deaths suffered by American soldiers in that tragic war. In tiny Windsor Locks, Connecticut, Italians, Irish, Poles, along with other immigrant groups in the early decades of the twentieth century often faced ethnic discrimination (particularly in the workplace), religious bias, and nativist attitudes, which often prevailed in communities throughout Connecticut. These newcomers, noted one former member of the General Assembly, possessed "strange customs, and shaky patriotism," which "menaced traditional American values." The critical question for a former state legislator J. Moss Ives of Danbury, whose views reflected the outlook of many Connecticut Yankees in the Land of Steady Habits, was "will old New England, her standards of living, her ideals, her customs and her laws survive the constantly increasing influx of alien blood?"[57]

Moreover, the problems of adjusting to life in a small Connecticut town, dominated by Yankee families often resentful of the new arrivals, conversely developed attitudes among the immigrants and their children of being outsiders. They struggled to be accepted as true Americans much less as social equals in a milieu that was still mired in generational connectedness to Connecticut's Puritan Protestant past. This prevailing disposition toward immigrants and their children was typical of the immigrant experience in Connecticut and in other regions of the United

States, and Ella Tambussi's sheltered world in Windsor Locks did not escape it.

Historically, Connecticut was inhospitable to immigrants from European homelands other than England. And the presence of German and Irish immigrants, prior to the Civil War, in the Land of Steady Habits, presented a challenge to Yankee domination in the state. The German immigrants brought Lutheranism and Catholicism to Connecticut in the 1830s. And the Irish, who streamed into the state in large numbers, also brought adherence to Roman Catholicism as part of their religious tradition. Connecticut's Protestant majority demonstrated a clear aversion to these newcomers by electing William Minor as Governor in the election of 1855. Minor, a member of the Know-Nothing party, spoke out clearly against immigrants in his inaugural address in 1855. Citing the fact that, "This large mass of aliens, some of them tinctured with the social Infidelity of continental Europe—very many of them blind followers of an ecclesiastical Despotism . . . without correct ideas of the duties pertaining to citizens of a republican Government . . . are totally unfitted to learn them." He went on to underscore his concern that those who emigrated to this country were the "majority of the inmates of our prisons and Almshouses . . . in many instances the Almshouses of the Old World have been emptied, their prison doors thrown open and the inmates of both transported . . . to our shores."[58]

Clearly, this anti-alien environment left an indelible mark on ethnic immigrants, who subsequently found their way to Connecticut's shores in the decades prior to the Civil War and also following America's tragic civil struggle. It was post-1865 when great waves of Italian immigrants came to America's shores and established themselves in various parts of the country and in Connecticut. Eventually, the deeply embedded anti-immigrant attitudes among Connecticut's citizens would find their way into every aspect of society and culture throughout the state. They would also leave an indelible mark on this young, first generation Italian-American girl who craved acceptance in a world straining to accept newcomers into its midst. For Ella, however, and many children of immigrants, education and schooling would be the path they pursued to become integrated into the mainstream of American life.

For young children, the process of attending school provides a transition to move from the parental matrix of friends to developing friends of their own.[59] By partaking in public school education, first generation children of immigrants held wide expectations and hopes of achieving a better life. Education and learning, it was believed, would also enable them to interact with other children in a setting that provided socialization opportunities and a chance to associate with their peers no matter what their ethnic or religious background. In Ella's world, however, her friends remained older adults, and she grew up to be most comfortable with them rather than with her own peers. Further, Ella's education shunned the public school system, touted as the "great melting pot" of Americanization, and her private school education facilitated educational pursuits on a path less traversed by most first generation immigrant children. It would be a road that led to invaluable educational opportunities and path-breaking experiences, which enabled Ella to achieve remarkable career success that went beyond what many in her immigrant community could anticipate achieving. In fact, years later she marveled at the achievements of "my hero" Dr. Ettore Carniglia a respected local Windsor Locks physician. Son of Italian immigrants, he studied at the Loomis School in Windsor, graduated from Harvard and Harvard Medical School. In Ella's eyes, he "broke discrimination barriers" and his example demonstrated the success first generation immigrants could attain in the land of opportunity.[60]

The eventual choice of a secondary school for Ella was largely the result of Mrs. Tambussi's friendship with a neighbor whose daughter was enrolled at the nearby Chaffee School, a private girls school in Windsor, Connecticut. Ella's mother decided that, if Chaffee was good enough for Josephine Preli, also the daughter of immigrants, then she would see to it that Ella enjoyed the same opportunity.[61]

Chaffee was considered an educational institution that catered to the daughters of prominent and wealthy families. It has been described as an "elegant place" with a "picture book campus" and as an outstanding preparatory school for exclusive private colleges.[62] And this step forward into Chaffee—truly an upward leap—placed young Ella Tambussi in a world quite apart from her blue collar Windsor Locks upbringing. In 1932, Ella won a scholarship to the Chaffee School, and this child of twentieth-century pilgrims "blossomed" there and achieved outstanding academic success at the school.[63]

She participated in the drama club and model League of Nations activities during her four years at Chaffee. "It was an excellent school, and the teachers there had a very strong sense of responsibility," she recalled.[64] But Chaffee's student body was comprised of mainly wealthy children whose backgrounds and social standing were worlds away from the working class background of the immigrant's daughter. So Ella's concerns about being accepted on a level of economic and social equality with her peers remained beyond her reach. Nevertheless, like her peers, Ella desired material possessions that many of her schoolmates could easily afford. But those desires for similar possessions, she noted, "wounded her mother who was struggling to make do." As a result Ella admitted years later, she felt a few of her classmates "treated her with patrician disdain."[65]

Despite the social snubs, Chaffee was for Ella Tambussi "an awakening." Years later, she told her family about an experiment she witnessed in science class in which the teacher used canned goods. Ella noted that she had never seen canned goods at home and was truly amazed at such commodities.[66] Her years at Chaffee aroused interest in areas that she had not previously come across. "I did not know the world of music (except for Italian opera), art and theater until I went to prep school." Chaffee provided a window of opportunity for academic and intellectual growth, including a simultaneous opening to a world of music, art, and drama for which she "developed an insatiable appetite."[67]

Many years later, one Chaffee alumna, two years ahead of Ella, remembered when Ella entered Chaffee. "Immediately she began to show a great prowess at leadership with a great big lot of common sense thrown in," wrote Harriet Fish. Even then she noted Ella Tambussi had an "interest in student-body conduct, current events, and analytical conversation," which made her stand out in the fifty-member student body.[68]

Ella's scholastic success and educational achievements enabled her to overcome any doubts she may have possessed about her intellectual capability in the classroom. At Chaffee she blossomed academically. Nonetheless, socially she remained the daughter of immigrants and apart from her more prominent and economically well-connected classmates. And that social distance engendered in her persona an emotional cutoff from people with whom she did not feel comfortable. As a result she developed few close relationships or friendships at Chaffee. This lack of feeling accepted in circles outside her own family remained part of Ella's character and personality throughout her life.

She did awaken, however, from her sheltered world in another important way. In the summer of 1932, shortly before entering Chaffee, she met Thomas A. Grasso a lifeguard at the beach at Sound View in Old Lyme, Connecticut, where her parents owned a modest summer cottage. Tom Grasso would become Ella's first boy friend, and she was enamored of the young, athletic Grasso four years her senior. "It was love at first sight. I was enchanted by him. He wrote poetry and painted. And that's pretty heady stuff when you are a growing kid," she explained.[69] In fact, Tom Grasso's artistic talent and interest in watercolor painting and pen and ink sketching of Old Lyme and the Long Island Sound shoreline, would last throughout his life.

At age eighteen, Hartford native Tom Grasso noticed Ella Tambussi as she sat on the beach in Old Lyme reading Shakespeare's *As You Like It*. He recalled that, "she had a nice figure and she wore a white bathing suit" and unlike other girls tanning themselves on the beach, "she seemed intent on reading not meeting young men." "She was cool, she treated me as if I were some dumbbell. When I asked her what she was reading, she replied, 'I'm reading Shakespeare.'" Grasso, who had been an outstanding football player on Hartford's Bulkeley High School team, immediately thought of Frank Shakespeare a nationally known football player at the University of Notre Dame. After that initial meeting, Tom Grasso recalled "I bothered her three or four times for a date," and eventually she agreed to his "persistent requests."[70]

Their relationship continued during Ella's years at Chaffee. Attending dances with her, young Grasso, who had attended Bates College in Maine for one year, was then enrolled at Central Connecticut State Teachers College in New Britain, Connecticut. He noticed how well mannered and well dressed the Chaffee students were and "all of them intelligent and educated as well and I wanted to be like them" and he vowed he would pursue an education in order to achieve an equal level of sophistication and intellectual achievement. Tom Grasso said it was Ella's intelligence and knowledge that "stimulated my curiosity" and gave "me the will to change my life." She would "read a book, talk about it, and then I would read it . . . and learn how to study."[71]

Ella and Tom's friendship was, at that point, a mixture of admiration and mutual affection coupled with desire and determination to achieve. And Ella emerged as a bright, intelligent, and achievement-oriented young woman who appealed to him. It was a friendship that grew and developed into a long-term romance and eventually marriage. It took them on a life-long journey far from that sunny beach in Old Lyme, Connecticut.

After Ella's successful years at Chaffee (1932–1936), she received encouragement from two sources to apply to Mount Holyoke College in South Hadley, Massachusetts. Her neighbor, Josephine Preli, whose enrollment at Chaffee had engendered Ella's mother's decision to enroll her daughter at the preparatory school, was a student at Mount Holyoke and shared her enthusiasm for that institution with Ella. Florence Sellers, Director of the Chaffee School, informed Ella of the unique opportunity

Mount Holyoke offered and encouraged her to apply to the prestigious Seven Sister School in nearby Massachusetts.[72] That decision proved to be one of the most important decisions Ella ever made. For the young woman from Windsor Locks, child of twentieth-century pilgrims, moving on to Mount Holyoke College was another leap forward from her sheltered Italian-American immigrant community. Ella's decision to attend Mount Holyoke enabled her to avail herself of a learning environment that would profoundly shape her life and future career.

❧ 2 ❧

ONE OF THE COUNTRY'S MOST WONDERFUL WOMEN

In the autumn of 1936, young Ella Tambussi moved on to college at Mount Holyoke in South Hadley, Massachusetts. Her matriculation there provided her with opportunities not only to receive an excellent education but also beneficial experiences, which would enable her to lay claim to and enjoy a great career. One hundred years earlier, in 1837, Mary Lyon founded Mount Holyoke Seminary to provide women opportunities for higher learning enabling them "to become full participants in the worlds they inhabited."[1]

At the Mount Holyoke College Centennial Celebration in 1937, speakers reminded the audience that the college "must empower women for a struggle to widen opportunity in the public world."[2] The college, considered one of America's most distinguished women's colleges, perceived its mission as one that prepared women to "be pioneers to go where no one else has been . . . and do what no one else has done."[3] This objective, instilled in Mount Holyoke's undergraduates, was the academic environment in which Ella Tambussi immersed herself in the fall of 1936.

In the year prior to her enrollment, the college adopted a new and experimental program of studies called the "two unit plan."[4] The new venture recognized individuals' aptitude, academic interest, and scholarly potential and permitted twenty incoming freshmen to focus on a specialized program of course work. Instead of concentrating on a broad, general liberal arts curriculum, the specially chosen young women would focus on two main subject areas.

By adopting the two-unit plan, Mount Holyoke also intended the young scholars to work closely with a faculty advisor. That advisor would counsel and recommend courses the student would engage in and would closely monitor each student's academic progress. The "two unit plan" enabled a young woman to "penetrate more deeply into her fields of interest"[5] than that which was done in the regular course of study, and to come to know their advisor as a mentor and friend.

First proposed in 1925, the two-unit plan had taken Mount Holyoke ten years to debate, finally approve, and implement. Seen at first as experimental and less regimented than the traditional curriculum, it was approved in 1935, and a contingent of twenty "two unit plan" students, including Ella Tambussi, began in the fall of 1936.

One faculty member, Professor Amy Hewes, who became Ella's mentor, had long spearheaded the drive to adopt the program. In her capacity as Chairman of the Economics and Sociology Department, she conceived the program as one that would not only be path-breaking and non-traditional but also would provide students with concentrated study and living arrangements where the young scholars would share the same accommodations in a campus house during their freshmen year.

The young women lived together in Sycamores, one of Mount Holyoke's oldest buildings, located a short distance from the main college campus. The group of twenty students would later discover that while their two-unit plan broke through old academic traditions, their living arrangements sustained some old customs that had not disappeared from the Massachusetts campus.

Student accommodations were divided along religious lines. "I was naïve," recalled Lucille Bernstein Ritvo one of Ella's classmates, "so I did not realize I was rooming with a Jewish girl because I was also Jewish." And Ella Tambussi, "being the only Catholic had the only single room."[6] In Ritvo's opinion, this arrangement was done to make it easier to adjust to college life by placing young women of the same religious faith together. In 1936–1937, approximately 6.5 percent of Mount Holyoke's student body was Jewish while Smith, Vassar, Radcliffe, and Wellesley enrolled more.[7] Ritvo recalled, however, no overt anti-Semitism among administrators, faculty, or students. Yet it is evident that homogeneous grouping along religious lines in living accommodations was very much in place in 1936.

Ritvo also remembered that Ella's room was at the top of the stairs in Sycamores, and when the girls went upstairs, Ella's "door was always open, her desk facing the door and she would always look up and be willing to exchange greetings." Many years later this former classmate and local political activist observed the same openness and friendliness during Ella's political campaigns. "Usually politicians try to shake as many hands as possible . . . Ella would let a line form to let you finish what you wanted to tell her," Ritvo emphasized.[8]

Mount Holyoke provided the intellectual rigor and scholarly environment that suited Ella Tambussi's ambitions. It was an institution characterized by nurturing, discipline, caring, and high expectations of female achievement. Placing Ella Tambussi within the Mount Holyoke experience, several observations need to be emphasized. First, among the college faculty there was a group of educators—predominantly female—who were outstanding in their chosen fields. Those female scholars were primarily selected to teach at Mount Holyoke because of their academic achievements, scholarly abilities, and teaching proficiency. And as a result, they emerged as role models for students. They were perceived as examples of what educated women could achieve; many faculty members attained national recognition and acclaim for their scholarship and leadership in various academic disciplines and social reform movements.

Second, as frequent participants in national and even international affairs, Mount Holyoke's faculty and administrators actively engaged in important events of the day. Emphasis on participation and service, a legacy of the college founder Mary Lyon, was pointedly brought home to each Mount Holyoke student by the breadth of the faculty's partaking in public affairs exemplified by Mount Holyoke's longtime President Mary Wooley. Miss Wooley presided over the college for thirty-six years (1901–1937),[9] and she had been selected in 1930 as "one of the twelve greatest living women in America."[10] In 1932, she was appointed by President Herbert Hoover to be an American representative to the Conference for the Reduction and Limitation of Armaments held in Geneva, Switzerland.[11] She was the only woman in the American delegation.

Mary Wooley graduated from Brown University in 1894 with honors in History and Latin. She was one of the first two women graduates from that institution of higher learning.[12] After teaching Biblical history at Wellesley College from 1895–1901, she was offered the Presidency of Mount Holyoke.

When she took the reins at Mount Holyoke in 1901, the college had an "enviable reputation for scholarship as well as a strong tradition of evangelical religion." The college had trained teachers who were scattered throughout the United States and missionaries who "carried its name to the world at large." Furthermore, the college had also gained a solid reputation in science education "equal to or perhaps superior" to other women's colleges.[13]

In her inaugural address in 1901, Miss Wooley spoke about "preparing Mount Holyoke women for lives of service."[14] Throughout her distinguished career, Wooley exemplified the principles set forth by Mount Holyoke's founder, Mary Lyon, who vowed that the college's purpose was to enable women to "enter the world and not withdraw from it."[15] And by her own example, Mary Wooley passed on to future generations of Mount Holyoke graduates, the importance of service to the community and nation. In 1936–1937, Ella's freshmen year, she observed in Mary Wooley's "life and her example . . . the symbol and substance of the activist woman."[16]

A third observation that emerges is that the all-female college provided its young students with an educational environment rich in intellectual fervor and excitement, and it emphasized service to society as a career goal for young women. Indeed Mount Holyoke pointed proudly to the public service career of one of its most distinguished graduates, Secretary of Labor Frances Perkins. She graduated from the college in 1902 and became the first female Cabinet member in President Franklin D. Roosevelt's New Deal administration in 1933. Later, Ella Tambussi, reflecting the Mount Holyoke emphasis on service, would become the first Mount Holyoke graduate elected to the Congress of the United States and also the first alumna elected governor of one of the states of the Union.

Frequent references to service also reflects a concept that Mount Holyoke and many American colleges embraced as a result of the impact the Progressive and social reform movement had on America in the late nineteenth century and the early decades of the twentieth century. Fundamentally, American institutions of higher education, at that time, perceived their role as one that would develop experts who would help the nation "solve . . . complex problems,"[17] which had arisen as a result of the industrial and manufacturing revolution that had transformed America by the turn of the century.

As more American women's colleges emerged in the early twentieth century, they took up that challenge by encouraging faculty to become activists, working to merge their academic work with a public role to help diminish and alleviate society's growing social problems. Serving as role models for students, the activist faculty would in turn help to encourage and develop young women of talent. Thus, as recent research has demonstrated, the development of achievement oriented young women is "directly proportional to the number of same sex role models to whom they have access."[18] At Mount Holyoke Ella Tambussi's interaction with outstanding women of academic achievement who combined distinguished classroom teaching and intellectual brilliance with a commitment to public service unquestionably impacted her life and subsequent career. In Ella Tambussi's case she "met, worked closely with and . . . was greatly influenced by several faculty members—one in particular, Professor Amy Hewes, Chairman of the Economic and Sociology Department."[19]

Amy Hewes, referred to by Ella many years later as "one of the country's most wonderful women,"[20] was a graduate of Goucher College and received her Ph.D. in Sociology from the University of Chicago in 1903 followed by advance study at the University of Berlin, Germany. (Her doctoral dissertation focused on The Part Invention Plays in the Social Process). She joined the faculty at Mount Holyoke in 1905 and remained an active member of the faculty until her retirement in 1943. She established the college Department of Economics and Sociology in 1909 and served as Chairman for many years. Furthermore, she lived for sixty years in the small town of South Hadley, Massachusetts, where her home became a favorite Sunday afternoon gathering place for tea and lively conversation with students.[21]

Professor Hewes emerges in Ella's life as another significant teacher and mentor, whose influence and impact on the impressionable young woman student was profound. Professor Hewes, according to Juliet Fisher Kidney (BA'34, a graduate assistant MA'37, and instructor in Economics and Sociology 1934–43) was during Ella's time at Mount Holyoke, "a good disciplinarian, rather officious but students respected her."[22] She was not only an admired teacher but her commitment to an active life of public service clearly distinguishes her legacy as an important influence on Ella's life. Amy Hewes' notable career demonstrates not only her skill as a teacher but also as an advocate for labor reforms — particularly child labor and women's rights in the workplace. And her scholarly achievements represent pioneering work by a woman scholar in the emerging fields of labor economics and statistical analysis.

Miss Hewes found time to engage in various civic and statewide public service activities, which the college encouraged faculty members to pursue. For example, in 1913–1915, she served as Executive Secretary of the first Minimum Wage Commission in Massachusetts, which was also the first in the nation. And later, during the Depression, she was appointed to the Massachusetts State Commission on the operation of the Minimum Wage Law, the Advisory Council of the Massachusetts Unemployment Compensation Commission, and the Advisory Council of the Massachusetts State Federal Employment Service.[23]

As a classroom teacher, she is remembered as one of the first scholars to "use statistical measurements to better understand social phenomena."[24] And in her many years of teaching labor economics, she demonstrated to her students the need to incorporate statistical analysis in their classroom work. She brought "problems of the work-a-day world into her classroom . . . her students always felt they were discussing human problems—problems of people with aspirations, frustrations, and fears."[25] She believed "strongly and conveyed to all of us the equality of people and the excitement of fighting for a better society,"[26] recalls Catherine Roraback, a graduate of Mount Holyoke College Class of 1941.

A respected scholar interested in labor reform movements, statistical analysis, and consumerism, Professor Hewes emerged as Ella's academic mentor and adviser during her years at Mount Holyoke. While Miss Hewes was deeply engaged in teaching and departmental activities, her work also enabled her to pursue research in fields of interest such as women's issues and working families' concerns, which were topics she actively pursued in the public and scholarly arena. Her work encompassed research that, for its time, was quite remarkable.

Professor Hewes was particularly interested in and focused much of her early research on factory workers—particularly women workers. Her monograph *Women as Munitions Workers*, published in 1917, examined the armament industry's expansion in Bridgeport, Connecticut, prior to and during the American participation in World War I. Miss Hewes' exceptional study focused on the work and working conditions of local Bridgeport women in the Remington Arms munitions plant. Four thousand women worked at the plant, and she documented the conditions under which those workers toiled. Her findings underscored the need for revision of Connecticut's factory laws, which had allowed women to work until 10 P.M. but fixed no hour in the morning when they might resume work.[27] Hewes also found that women were working near explosives, which placed them near potentially dangerous situations, which could lead to accidents and exposure to industrial poisons and potential illnesses.

Her research, undertaken with support from the Russell Sage Foundation,[28] was a clarion call for Connecticut to revise its labor laws aimed at protecting women in the workplace. Miss Hewes' investigative results, reported in the *New York Times*, recommended prohibiting night work for women, reducing the daily work hours from ten to eight, and protecting women workers against industrial poisons and diseases.[29] Her methodology included utilization of research techniques such as mass data analysis and personal interviews with a number of women who worked in the Remington factory. Amy Hewes' activities exemplified the expectation of Mount Holyoke's President Mary Wooley that faculty should engage in scholarly research that would ultimately benefit the public good.

Dr. Hewes' research approach also characterized the type of assignments she required of her young Mount Holyoke students. In 1935, for example, her statistics class collected and analyzed data on the cost of living in the city of Springfield, Massachusetts.[30] Between 1935 and 1938, her students investigated housing in South Hadley, Massachusetts, utilizing "analytical methods and gathering and interpretation of mass data."[31] Professor Hewes, in her department's Annual Report to the college President, noted that the housing study caught the attention of Professor William Witte, Chairman of the Economics Department at the University of Wisconsin, who called it a "high grade statistical piece of work and an interesting sociological study."[32]

Professor Hewes' 1939–1940 Annual Report took note of Ella Tambussi's High Honor Senior Thesis, "Workmen's Compensation in the United States."[33] In June 1940, she wrote to a friend, Margaret Wiseman of the Massachusetts Consumer's League, noting that while Ella Tambussi was not able to "secure very extensive material on cases . . . the paper is a very good, up to date presentation of the subject."[34]

Ella's study cited the need for establishing compulsory state funding for workmen's compensation and called for the elimination of private insurance companies from covering workers noting that insurers were "responsible for increased litigation and delays in enforcing the workmen's compensation laws which have proved disastrous to the injured workers."[35]

Her second proposal suggested a uniform federal workmen's compensation law citing "a virtual hodgepodge in which no progress toward standardization has been made."[36] Ella's choice of thesis topic and lifelong interest in labor issues reflects the influence Professor Amy Hewes exercised as her academic mentor.

In the summer of 1939, after Ella completed her third year of study, the relationship between the student and mentor entered a new level of collegiality. Since 1921, Professor Hewes had been a member of the faculty at the Bryn Mawr College Summer School for Women Workers in Industry. This program originated under the leadership of M. Carey Thomas, President of Bryn Mawr. She appointed Bryn Mawr undergraduate Dean, Hilda Worthington Smith as director of the school. Women selected to attend the summer program were members of the trade unions and they were invited to study at the suburban Philadelphia campus for six weeks of classroom learning. There, with the financial assistance of scholarships offered through the Women's Trade Union League and the YWCA Industrial clubs, women attended summer classes. They included lessons in economics, government, history, the history of trade union movements,[37] and also courses in pottery making, dance, theater, and public speaking. The aim of the Bryn Mawr school was "to offer young women in industry opportunities to study liberal subjects and to train themselves in clear thinking to stimulate an active and continuing interest in the problems of economic order; to develop a desire for study as a means of understanding and of enjoyment in life."[38] In addition, the school aimed to enlarge women's "influence in the industrial world, and increase the happiness and usefulness of their lives."[39]

The summer school students were "instructed by mainly female faculty from independent colleges,"[40] who were accompanied by student assistants selected from Seven Sister Colleges. Professor Hewes devoted nineteen consecutive summers (1921–1940) as a faculty member at Bryn Mawr and its successor school Hudson Shore in West Park, New York. Every summer she selected Mount Holyoke students to accompany her to the labor school, and Ella Tambussi was chosen by Miss Hewes in 1939 to assist her at the Hudson Shore Labor School.

The university assistants were "economics and sociology majors" with a "sympathetic interest in the labor movement" noted a Hudson Shore school flier circulated in 1940.[41] Ella's background fit perfectly with the school's descriptive brochure. Her experience at Hudson Shore opened up an interesting phase in her life. In later years she never talked about it, and it never surfaced in her public career, in her campaign literature, or in her public discourse. In fact, for reasons that seem clear now, her involvement that summer left an indelible mark on Ella Tambussi that she wanted few to ever uncover.

In the summer of 1939, the Bryn Mawr Summer Labor School relocated to West Park, New York, to the expansive summer home of Hilda Smith who had been the long time director. The school, renamed Hudson Shore Labor School, enrolled about sixty young women from mostly urban, industrial centers like New York City, Philadelphia, and cities throughout New England. Most students were immigrants or children of immigrants, and most did not have an education beyond the sixth grade. Limited schooling, in fact, was a criteria for admission. The young women came from a variety of trade unions, and a large number of the students "were in their thirties and forties."[42] They attended daily classes including how to organize and run a meeting, basic biology, English language, elementary science, economics, and social psychology. And since the students also ate their meals with the undergraduate assistants like Ella Tambussi and with college faculty, "by example they even learned table manners."[43]

In addition to being Amy Hewes' teaching assistant for seven weeks that summer, Ella worked in the school library.[44] Both tasks, for which there was no compensation, brought Ella into daily contact with women whose toil often took place in garment factories or grimy textile plants. Her experience that summer, she wrote, was "a chance to learn more at firsthand about the working women of the nation and about the attitudes and plans of young workers."[45] But that brief recollection about Hudson Shore was her only public reference to her time at the school. Yet it was an experience she never forgot, and she hoped others would never discover. Years later, Ella's son James Grasso would remark that his mother "lived in fear" someone would find out about her summer at the Hudson Shore "socialist school."[46]

As they did other trade union–supported schools, such as the Southern Summer School at Sweet Briar College in Virginia, some critics portrayed Hudson Shore as a training ground for militant labor activists. In fact, in 1935, the United States House Un-American Activities Committee charged that, "communists had captured and controlled workers education at the labor schools."[47] Hudson Shore, like the federal government's National Youth Administration network of workers' educational schools, was seen as sensitive to the needs of workers — more mainstream, more democratic — but it did not escape the public skepticism and strident criticism from political critics of the New Deal who emerged during the supercharged political atmosphere of the 1930s and 1940s. While not directly tied to the New Deal social programs of that era, the labor school workers educational programs, communal environment, and activist union connections, increased fears among political critics that young people were being educated and trained to become militant, radical, leftist-leaning socialists or communists. As events on the international scene demonstrated, those fears became more real in the minds of some Americans reflecting anxieties over the expansion of socialism in Western Europe and communism in the Soviet Union. Thus, the labor school movement in the United States became associated — in some critics minds at least — with educating and training radical labor agitators.

The nation's First Lady, Eleanor Roosevelt, was closely identified with the Hudson Shore School and she contributed financially every year to help support it. She resolutely answered critics who often criticized it and its predecessor school at Bryn Mawr as radical and communistic leaning by firmly responding it was not "communistic."[48] Mrs. Roosevelt was a longtime supporter of workers education and a close friend of Hilda Smith, whose family estate in West Park, New York, housed the school directly across the Hudson River from Roosevelt's Hyde Park home. Mrs. Roosevelt often hosted the Hudson Shore students for a one-day outing, including swimming, refreshments, and a picnic at her Val-Kill cottage. In 1940, Juliet Fisher Kidney, one of Professor Hewes' assistants that summer, remembers visiting Val-Kill with the Hudson Shore contingent and using Mrs. Roosevelt's bathing suit which "she threw over the transom in the bath house. It was still wet and still had the price tag on it,"[49] she noted. Another Hudson Shore assistant from Mount Holyoke, Catherine Roraback, recalled that in 1940 one week before the Hudson Shore students went to Val-Kill, they sent home for better clothes to wear when they met Mrs. Roosevelt. Yet, when the day came, July 19, 1940, and the thirty young women arrived at the First Lady's cottage, "Mrs. Roosevelt walked out in a bathing suit and greeted the students and said, "Where are your bathing suits?" "We don't have any," replied the young ladies. "Well we'll find some around here," said Mrs. Roosevelt. Next, she was "talking to them by the pool and they were absolutely enthralled."[50] The indefatigable First Lady had just returned from Chicago where she had addressed the Democratic National Convention the previous evening.[51] Despite widespread public criticism, Mrs. Roosevelt always demonstrated genuine, sincere, and continuing interest and support for workers educational programs across the country with particular interest in the Hudson Shore endeavor.

Yet there is a wall of silence on Ella's part about her experiences during the summer of 1939. She later viewed that period as having exposed her to a radical, socialist-oriented activity that she feared would be used against her politically. In later years, if her association with Hudson Shore became public, she may have been tagged as a radical, activist, liberal young woman. "It would have killed her politically," remarked her husband.[52] But there was also a more personal reason why she blotted out that summer of 1939. She met someone with whom she became infatuated. She fell in love with a thirty-five-year-old Hudson Shore male staffer of Italian heritage, Joseph Rotondo, from Union College in Schnectady, New York.[53] (He later married a Mount Holyoke graduate.) Ella's relationship with Joseph Rotondo came to be much talked about that summer, and it created a crisis in her relationship with Tom Grasso. The mere reference to Ella's other suitor would provoke, many years later, threatening responses from him.[54] He never forgot his rival's entreaties to Ella to marry him. Both James and Susane Grasso, Ella and Tom's children, recall that it was a topic that was never discussed openly within the family circle.

While the storm clouds gathered on the international scene during those fateful summer months of 1939, when Germany, Italy, and Japan were on the march and the world was on the brink of another disastrous world war, the relationship between Tom Grasso and Ella Tambussi hit a dark and uncertain time. In the ensuing months Ella's summer romance at Hudson Shore became a topic of Mount Holyoke gossip. Besides Tom Grasso, Ella's mother and Professor Amy Hewes also knew of Ella's new romantic interest.[55]

As a result, Tom found himself spending more time in South Hadley pursuing Ella in view of the competition he faced. Since he was enrolled in a Masters Degree program at Springfield College not far from South Hadley, he said he "almost became a student at Mount Holyoke, I was up there so many times."[56] He was there trying to woo Ella back into his life and his future.

❧ 3 ❧

THE WHOLE DAY . . . A ROSY GLOW

Tom Grasso would eventually win Ella's hand in marriage. His persistent and tenacious quest to marry her, however, would take years to accomplish because Ella put off marriage until she completed her graduate academic studies at Mount Holyoke. He availed himself of assistance from Ella's mother, who "put her foot down" and convinced Ella to marry Tom Grasso and not pursue the entreaties of her other suitor from Union College. Mrs. Tambussi preferred Grasso because she had known him for many years and felt a level of comfort with him but not with Ella's admirer from Hudson Shore. It was a debt to his future mother-in-law Tom Grasso felt deeply throughout his married life.[1]

On June 10, 1940, Ella graduated with a B.A. degree magna cum laude. It was a joyous and proud day for her parents to see their only child receive honors and recognition from one of America's outstanding institutions of women's higher education. As an undergraduate, she had excelled academically, maintaining her Williston Scholarship for all four years, and in her junior year she had been elected to Phi Beta Kappa. At the end of her senior year, she ranked among the top five in her class.

It is important to note that Ella often said years later that she frequently felt socially distant from her classmates because of her economic and social background.[2] "My mother," recalls Ella's son Jim, "had only two or three skirts and three sweaters at Mount Holyoke."[3] She took on "babysitting chores" to earn money primarily with Mt. Holyoke College

Professor Valentine Giamatti's family. Years later, Professor Giamatti's son, A. Bartlett Giamatti, became President of Yale University.[4]

Despite that social and economic separation from her classmates, Ella's years at Mount Holyoke College were years of preparation for what was to come in her public career. At Mount Holyoke, her intellectual horizons, self-confidence, initiative, inner-strength, and aggressiveness were energized and solidified by the stimulating and thought provoking academic environment she encountered. Her persona was molded and shaped by the role models she observed, and the nurturing faculty relationships she developed. Likewise, her career path was determined in large part by the enlightened Mount Holyoke emphasis on public service and responsibility to others; and it was there she developed her passionate conviction, sharpened by the Depression era economic turmoil, that a relationship between politics and government deeply affected the lives of people.

One Mount Holyoke classmate remembered Ella as a "strong, clear spoken, straight standing girl in her blouse and long wool skirt who seemed to set the air around her vibrating with purpose and life."[5] While another contemporary recalled Ella as "something of a loner,"[6] the 1940 Mount Holyoke yearbook, *Llamarada* reveals that Ella participated in several extracurricular activities. She was President of the American Student Union chapter, served as Vice President of the International Relations Club, and was active in the Student Industrial Club.

The American Student Union (ASU) chapter at Mount Holyoke was the organization that promoted campus-wide discussions about political issues, U.S. foreign policy, and contemporary issues.[7] It sponsored lectures and forums, all of which aimed to generate student interest in current events of the day. It was cited as one of the "most active clubs on campus."[8]

The national ASU, formed in 1935, was a "coalition of socialists, communists, and liberals" which at its peak numbered around "twenty thousand members out of a student population of over one million" across the country.[9] One comprehensive study of student movements of the 1930s concluded that student movements, including the ASU, "received . . . major impetus from the anti-war movement" of the pre-World War II period.[10] The ASU and other student groups (the American Youth Congress for example) were frequently outspoken supporters of President Franklin D. Roosevelt's noninterventionist policies and were also vocal opponents of Fascist governments in Mussolini's Italy and Hitler's Germany. While communists were noticeably prominent in the student movements of the thirties, including the ASU, they were increasingly less dominant in the late thirties, after the Soviet Union's foreign policies shifted and became more pro-German. Students opposed the turn-about, and the communists influence within the ASU diminished when the Russo-German Non-Aggression Pact was signed in 1939.[11]

The Mount Holyoke ASU chapter, which Ella headed, encouraged and supported opportunities for students to become informed about contemporary domestic and international issues. A review of the list of campus speakers at the college, during the years 1936–1940, reveals an array of guests including socialist Norman Thomas and leftist editor Granville Hicks, whom Ella recalled told the students "he left the Communist Party because of the Russo-German Pact."[12] In addition, Mount Holyoke faculty frequently spoke to the campus community on topics ranging from Fascism and the Civil War in Spain, to issues regarding Germany and isolationism.[13]

While those efforts attempted to generate campus interest in international and domestic political issues and controversies, many Mount Holyoke students showed little support for America's intervention in events taking place in far distant places in the world. With little overt campus interest in international problems, it is not surprising to find that students at the college, who were polled in the spring of 1938, showed overwhelming support for President Roosevelt's noninterventionist policies.[14] By a convincing margin 350–26, the Mount Holyoke student body demonstrated approval of the national administration's stand against intervening in the increasingly dangerous European and military controversies.[15] The Mount Holyoke student poll results were consistent with national polls of college students throughout the 1930s, which revealed Roosevelt and his policies were held in high regard among the younger generation.[16]

Despite the lack of interest in international politics on the part of many students, for young women like Ella Tambussi whose interests were decidedly focused on the economy, politics, international affairs, and labor issues, these were stimulating and provocative times. Many years later she noted "Holyoke never seemed isolated from the serious events that were taking place at home and abroad."[17] These were the years during which she formulated her beliefs and opinions on a range of issues confronting the United States: the question of American military rearmament, the U.S. relationship to the League of Nations, the expansion of Fascism in Europe, the collapse of the American economy, and the plight of the working man and woman in the United States. It was during that period that she, like many other campus intellectuals of the 1930s, associated herself with the New Deal, which "stimulated interest in current affairs, politics, and the social sciences."[18] This was the juncture in her life when she solidified her views on political, social, and domestic economic issues favoring governmental programs of assistance to the poor and jobless, while maintaining strong sentiments for using America's moral and humanitarian persuasion and influence to counter the anti-democratic forces that were threatening the precarious balance of power in Europe.

Ella's apparent frustration with fellow students appeared in a "Public Opinion" column she authored in the *Mount Holyoke News*, October 20, 1939. Ella lamented student disinterest in contemporary issues such as civil liberties being curtailed in Europe, or the "red raid" in Chicago led by the Dies (Un-American Activities) Committee of the U.S. House of Representatives. Neither of those problems seems to have aroused campus reaction. It led her to scold fellow undergraduates by saying "All the knowledge we so avidly pursue is knowledge—for what—if we do not intend to make practical application of what we learn to everyday problems."[19]

Most observers would not have predicted at the time that Ella was preparing herself for the career path her life would follow. However, one Mount Holyoke professor, John Lobb, a member of the Economics and Sociology Department faculty, years later recalled that he felt she indeed was "preparing herself for the opportunities and work that came her way throughout the rest of her life . . . Certain students stand out in one's memory for their accomplishments, their personalities, and their ambitions. It is so with Ella Tambussi."[20] He went on to describe her as one who "concentrated her studies in Labor Relations and Statistics with a keen interest and curiosity in Cultural Development of Society . . . Together with . . . a strong awareness of Political Science and politics."[21] In retrospect, it seems evident the foundation for Ella's political outlook, intellectual growth and social conscience was being shaped during those formative years at the Mount Holyoke campus.

There is also a clear indication of what Ella believed her academic studies prepared her to pursue. In an article she wrote for the *Mount Holyoke Alumnae Quarterly* in 1941, entitled "Building a Background for a Practical Life," she noted that what appealed to her about Mount Holyoke's academic environment and the two unit plan of study, was the independence and individual initiative offered to the willing student.[22]

Her article mentioned the academic courses she chose and the papers and reports she generated, especially about the "integration and assimilation of the Italian people in my home town."[23] In her junior and senior years her course work in history and economics was followed up by independent work in "various fields of economics," which included "personal investigations" where she "visited factories and met the directors and attended trade union meetings with workers."[24] These visits to factories, part of the Mount Holyoke undergraduate Student Industrial Club activities of which Ella was a part, remain vividly etched in the memory of Catherine Roraback '41, a Mount Holyoke contemporary of Ella's. She recalled going to textile factories in the Holyoke area because Amy Hewes wanted "us to know first hand what it was like to be a factory worker." And Roraback remembers visiting factories "somewhere near Holyoke," and "I can remember the noise of those machines even today . . . something I'd never heard . . . the atmosphere of the place."[25] Also, in extra-curricular hours, Ella noted that, "I worked out educational and recreational projects with a group of industrial girls at the Holyoke YWCA."[26] She acknowledged the benefits that type of academic and practical education offered, seeing it as the "better method of learning." And she concluded that, "I hope that I did not acquire mere facts through my two-unit study, but also initiative and independence in scholarship. Surely such habits will be of use in the world today."[27]

What is also revealing about Ella's years at Mount Holyoke is her exposure to female role models whose influence was manifested so often at the college. Many years later, on June 1, 1975, when she returned to campus as the Commencement speaker, she recalled the "visibility of women on the faculty, on campus as guests of the college, functioning as what we know to be role models today."[28]

She mentioned the appearance of Anna Rosenberg who had been a close associate of Franklin Roosevelt.[29] There were many other leading artists and thinkers who came to the campus. They included Elizabeth Arden, Muriel Rukeyser, Dame Myra Hess, Nadia Boulanger, Annie Jump Cannon, Cornelia Otis Skinner, and Lottie Lehman, among others. In addition, historian Mary Beard spoke at Mount Holyoke's Centennial celebration in 1937, and Secretary of Labor Frances Perkins, a Mount Holyoke graduate and the first woman Cabinet member, also appeared during Ella's undergraduate years.[30] It was an impressive list of role models, of successful, achieving women.

At the department level, the Economics and Sociology Department hosted an impressive number of specialists in related fields who spoke to students majoring in Economics and Sociology. Those lectures and occasional luncheon-dinner conferences encompassed a broad array of themes and topics and were seen as supplementing and enriching the academic work the young women were carrying out in the classroom. In 1938–1939, the speakers and topics included Elizabeth Nord (organizer for the T.W.O.C), who spoke on "The Wagner Act in Action"; Julia Chapin (Holyoke State-Federal Employment Office), "Operation of a State-Federal Employment Office"; Robert Watt (Employees Representative for the United States in the International Labor Office), "Industrial Relations in Great Britain and Sweden"; Clara Dzubin (Briarcliff School Faculty), "Everyday Life in Soviet Russia"; and Professor Robert Heaton (University of Minnesota) "Clio in Overalls."[31] In 1939–1940, the list of speakers, while shorter, was no less impressive and the topics remained far-reaching. Included in the list was Professor Werner Bohnstedt (National University of Panama) "Social Life and Institutions in Germany Today," Dr. Marie Munk (formerly with the Berlin, Germany, Municipal court) "German Women at Home and at Work," and John Foster (Business Manager of Hospitals, Eighth Route Army in China) "Reorganization of the Economic Life of China."[32] While the topics were wide ranging, there is no doubt that the Department purposely invited specialists in various fields in order to spark students intellectual and scholarly interests but also to encourage their aspirations to pursue various public and professional opportunities once they earned their degrees.

In the Department's Centennial Year Report (1937), it was noted that the faculty wanted their majors to realize that former students "are continually blazing new trails for those who will follow."[33] As if to emphasize the point, a gathering took place on March 19, 1937, notable for its vocational focus, when the department hosted a banquet for undergraduate majors on the subject of Professional Experience.[34] The guests included Eleanor Sauer '36, a graduate student at Columbia University, Eleanor Neill '27, employed by the WPA in Washington, and Madeline Hoagland '30, a social worker. All of the women were alumnae of Mount Holyoke and also former Economics and Sociology majors. Another gathering of alumnae occurred in 1939, and the subject was Choosing a Vocation. The guests were Mary Tuttle '37, a medical social worker, Dorothy McKenna '39, a business manager in New York, and Doris Pullman '39, Editorial Research Assistant in New York.[35] It is reasonable to conclude they were seen as blazing new trails in fields of endeavor that the faculty judged worthy career paths their young scholars might pursue.

By presenting these enrichment activities, the college sought to dispel any doubts in the students' minds that finding a mate and having children were the only options awaiting them. Careers in the world — outside the home — would provide a chance for service "to become full participants in the worlds they inhabited" as Mount Holyoke's beloved President Mary Wooley had urged during her tenure as President of the college. It was a not so subtle way to demonstrate to young women that their ambitions include choices: marriage, a professional career, or both.

Another point Ella raised in her commencement speech in 1975, was her pointed reference to a remarkable Farewell Letter that one Mount Holyoke faculty member wrote to Ella's graduating Class of 1940.[36] Professor Jeanette Marks published her exhortation to the graduating seniors in the student newspaper the *Mount Holyoke News* on June 10, 1940. In that letter, Professor Marks reminded the graduates that there was for women "a greater opportunity to serve than women have ever known."[37] In one particularly memorable phrase that would resonate with Ella Tambussi, Miss Marks urged the graduates to become "applied students of public affairs, refusing to use our influence by deputy."[38] "Those were stirring words for future leaders to hear," Ella said in that 1975 commencement address.[39] In truth, her own life and career would more than live up to the challenge placed before Ella and her classmates on that graduation day in 1940.

The idea of public service and responsibility to others appears as a recurring, oft-stated ideal to which educated women were expected to aspire. This was particularly true at Mount Holyoke and its sister institutions, which emphasized strong nurturing, caring, discipline, and high expectations of its graduates.[40] At the campus in South Hadley, Massachusetts, a vital part of the faculty's role was to help each young woman "discover and strengthen her talents" so as to achieve "fulfillment of informed and creative involvement in the world."[41] In other words, the expectation for Mount Holyoke graduates was that they should aim for public involvement to improve, in some way, the common good, and that objective was seen as integral to the life of an educated woman. By employing outstanding women faculty and bringing successful women to campus, the college continually reminded students of the contributions women were making at various levels of American society. And the nurturing environment at the South Hadley campus encouraged Mount Holyoke's "uncommon women" to endeavor to remove "barriers to their presence"[42] in a world where women's contributions were not always welcomed or recognized.

In 1940, unlike some of her classmates, Ella chose to remain at Mount Holyoke to pursue a Master's Degree in Economics. By doing so, she put off an immediate career choice and marriage. Ella's mentor, Professor Amy Hewes, was unquestionably responsible for convincing Ella to remain at the college. She not only directed the intellectual and scholarly pursuits of Ella Tambussi, she was largely responsible for the career path Ella pursued. Many years later in 1972, when Ella was a member of the United States House of Representatives, she emphasized that it was Amy Hewes, like Sister DeChantal years before, "who opened the windows of my mind to a new and exciting world."[43] "I loved her (Amy Hewes) dearly," Ella wrote. [44]And it was Amy Hewes' teaching, "relating learning to the world around me," that was the college experience that imparted special encouragement and confidence and "whetted my appetite for public affairs."[45] In many ways, being among the Hewes' elect was like having a second mother: a mother/teacher who encouraged and influenced her daughter Ella to pursue a career path of public service. Miss Hewes, by her own distinguished career as an academic, scholar, and social activist, stands out as an exceptional role model and mentor for Ella Tambussi. They remained friends and admirers until Professor Hewes' death in March 1970.

Also in 1940, with Professor Hewes' encouragement, Ella accepted an offer of a fellowship for graduate study, which also entailed teaching in the Statistics Laboratory (1940–42) within the Economics and Sociology Department. In that position, she was the departmental assistant to Professor Hewes, as well as to the other department faculty members. "It was during these years that the faculty had an opportunity to observe her drive, her determination, and her ability in taking on new responsibilities. I know of no student since then who so well fulfilled and carried out the . . . duties of the job," recalled faculty member John Lobb.[46] Ella's assistantship contributed enormously to further strengthening the personal bond that had developed with Amy Hewes. Professor Hewes and other faculty members recognized certain qualities in her persona including her intelligence, energy, enthusiasm, and determination. Amy Hewes nurtured her young protégé's confidence and ambition believing that she would have a bright and successful future with "a decided capacity for leadership."[47]

As a graduate student, Ella wrote her thesis on the Knights of Labor. It was an "attempt to find in the history of the Knights of Labor explanations of the role they played" in American labor history. She emphasized that it would be a "study of their social philosophy, of the ideals, and methods, and theories which they advocated."[48] Ella's choice of thesis topic, like that of her senior honors thesis, reflects Professor Hewes' own scholarly interests in labor union history as it related to the working men and women of America. While the thesis did not unearth any new information about the Knights, it remains a fine overview of the militant union and it also traces the continuation of the Knight's aims and programs through various labor organizations that came along after the union's demise.

Many years later, Ella referred to her six years at Mount Holyoke with fondness, "reverential gratitude"[49] and respect. "I did all sorts of blissful things. There were some real giants on that faculty, early leaders of thinking about the consumer movement and about world economics."[50] And she added, "there never would be enough lines or enough pages to express my delight and appreciation for the adventures in living—Amy Hewes making the worker's movement alive and vibrant—Red Hawkins making Economic Theory real—reading the Divine Comedy with Miss Duane and reaching Paradise as spring burst all over campus."[51]

She emphasized that at Mount Holyoke, "I was always taken seriously, first as a student and then as a teaching assistant and graduate student." At Mount Holoyke, Ella said "I was encouraged to think of my life not as something that would happen to me, but as something I would shape for myself. We were encouraged in the view that to share a passion for helping others was a joy and not a drudgery." And she added, "the gift of Holyoke to its graduates then and now are a taste for autonomy, a capacity for commitment and the self-confidence that keeps us moving from one task to the next."[52] For Ella Tambussi, the six years spent at Mount Holyoke were enormously satisfying and rewarding. The long hours of intense study, the fascinating opportunities to visit and observe factory and industrial labor, to savor the provocative and thoughtful words and ideas of faculty and campus speakers, all combined to provide Ella with an outstanding education and preparation for what was to come in her life.

In one sense, leaving Mount Holyoke tested Ella's "capacity for commitment" because soon after leaving South Hadley, Massachusetts she married her "best friend" Tom Grasso. The wedding occurred several weeks after she received her Masters degree. An account of the ceremony, reported in the Hartford *Times*, noted that the nuptial mass took place on August 31, 1942, at St. Mary's Church in Windsor Locks.[53] Ella would recall her wedding day as the best day of her life. "It was a gorgeous end of summer day. All of my family and friends were at church and at the dinner . . . The whole day was a rosy glow, affectionate good wishes, and good fellowship unmarred by even one small cloud."[54]

For Ella and Tom Grasso, that memorable day was the beginning of a nearly thirty-nine year marriage that would take them on a journey that would have been unimaginable for two young people whose paths crossed on that sunny beach in Old Lyme ten years earlier.

In 1942, twenty-eight-year-old Tom Grasso secured a teaching position in Windsor, Connecticut, and five years later he took a similar post in the East Hartford, Connecticut, school system. He remained there for many years eventually rising to become a school principal and retiring from the East Hartford school system in 1973.

Ella, age twenty-three and newly married, was determined to utilize her knowledge and skills in the public sector and she accepted a position on "the lower rungs of public service" as an Interviewer Grade 1 for the State of Connecticut's Employment Service.[55] She earned the "magnificent sum of $1440 per year."[56]

Ella's decision to undertake employment in the public sector was a fateful choice. It placed her in a state government department, which was a front line agency that dealt with Connecticut's labor needs in the midst of wartime mobilization. It was, however, a position where she could apply her knowledge of labor and personnel relations and eventually utilize her skill at statistical analysis, particularly when she became the Assistant Director of Research in the office of Manpower Research.

Prior to World War II, during Ella's years at Mount Holyoke, Connecticut like the rest of the nation suffered through a serious economic collapse. And the State of Connecticut's Employment Service had been established to assist workers find employment suited to their background, skills, and employability.

Yet the economic misfortune of the 1930s demonstrated how wedded Connecticut's economy was to industry and manufacturing interests. As those major components of the state's economy declined, Connecticut's overall prosperity suffered. By 1932, 25 percent of Connecticut's workforce was unemployed, and Connecticut's cities and towns attempted to put the unemployed to work on municipal projects, such as repairing streets, painting municipally owned buildings, and even constructing a city owned golf course in Bridgeport.[57] While wages were minimal—50 cents an hour in Bridgeport—it was one way that towns and cities tried to help or assist many of their own citizens to eke out a subsistence living.

Connecticut's state government had long been in the strong grip of industrial, manufacturing, and conservative business interests. Those "captains of industry" envisioned a minimal role for government in any effort to combat the effects of the state's economic collapse. In 1930, Republican Governor John Trumbull established a Connecticut Unemployment Commission to determine what the state could do to combat the economy's depressed state.[58] James Hook, President of Geometric Tool Company in New Haven and Chairman of the Unemployment Commission, reported to the Governor that, other than collect data or exchange information with the cities and towns, there was little the state could do. "On this matter, my mind is pretty much of a blank," admitted Hook in January 1932.[59]

In the early 1930s, the economies of the forty-eight states were slowed to a virtual standstill. In Connecticut, with hundreds of thousands unemployed, banks foreclosing on mortgages, and individuals begging on street corners, local mayors petitioned the Connecticut governor to consider relief programs to help the plight of cities and urban areas of the state.[60]

For most people who lived through the stresses of the Great Depression of the 1930s, and for many young people like Ella Grasso who grew up during that period, the Depression had a "significant impact," which left an indelible mark on their lives.[61] "I'm a child of the Depression," Ella often explained, though her family seems not to have suffered great hardship during this period. [62]Her parents, she said, "lived tenaciously . . . we were pressed, other people were destroyed. We ate, other people starved." Unfortunately, she witnessed many instances of heartache and despair within the small Windsor Locks community and she vividly described her recollection of those bleak and dreadful times. "One day my mother and I were walking home . . . It was just dusk and in our little town of Windsor Locks there was such a chill in the air that it was horrible . . . The lights in the houses seemed to be dimmer and the banks had closed. This was a absolutely traumatic because every penny that anyone had been able to save was there."[63]

She went on to describe what she witnessed first hand among her neighbors and friends. "I watched a family being evicted from their home. I knew the kids. I had gone to school with them and suddenly they were out and everyone looked at them strangely until other families were evicted too."[64]

Like so many others who lived during that era, Ella was deeply affected by what she witnessed happening around her. "We learned that you could make do with very little and how to make a little bit go a long way," she recalled.[65] It left her, as it did so many, with a cautious outlook about the vagaries of American capitalism and its roller coaster–like effects on the economic well being of the citizens of this democratic nation. "The Depression sparked a social consciousness among the educated," and it was at that point Ella "learned the values of frugality . . . and she got her compassion for the poor and underprivileged."[66] The Depression, Ella recalled, "was a time I will never forget. There was such poverty . . . It was a devastating experience."[67] It was the seminal event in her life that deepened her commitment to serve others whose lives were irrevocably changed by the loss of a job, loss of a home, or even the loss of their human dignity.

Having grown up in a small, largely immigrant community, Ella witnessed how a community of that makeup nourished, supported, and helped neighbors during difficult times. Her growing awareness led to conviction that, in a stressful, bleak, and overwhelmingly harsh economic climate, government must replicate on a larger scale what local communities tried to do for themselves. As a result, in the long term the Depression impacted her views on government and its role in people's lives.

Ella noted that prior to the Depression, government's role was hardly visible, and it rarely intruded in people's lives.[68] But that posture changed in Connecticut after the gubernatorial election in 1930. In that pivotal vote, Connecticut's electorate turned to a Democrat, Wilbur Cross of New Haven, to take up the burdens of the governor's office. They hoped he would bring new leadership and a sympathetic ear to the highest levels of Connecticut's governmental structure. Cross, who had been an academic most of his professional life, including Dean of the Yale Graduate School, had never run for office prior to becoming the Democratic nominee for Governor in 1930.

Elected as the state's seventy-first Chief Executive, Wilbur Cross was a political conservative who possessed shrewd political instincts. He realized that the unemployment situation was the primary problem facing the state. And while he was initially not a champion of expanding governmental powers, Cross understood that state government had to offer some form of relief to its citizens.

As Governor, he created Connecticut's Commission on Relief, which established for the first time a coordinated relief effort to assist local towns and cities and nonprofit groups, which faced the enormous task of housing, feeding, clothing, and finding means of employment for its needy citizenry. The Governor's relief efforts, referred to as Connecticut's Little New Deal, while modest in scope, foretold the national program that would characterize President Franklin D. Roosevelt's New Deal program of the First Hundred Days in the spring of 1933.

In the fall of 1932, Roosevelt, then Governor of New York, campaigned in Bridgeport, and Governor Cross introduced him to a throng of eager citizens. In what came to be called the Forgotten Man Speech, Cross urged Roosevelt not to forget the man who "is the simple, honest laborer, ready to earn his living by productive work . . . He works, he votes, generally he prays . . . but he always pays . . . All the burdens fall on him or on her, for it is time to remember that the Forgotten Man is not seldom a woman."[69]

Wilbur Cross reminded Roosevelt that, "when you take up your abode in the White House . . . remember the Forgotten Man to whom you will owe your election. Give him . . . Fair and honest treatment."[70]

As Connecticut's Governor would soon realize, Roosevelt's New Deal program for the Forgotten Man championed new policies and programs that shifted much of the control and direction of relief and recovery efforts to the federal government in Washington. It was the national government that for the first time took command of the nation's economic policy of Relief, Recovery, and Reform. The New Deal, however, would require the state government's involvement and cooperation to carry out many programs at the state and local level.

Cross's four consecutive electoral victories were testimony to his popularity, and they were instrumental in invigorating Connecticut's Democratic Party. For the first time since 1914, a Democrat sat in the Governor's chair. And in 1932, when Cross was reelected, Augustine Lonergan, also a Democrat, was elected to the United States Senate, the first Democrat to serve in the Senate since the 1870s. And in 1934, with Cross again the party's standard bearer, the Democrats won all statewide offices, four of the six congressional seats, and elected another Democrat Francis Maloney as a United States Senator.[71] The result of these Democratic victories was the downfall of the Connecticut Republican Party machine led by its State Chairman J. Henry Roraback, who had dominated Connecticut's political scene for two decades.[72]

What occurred in Connecticut was the emergence of the Democratic Party appealing to urban voters, immigrant groups, ethnic minorities, labor unions, and workers in factories and industries. These were the same groups that were part of the national constituency to whom the New Deal aimed many of its policies and economic revival efforts.

In addition to enhancing the Democratic Party's emergence in the state, Cross's legacy included the special effort he made to interest young people in public affairs. In a speech that reflected his beliefs on this matter, the Governor remarked that, "there can be no doubt that among the more recent college graduates . . . the present depression is acting as a spur upon interest in public affairs." He went on to state that, "for the first time, in many years, young people are beginning to realize that national policies directly affect them."[73]

Besides his personal popularity, Governor Cross possessed an insightful understanding of the challenges public service presented. He realized that it would be a long road for young people who enter "upon a political career before they can reach a conspicuous post."[74] And he cautioned that the "present situation is a still stronger challenge to robust American youth . . . for the political scene is no place for the anemic dilettante who is unwilling and unable to learn how to meet the hard blows and stubborn opposition."[75]

In a strikingly similar manner to that which Ella Grasso encountered at Mount Holyoke, Wilbur Cross issued a summons to young people to undertake careers in public service. "From my brief experience in state government," Cross emphasized, "I have learned one thing that our democracy needs today above all others. It is the energy of intelligent, aggressive and well-trained young men and women in practical efforts for the public welfare."[76]

For her part, Ella Grasso would heed the call that Mount Holyoke instilled in her and that Connecticut's Governor Wilbur Cross placed before young people: to serve their fellow man through a career in public service. She awakened to the realization that government's traditional role of non-intrusion in people's lives had changed dramatically. She became aware that state and federal government programs and policies "served a very real public purpose," and that while some government programs such as the "WPA and food programs were not well managed . . . they were certainly well intentioned." And she added, "I think that was the first time I realized that the machinery of government can be used for the service of the people."[77] Thus it was the Depression and government's role in responding to public distress that put in place what became part of her thinking. There developed in Ella's thinking a "very

real sense of a relationship between politics and the lives of people—
that what happens to us was affected by government and I wanted to be
part of that government."[78]

Arguably, one of the best training grounds for middle class, politically
inclined women to learn about government, to understand, discuss, and
comprehend the relationship between politics and government was the
League of Women Voters. This would be the organization to which Ella
Grasso would turn to enhance her understanding of an array of public
issues. The League would provide her, and many other women, an outlet
for the politically interested, community oriented woman to participate
in activities outside their home.[79]

The emergence of the Connecticut League of Women Voters came
after a long and difficult uphill struggle to have women's voices heard
in the Land of Steady Habits. The contentious political environment in
Connecticut was dominated by "male politicians who wanted to keep
their power and by politically minded women who wanted to advance
their causes."[80]

The women's movement in Connecticut was organized in 1869 with
the founding of the Connecticut Women's Suffrage Association led by
Isabella Beecher Hooker. A protracted struggle ensued between women
suffragettes and male politicians in the state before women achieved
many of the reforms they desired. Indeed it would take the movement
nearly forty years before gaining major reforms in the state of Connecticut. Agitation for achieving those reforms was carried out in the early
decades of the twentieth century by women such as Catherine Luding-
ton and Katherine Houghton Hepburn. Their initial successes included
establishing day nurseries and traveling libraries, serving on school
boards, and lobbying the Legislature.[81]

In 1919, when the United States House of Representatives passed the
women's suffrage amendment, four of Connecticut's five Congressmen
voted with the majority. In June 1919, however, when the United States
Senate passed the suffrage amendment, Connecticut's two senators voted

"no."[82] Despite their opposition, the full Senate passed the Amendment, and by the summer of 1920, the required thirty-six states ratified the 19th Amendment, and women gained the right to vote. Sadly, Connecticut was not among those first thirty-six states.

In the immediate aftermath of ratification, thirty-four Connecticut women vied for public office as candidates for State Representatives in the 1920 election. Four women won: Helen Jewett (D-Tolland), Mary Hooker (R-Hartford), Emily Sophie Brown (R-Naugatuck), and Lillian Frink (R-Canterbury).[83] By 1931, forty-seven women had been elected to seats in the Connecticut legislature.[84]

After securing the franchise, women's organizations pondered how they would develop, influence, and affect legislative programs and government policies. One entity that would carry on with a large part of the organizational and lobbying work in the public sphere was the League of Women Voters.

During the 1920s, and later during the Depression years, women lobbied through the Connecticut League of Women Voters to gain legislative approval for a number of measures central to women. Among the legislative enactments during Governor Cross's tenure was the elimination of sweatshops, restriction of hours of work for women and children, and eventually, in 1937, women gained the right to sit on juries.[85]

Ella Grasso, in the 1940s and 1950s, turned to the Connecticut League of Women Voters, which became for her the "best political internship possible for an aspiring politician."[86] She helped establish a League unit in the town of Suffield, Connecticut, adjacent to Windsor Locks where she and Tom Grasso lived. Membership in the League, she later explained, was a "great privilege. My activities with the League have influenced my life tremendously—providing me with incentive and encouragement."[87] As a League member, Ella learned a great deal about the structure of Connecticut government and about the issues that faced Connecticut and its citizens. As she explained, it gave her "the most detailed and intimate exposure to the workings of local government."[88]

Furthermore, she noted that being in the League "teaches you to understand issues, to formulate programs, and to learn legislative procedures," and "you must also learn how to use facts to influence legislation or legislators. So this was a very good experience in how to be a good lobbyist. And I like to think that lobbying in the public interest is the best kind of lobbying."[89]

During those years as a League member, she learned "three political facts of life" that stayed with her throughout her political career: "one, if you keep talking about something long enough it suddenly was an idea whose time has come; second, I learned the importance of the media; and last, I learned the importance of enlisting the support and help of constituents."[90]

Interestingly, years later she confided another benefit she acquired from participation in the League. In those years, she explained, she was reticent about speaking in front of the public. However, she credited the League not only for training her on the issues but providing the opportunity to speak publicly about them, and she added that once she got to speak with some frequency "it just came more naturally."[91]

The fact that the League of Women Voters played a major role in shaping the political careers of many women is well documented. Former United Nations Ambassador Jeane Kirkpatrick, in a monograph entitled *Political Women*, concluded that nearly 40 percent of the nation's female office holders in 1970 had been active in the League prior to holding public office.[92] In a manner of speaking, the League of Women Voters served as a "kind of farm club" for women politicians and "Ella Grasso was one of those individuals."[93]

As a non-partisan organization, however, the League requires members to resign their affiliation if they enter partisan politics. Ella complied and explained that when an individual wants to "translate programs into action, then you have to learn to work within the political structure."[94] And she added that, "I think that is why I went into government because I realized early on that if I was concerned with problems, the best way of getting them solved was to be part of the decision making process."[95] For Ella Grasso, stepping into the world of politics was a major step that would place her in a public arena characterized by one male politician as a "world of sharks."[96]

4

INVOLVED IN THE MAKING OF
A GOVERNMENT

Soon after their marriage, Ella and Tom Grasso took up residence at 13 Olive Street in Windsor Locks across the street from her parents' home at 12 Olive Street. That decision would prove beneficial because as their children were born, Susane in 1948 and James in 1951, Ella's parents would be nearby to assist with their care and well-being. "I was fortunate," Ella explained, "to live near my parents like an extended family situation. Some of the concern for the children's care and the management of the household was lessened by the exchange of duties."[1]

In Ella's mind, the Olive Street neighborhood "was an area of modest, well-kept homes, carefully tended lawns and a genuine sense of neighborliness."[2] The neighborhood included Ella's Uncle Nat (Natale) Tambussi and his wife Rose and their family, and neighbors "all around" who knew Ella "since before she was born."[3] "My children," she explained, "were living in a familiar neighborhood . . . where their mother had been born. So it was almost like a little enclave and I had no qualms."[4] "I was lucky to live on Olive Street," she noted, "like all working mothers I worked hard at my being true to my responsibilities." Furthermore, Ella emphasized, "all my neighbors were family so my children were protected."[5] She noted in talking about her parents that, "close family ties were precious to me. Our two families shared everything. Often, my mother and I would meet in the street halfway between our houses to exchange dishes of food."[6]

Clearly, that close proximity enabled Ella to eventually undertake a full-time commitment to public service. Not only did they exchange dishes of food, Ella's parents also became their grandchildren's baby-sitters. "If there was a late meeting or late dinner," recalls James Grasso, "my sister and I would be shipped across the street to my grandparents to sleep in my mother's childhood bed in my grandparent's house." In fact, "my grandfather would take us to school and would take us back from school and stay with us until our parents came home." This provided his mother with "more ease of movement than other people had" at that time and enabled Ella to pursue her career in politics and public service in which she "found satisfaction."[7]

A large part of Ella's parental responsibilities and duties fell onto the shoulders of her parents, and it remained a vital factor in allowing Ella to pursue her career in politics without worrying about household duties such as preparing meals or watching over her children at night as they were in good hands with their grandparents. While Ella wrote that, "I don't think my children were neglected, physically or emotionally," the support network she had of having her parents close by clearly was enormously helpful in her absence.[8]

She pointed out that "I did not need to worry about where I would leave my children when I was not there. I did not need to worry that I might not have prepared dinner properly because my mother would have started it before I got home. I think it made for removal of lots of frustrations and problems that other couples do have to face now."[9]

Having grandparents nearby "meant that my brother and I had a constant source of real safe, real loving childcare," explained Susane Grasso, Ella's daughter. "If it hadn't been for my grandparents . . . my mother would have had a much different destiny . . . there is no question."[10] And since Ella was considered a "horrible cook,"[11] eating meals prepared by Ella's mother was probably more appealing to the Grasso children.

Six months after her initial employment with the State Employment Service in 1942, Ella moved into a position as Assistant Director of Research for the War Manpower Commission in Connecticut, which had taken over the responsibilities of the Connecticut State Employment Service.[12] She served in that capacity until 1946, utilizing her skills and talents in the field of labor statistics.

Then, for six years during the post–World War II period, Ella "withdrew from my lifestyle of participation and involvement, quit my job and vegetated." This fallow period may be explained because this was the time period when she had her first child, her daughter Susane (1948), and felt some family pressure to stay at home and start a family. Her son James would be born in 1951. Traditionally, Italian mothers focused on domestic duties, and Ella fell into that pattern. However, "this phase was short-lived and never repeated."[13]

While employed with the War Manpower Commission, Ella became acquainted with Chester Bowles who headed the state Office of Price Administration and who later went to Washington to head the national office. It was an association that would later lead Ella to become politically involved in the Democratic Party. When Bowles ran successfully for Governor in 1948, and unsuccessfully for reelection in 1950, Ella supported him in both election runs. He campaigned on a liberal, pro-labor platform, and that served to draw Ella's interest, attention, and support. The Democratic campaign platform, which "impressed" Ella, called for an increase in the minimum wage, an extension of workmen's compensation insurance, and a statewide effort to build low cost housing.[14]

Chester Bowles' gubernatorial programs and reform efforts commenced in January 1949 and led to legislative turmoil. Bowles himself, looking back on his gubernatorial years, wrote that "we tried to do too much too quickly."[15] His liberal bent went against the grain of Connecticut's conservative Land of Steady Habits tradition. He surrounded himself with "bright young people," a brain trust, which prepared an agenda that attempted to accomplish a great deal in a very short time.[16] These ambitious aides, several of whom went on to distinguished careers of their own, included Edward J. Logue (later President of the New York State Urban Development Corp.), Abram Chayes (later General

Counsel for the U.S. State Department and Professor of Law at Harvard University), Joseph Lyford (formerly a *New York Herald-Tribune* staff writer), and Penn Kimball (formerly of *Time Magazine*).[17]

Among the first legislative efforts Governor Bowles proposed was to end segregation in the state National Guard. That measure passed the General Assembly and Connecticut became the first state to desegregate its military units.[18] He proposed a bond issue for new dormitories at the University of Connecticut campus, and he urged expansion of powers for the state Interracial Commission to enable it to examine complaints of discrimination in public housing, hotels, and restaurants. In addition, his agenda included government reorganization and consolidation of state agencies, creation of a state Housing Department, spending increases for state mental hospital expansion, and a school building bond issue of $25,000,000.[19] But his proposal to abolish the state sales tax and replace it with an income tax created a political firestorm and strong political opposition even within his own political party's legislative ranks. His tax proposal was doomed, and in Bowles' judgment, "it never had a chance."[20] The resulting turbulence produced "more political fireworks than any comparable period in the century."[21]

The result was Bowles' defeat in the 1950 election and a firm Democratic and Republican Party credo was born: publicly supporting an income tax was the death knell for any statewide candidate. Despite Bowles' election loss, Ella formally joined the Democratic Party in 1951 in her hometown of Windsor Locks.[22] She had originally registered as a Republican, like her father, when she became a voter. Eventually, she switched and became a registered Democrat because of the party's stand on issues raised during Bowles' tenure as Governor.

During the Bowles' years, Ella's interest in running for elective office was stimulated, and in 1952 she sought the Democratic nomination for state representative from Windsor Locks. Two years before that, the town had become eligible for a second legislative seat, which the Connecticut Constitution provided once the population of a town topped

5,000 people. (The 1950 census revealed a population of 5,221). Her husband encouraged her to make the bid for the state legislature, and he noted, "there was never a regret"[23] about that initial decision to seek public office.

She found herself, however, in a "bitter primary fight," against her neighbor Gladys Lynskey. The issue that was used against Ella "was the fact that she had been a registered Republican and only joined the Democrats a year before."[24] The primary was "difficult because of the intimacy but it ended up being a healthy experience,"[25] Ella noted, because she won and would go on to win the general election for the legislative post. She campaigned in the general election with fervor and enthusiasm, focusing on issues that she had become familiar with during her participation in the League of Women Voters. The issues included abolishing the inefficient structure of county government, eliminating duplication of services offered by the state and local governments, and streamlining the often archaic, patronage-laden court system. All of those issues became focal points of her campaign discourse, and they would become the basis for her legislative agenda once she reached the grand halls of the State House of Representatives.

Ella described her first two years in the state legislature as the time and place, where she served her "apprenticeship in government,"[26] as "absolute bliss."[27] Ella was one of forty-three women elected to the Connecticut House of Representatives in 1952. There were, however, no women elected to serve in the upper chamber that year. In 1953, the House of Representatives and the Executive branch were in the strong grip of the Republican Party, however the Democrats controlled the Senate 19–17. So, as a lowly freshman legislator and member of the minority party, those first two years would seem less than blissful to any objective observer. But those years proved useful to Ella as she learned the legislative process—a process she mastered quickly.

During her first years in the General Assembly, Ella introduced a number of bills on the issues for which she had campaigned. Although the House of Representatives did not pass those bills, she was encouraged to introduce them and testify before the appropriate committees, and she deluged the press with news releases outlining the benefits of her proposed legislation. One issue that garnered widespread notice for Ella Grasso was the GOP-led removal of pasteurization dates on milk bottle caps. Ella led the fight to have them put back on bottle caps, submitting a petition with the signatures of over one thousand housewives demanding that dates be put back on caps.[28] Her efforts on that issue were successful; the dates were restored to the bottle caps.

Her hard work as a freshman legislator was noticed by members of the Laurel Club, a group of reporters who covered the State Capitol for various state newspapers. She was later chosen as the "Most Hardworking Legislator" and "Best State Ticket Material," noteworthy honors for the Windsor Locks native.[29]

She was, in her own words, "just a one man army."[30] In reality, Ella Grasso was the "star of that freshman class," [31]and she came to the attention of the Democratic State Chairman John Moran Bailey. One of John Bailey's strengths as a party leader was that he "did have a real eye for talent,"[32] and in recognizing Ella's abilities he recognized her as a "coming star."[33] The Chairman's recognition would transform her career. He became Ella Grasso's political mentor, as had Sister DeChantal and Professor Amy Hewes become academic mentors at pivotal stages earlier in her life.

John M. Bailey had been elected Connecticut Democratic Party Chairman in 1946. The only son of a wealthy Hartford physician, he was educated at Catholic University in Washington, D.C., and received his law degree from Harvard. Politically active in the cauldron of the Connecticut capitol city's political battles, Bailey had become a protégé and later rival of Hartford's long-time Democratic boss Thomas Spellacy.

Bailey took notice of the energetic, quick thinking, and smart thirty-four-year-old legislator from Windsor Locks. He saw a woman of intelligence with a "good brain,"[34] who not only knew the issues but also projected a sense of political acumen unusual in a first term legislator. John Bailey "saw in Mrs. Grasso a bright, aggressive yet personable figure of tremendous appeal to voters as a woman and as a member of a rising ethnic group that was challenging the political supremacy of the incumbent Irish."[35] Bailey encouraged Ella's legislative initiatives in her first legislative session, even though he did not support her reform proposals. The pragmatic Bailey, as one veteran Connecticut politician observed, "would never hold it against you" even though he disagreed with your proposals."[36] He thought of her as representative of the "highly educated and socially concerned segment of his party."[37] Another observer said he was drawn to her because of her "brainpower and he was looking for a Democratic Clare Booth Luce — a woman who could win."[38] (Mrs. Luce, a Republican, had been elected to the national House of Representatives in 1942 from Fairfield County — the first Connecticut woman ever elected to the Congress of the United States).

The Bailey-Grasso friendship, mutual respect, and political alliance grew rapidly during that 1953 legislative session. So vibrant and productive was the political chemistry between them that Bailey, years later admitted that, "Ella helped put this whole thing together for the Democrats back in '53."[39] It was a symbiotic relationship that James Grasso, Ella's son, characterized many years later as "purely platonic," but she "idolized him."[40]

Symbolic of their mutual admiration and evolving working partnership was the fact that John Bailey provided an office for Ella Grasso in his law firm in downtown Hartford close to the capitol. There, largely out of sight, Ella put together the Democratic strategy for the 1954 gubernatorial election. Among other things, she wrote position papers and press statements and became the "chief architect" of the 1954 Democratic Party platform.[41] In fact, "by 1954, when it came to the platform Bailey put great faith in . . . Ella Grasso of Windsor Locks. He . . . trusted her as a sound and practical political thinker."[42] The 1954 Democratic platform was "designed to please various pressure groups including organized labor, state employees, farmers and educators."[43] The platform proposed additional aid to towns for school building projects and teacher salary raises; more medical, dental, and veterinary education facilities; increased workmen's compensation and unemployment compensation; and increased salaries for state employees.[44] In addition, the platform called for a statewide "Constitutional Convention to rewrite the charter to change representation in the State Legislature; abolish counties and governmental units; abolish minor court system and set up a new 'career' system; and establish a direct primary system for nominating political candidates."[45]

This was the time period Ella Grasso learned the art of politics at the side of the state's dominant political party leader. During her political apprenticeship, she learned about the state party organization, met and became acquainted with local Democratic Party leaders from around Connecticut, and observed the consummate political skills Bailey exercised in his dealings with Democratic legislators, elected officials, and party stalwarts. In those days, Ella said she learned an important lesson. "The most important lesson I learned from John Bailey was patience," she explained. "The objective may not be secured in a day or a week, but you may work toward it. Don't panic under pressure."[46]

She would take heed of Bailey's advice in the months leading up to the Democratic state nominating convention in the summer of 1954. Ella told John Bailey that she wanted to run on the Democratic ticket for Secretary of the State. Bailey, however, explained he had made a commitment to run State Representative Elizabeth Zdunczyk (D-Southington) for that position. "Do me a favor," Bailey reportedly told Ella, "postpone running and run in the next election." Ella complied with his request and Mrs. Zdunczyk, Bailey's candidate, went on to defeat in her 1954 run for Secretary of the State.[47]

Looking back on this period in her life, there seems little doubt that Ella, the quick study, also became Ella, the political wholesaler—a person whom one veteran Connecticut politician characterizes as an individual who "makes his reputation on issues, on philosophy, and major policy."[48] She became Bailey's "issue philosopher."[49] John Bailey was the political operator "who loved the wheeling and dealing side of politics." He "left the issues to others," and Ella "moved into the issue role."[50]

In that issue role, she worked alone, and it would prove to be a fast track road to getting ahead in the rough and tumble political environment. It was during this time, as John Bailey's confidante, political ally, and "strong right thinking arm,"[51] that her eyes were opened to the hard realities of the male-dominated political world so skillfully controlled by Chairman Bailey. This was the moment when, as a woman new to public life, Ella Grasso emerged as a young political operative who would follow advice Eleanor Roosevelt once proffered to women thinking about entering politics: "Get into the game and stay in it";[52] and "All women in public life needed to develop skin as tough as rhinoceros hide."[53] It was advice Ella Grasso took to heart, building a life and career in politics where strength, determination, firmness, and toughness are necessary ingredients of success. "And through her close association with John Bailey, a Bailey-Grasso partnership developed, that enabled Ella to come along fast in the state's political world because of her ability to be useful in a great many ways to the state party leadership."[54] She learned to "play the game as men do," following the sage advice Eleanor Roosevelt suggested in an article she wrote in 1928. In reality, she used her skills and talents not only for the benefit of John Bailey and the Democratic Party, but also for Abraham A. Ribicoff, who would become the Democratic Party's standard-bearer in the gubernatorial election of 1954, and later for Ribicoff's successor John Dempsey.

During that election campaign, Ella was behind the scenes developing public policy ideas, writing speeches for Ribicoff, and offering campaign proposals on issues that would become the basis for the successful Democratic statewide campaign. "I was able to become involved in the making of a government," she told a reporter. "That was the year Abe Ribicoff ran for Governor . . . and I helped bring him up to date on all the things happening in Connecticut."[55]

The year 1954 appeared to be a year when the Connecticut Republicans would win reelection and hold on to the statewide office they had won in 1950. Governor John D. Lodge, the scion of an old Massachusetts family, was popular, and he and his Italian-born wife, Francesca, had made a positive impression on the Connecticut electorate. But Lodge, the first Connecticut Governor to serve a four-year term, had pushed through several unpopular tax increases, including a new corporate tax from 3 percent to 3.75 percent and sales taxes from 2 percent to 3 percent.[56] He also became embroiled in an ongoing, intraparty political fight between the conservative wing of the state GOP and the more moderate wing that he led. But it was the general issues of taxation that were the "most troublesome for Lodge," according to Meade Alcorn, a leading Connecticut Republican and the Republican National Committee Chairman.[57]

On the Democratic side of the aisle, the party's gubernatorial nominee was former Hartford Congressman Abraham A. Ribicoff, who had run unsuccessfully for the U.S. Senate in 1952. However, Ribicoff showed "unusual vote getting ability"[58] in that election, and as a result was selected to lead the party ticket in 1954. Interestingly, a young U.S. Senator from Massachusetts, John Fitzgerald Kennedy, presented the keynote address at the 1954 Democratic State Convention in Hartford.[59] It would mark the beginning of a long political and personal alliance between Ribicoff, Bailey, and a future President of the United States.

On Friday evening, June 25, 1954, the young Massachusetts Senator, accompanied by his wife, spoke to a "well filled" auditorium in Hartford's Bushnell Memorial Hall.[60] Kennedy, in his keynote speech, focused his remarks on foreign policy taking issue with the "lack of a strong foreign policy"[61] in the Eisenhower administration, particularly in the area of Indochina policy. "I challenge anyone to say what the policy of the United States is or has been in Indochina during the past several months. If there is such a policy neither the American people nor the Indochinese nor the French nor our enemies know it."[62] Little would he or his audience know how vastly important that part of the world would become by 1961, when Kennedy himself became the President of the United States.

The 1954 election campaign focused on issues that were of paramount interest to Ella Grasso. They included sweeping constitutional reform proposals such as abolition of county government, equitable legislative representation, reorganization of the state court system and a call for direct primaries for political party nominations. The Democratic Party platform was largely the handiwork of Ella Grasso, whose impressive writing skills and sound political judgments Bailey trusted to create a reasonable platform that would have widespread appeal to the Connecticut voter. "I recognized her as a woman," said Bailey, "who was very devoted to the Democratic Party and its principles. She was always willing to work. She was very helpful to me in my position as State Chairman. A very capable writer, she was always good with words."[63]

Ella also served as "Bailey's bridge to the liberal good government element of the Democratic Party that he wanted kept within the Democratic fold."[64] She strategized, wrote position papers and speeches for Ribicoff which reflected her adroit and creative writing talents, and she immersed herself, along with Herman Wolf, a veteran political publicist, in the Ribicoff campaign. For his part, Ribicoff remembered the 1954 campaign as a "small, lean campaign" and the staff came down to "one person — young Ella Grasso and she was superb. I depended on her completely for the platform, the issues and the backup leading to that election in November."[65]

Abraham A. Ribicoff won the 1954 election for Governor by a margin of 3,115 votes. It is important to emphasize, however, how significant that Ribicoff victory was that year. While the other statewide office remained in Republican hands, the General Assembly split with the House of Representatives in Republican control 187–92 (including forty women) and the Democrats controlling the Senate 20–16 with Florence Finney (R-Greenwich) becoming the only female in the upper chamber.[66]

Ribicoff became the man who, as Governor, would drive the machinery of government and would be in a position where he could do the most good for the greatest number.[67] Ribicoff's victory also provided the impetus for the Connecticut Democratic Party, under John Bailey's leadership, to build a strong statewide organization that would become, in the words of journalist and veteran political observer Theodore White, the most formidable, successful and "efficient Democratic machine of the Atlantic Coast."[68] Within that organization, there was no one closer to John Bailey than Abe Ribicoff, and there was no one closer to both of them than Ella Grasso.

Abe Ribicoff never tired of saying publicly and privately that he attributed his success in politics to John Bailey. "John was indispensable. I don't think without John Bailey I would have achieved my political success."[69] And one element of his success was that "Bailey took care of the politics. I didn't bother with the politics. They would go through John Bailey to me and I would go through John Bailey to them. But it was a wonderful working relationship and it indicates that you can have successful governmental leadership and use the best of politics and that's when it works.[70]

Ribicoff also attributed his success to the important role played by Ella Grasso. She had been reelected to a second term as State Representative in 1954 and became an Assistant Democratic Floor Leader, the first woman to hold that position in the lower house of the General Assembly. Ella assumed a critical role as the new Governor's "most important unofficial braintruster."[71] In that role, she was "very valuable,"[72] Ribicoff explained. "Ella Grasso was a very superior person. Intellectually Ella was top of the line. I would often use Ella to write legislation,"[73] Ribicoff stated. Further, he pointed out that "There was a small handful of people who were in on the functions of the state, politically and legislatively and from an executive standpoint. I would say there was no one closer than Ella."[74]

For ambitious Ella Grasso, those years of Ribicoff's first term were exciting and stimulating. As Bailey and Ribicoff's protege and trusted confidante, Ella was also earning plaudits from State Capitol reporters and journalists. In 1955, she was chosen as the "most hardworking" legislator and recognized as "Best State Ticket Material."[75] And she was seen as one of Bailey's "greatest students."[76] It was also a time when she would absorb lessons that would be of inestimable value for a future governor. Among those lessons Ella learned how vitally important it is for a Governor to have a strong party leader who could effectively maintain party discipline, especially among the legislators, and serve also as a conduit to local party officials and who would oversee and monitor the progress of the party's legislative agenda. In addition, that leader would keep the lines of communication open to state legislators and party stalwarts, and would attend and monitor legislative caucuses and the General Assembly on a daily basis. This was the Bailey formula and it proved successful.

As a result of her association with Governor Ribicoff, Ella also came to understand the significant power that emanates from the Executive Office of the Governor and how that power and the individual who wields it can be most effective. She also learned the "importance, the integrity of compromise, the necessity to get varying opinions, varying points of view"[77] in order to save the basic idea on key legislative matters. For Ella Grasso, it was clear evidence of her belief, formed during her years at Mount Holyoke and made clear during the economic collapse of the 1930s that there is a close, interdependent relationship between government, politics, and the economy and people's livelihood depend on positive leadership which must come from government and political leaders.

Her association with Governor Ribicoff and John Bailey resulted in Ella's desire to exercise and expand her role in Connecticut's government. She reminded John Bailey of his earlier promise to support her bid for statewide office in the next election. In her late thirties, she emerged from her political apprenticeship as a "seasoned" politician with a firm understanding of Connecticut's governmental and legislative processes, sharpened political skills, determined political ambitions, and an ability to articulate the issues to the electorate. A respected member of the Fourth Estate, who covered the political news at the State Capitol for one of the state's major newspapers, noted in early 1955 that Ella Grasso "has been frequently mentioned as a possible nominee in 1958 for Secretary of the State."[78]

One way to lay the groundwork for a potential run for statewide office was not to run in 1956 for a third legislative term in the state House of Representatives. Freed up from legislative duties, she would be able to devote time to develop statewide support for a possible run in 1958 for Secretary of the State. Chairman Bailey urged her not to run for a third term and once again she accepted his advice. However, she did remain Chairman of the Democratic State Platform Committee, a post she retained in every election through 1968. Also, he insisted that Ella, in 1956, run for one of two slots on the Democratic National Committee, a post that would give her statewide recognition and would help lay the groundwork for her eventual candidacy for Secretary of the State. She defeated Dorothy Satti of New London 35–2 for the national committeewoman post. Satti was the wife of the New London Democratic Party leader who "was out of favor with the state leadership."[79] A keen observer of the Connecticut political scene confirmed that Mrs. Satti's removal was a "slap at Satti" by John Bailey.[80] Consequently, Ella set out to visit various Connecticut cities and towns befriending key Democratic leaders in those localities, and at the same time gain statewide recognition. While she later reported that she found the National Committee seat an "anesthetizing bore,"[81] her election to the post "cheered" one person in particular: her beloved Mount Holyoke College mentor Professor Amy Hewes. Miss Hewes, who was hospitalized at the time, received the news of Ella Grasso's election while recovering from a fall.[82] Ella's election to the DNC seat brought enormous pleasure and satisfaction to the former Mount Holyoke faculty member. It was Amy Hewes who had been one of the first to recognize Ella's leadership potential and her outstanding abilities and keen intellectual competency.

The National Committee position allowed Ella to work unfettered on Ribicoff's legislative program, to continue participation in his brain trust, to edit and publish the state Democratic Party Newsletter, to keep track of the party's legislative proposals in the General Assembly and all the while work alongside John Bailey on policy matters. Therefore, the two-year interregnum between 1956–1958 was pointedly aimed at further refining her political skills and strengthening her ties to local politicians, and working to gain statewide organizational support for her bid to be the Democratic nominee for Secretary of the State of Connecticut in 1958.

Ella's desire to run for that statewide position was consistent with Bailey's ticket balancing formula. Ever conscious and aware of Connecticut's ethnic diversity, largely concentrated in the state's urban areas, Bailey carefully assembled a statewide ticket that was specifically aimed at attracting diverse ethnic, geographic, and gender support while also including some longtime Bailey allies.[83]

The 1958 Democratic ticket remains one of the best examples of Bailey's political strategy to run candidates who would appeal to a broad spectrum of Connecticut voters and who would exemplify the ethnic makeup of the electorate. Obviously, Governor Ribicoff would again head the ticket and he was the first person of Jewish ancestry to win the Governorship of the State of Connecticut. He would be joined on the slate by Irish-born John Dempsey of Putnam to be a candidate for Lieutenant Governor. In recognition of the growing Italian voting bloc among the electorate, the Democrat ticket would include two candidates John Speziale of Torrington for State Treasurer and Ella Grasso of Windsor Locks for Secretary of the State. The under-ticket was rounded out by the choice of Albert Coles of Bridgeport for Attorney General and Raymond Thatcher of East Hampton for State Comptroller. The choice of Coles represents Bailey's recognition of the need for candidates from one of the state's urban centers and Thatcher was a longtime ally of Bailey's from a small town. This carefully balanced slate of candidates stands out as a clear example of the careful attention Bailey gave to the political appeal of a carefully balanced ticket reaching virtually all geographic regions of the state and including various ethnic representation that would enhance the appeal of the Democratic Party candidates at the polls that November.

Even the makeup of the Congressional slate of candidates reflected Bailey's masterful ticket balancing strategy. For the U.S. Senate seat Thomas J. Dodd (Irish); for the U.S. House of Representatives Emilio Q. Daddario (Italian), Robert Giaimo (Italian), Frank Kowalski (Polish), former Governor Chester Bowles (WASP), Donald J. Irwin (WASP), and John Monagan (Irish). The result of the 1958 election was a Democratic Party sweep of all congressional seats, all statewide constitutional offices, and majorities in the General Assembly- including a slim three-vote majority in the State House of Representatives for the first time in sixty years.[84] Ella Grasso was victorious in that electoral landslide and the daughter of twentieth century pilgrims became Connecticut's sixty-fourth Secretary of the State.

The 1958 election victory was a signal triumph for John M. Bailey's Democratic organization. It was both a decided vote of confidence in Governor Abraham A. Ribicoff and a stamp of approval of his administration's programs and policies. At the same time it underscored the Democratic Party's emergence as the majority party under Bailey's leadership, which proved to be a major turning point that ushered in a long period of Democratic Party rule in both the executive and legislative branches of Connecticut's state government. Ribicoff's reelection, by a precedent setting margin of 246,000 votes, would enable him to more easily implement his party's campaign promises with a working majority in both legislative houses.

Ella Grasso's election by a plurality of 150,366 votes over Mary Fahey (R), as the state's eighth woman Secretary of the State and the first woman of Italian ancestry to win statewide office, was a proud moment. Since the 1938 election, the position of Secretary of the State had been viewed as the traditional woman's place on the statewide ticket. That year, the first woman to hold the office, Republican Sara B. Crawford of Westport, won her party's nomination and went on to win the office in the November general election. Subsequently, six women held the position in succession with one exception. In 1945, Charles J. Prestia (D) of New Britain was elected to the position. The office was not perceived as a launching point for furthering one's political career. In truth, the Secretary's position, which paid an annual salary of $8,000, was statutorily designated as the chief elections official for the state with other limited authority. One reporter saw it as a job that "has more glamour than power, but it has distinct advantages for the ambitious person canny enough to make the most of it."[85]

Ella Grasso was certainly ambitious. She was determined to succeed and prosper politically in an office, which "opened a large window . . . on the world of Connecticut."[86] She began that endeavor by providing the Secretary's Capitol office as a daily meeting place for the State Chairman, Democratic legislative leaders, and Ella herself to converse, plan, and strategize the party's legislative agenda.

That agenda was ambitious, although controversial. It included abolishing county government, reapportionment of the legislative representation through a constitutional convention, reconfiguring the state's judicial system, and providing for reorganizing several government agencies. The Democratic Party had included these proposals in its campaign platform in 1954 and again in 1958 and they were principally Ella's ideas. The reform proposals reflect a lesson she learned while a member of the League of Women Voters—if you keep talking about something long enough it suddenly was an idea whose time had come. As anticipated, she reminded John Bailey, Governor Ribicoff, and the General Assembly's legislative leadership that since the Democrats controlled both houses of the legislature their responsibility for implementing the party's promises was now in their hands.

Her approach was that leaders had "no excuse not to live up to the party's platform promises."[87] Ella "shrilled-voiced it to us continually," recalled Bailey, and in so doing she had assumed another role that of the "Conscience of the Democratic Party."[88] In her eyes, the "test of responsibility comes in the translation of platform into program into action."[89] Indeed, one of the most rewarding experiences in political life, she said, comes when the "items of the platform on which I campaigned for public office, introduced support legislation, . . . become law."[90] "It was an exciting time," she recalled. "There was the challenge and the opportunity and we Democrats had to keep faith with all the things we had said. We had called county government obsolete; now we had to do away with county government. We had said the court system especially the municipal plan with judges going in and out of office according to which party controlled the executive branch- should be replaced with a permanent system. Now we had to do something about it."[91]

Forty-year-old Ella Grasso was where she wanted to be: holding a position in government where she could have the "greatest opportunity to work with citizens, to help with all kind of informal lobbies, to be sure that good legislation was achieved."[92] It was an office that she would utilize to effect substantial change in Connecticut's government and further her own political ambitions. She was truly "involved in the making of a government."[93]

❧ 5 ❧

WORKING IN THE VINEYARDS

Ella Grasso embarked on her tenure as Secretary of the State with her usual high energy, enthusiasm, commitment, and determination to succeed and excel at the tasks and challenges that lay before her. Inheriting an office that was the vital record-keeping agency for the state, the Secretary of the State came into contact with lawyers, business leaders, and corporate executives, as well as local election officials, namely Town Clerks and Registrars of Voters.

Large numbers of lawyers and businessmen customarily appeared in the Secretary's office to file trademark papers, security agreements, incorporation papers, and other legal documents required by state law. Contacts with Town Clerks and Registrars of Voters of the 169 towns and municipalities was another vital component of the Secretary's duties, since local municipal officers implemented the election laws, and the Clerks and Registrars also carried out legislative mandates that the General Assembly passed concerning voter qualifications, voting procedures, and election laws.

The Secretary of the State's office is also an office of unlimited opportunity to build a base of public service — not only in the areas spelled out in Connecticut's Constitution and Statutes but as a base from which one could build widespread public and voter recognition for an ambitious incumbent determined to advance politically. "It is a great office for doing that if you've got the energy . . . and she did," noted Washington *Post* columnist David Broder. He frequently visited Hartford to confer with John M. Bailey about the Kennedy campaign strategies for the 1960 election and recalls visiting Ella Grasso in her state capitol office. Her energy and enthusiasm for politics and public service was quite evident to that keen observer of the political scene.[1]

Ella's second floor office in the State Capitol, across the hall from the Governor's Executive Chambers, became a meeting place for concerned civic organizations and groups to gather since accommodations for organizations was virtually non-existent elsewhere in the building. "I gave space to the League of Women Voters," Ella explained, and her office was dubbed a "people's lobby" bringing visitors, good government organizations, and people unfamiliar with the legislative lobbying process to the Secretary's domain. "Everybody who wanted to have a meeting place and didn't know where to go came to my office," she recalled.[2] Her office was also a "gathering place for reporters . . . she . . . understood every facet of government," noted a Bridgeport *Post* editorial writer. In fact, she would willingly explain the most complicated statute or legislative proposal in layman's language. Ella was the interpreter for the press."[3]

Additionally, when the General Assembly was in session, her office was used daily by the Democratic Party's legislative team and party chairman John M. Bailey. It was conveniently located on the same floor as the House of Representatives with the Senate chamber one floor above and was a convenient location to discuss the legislative agenda for the day. Her office became known as "Ella's Place,"[4] and it "came to resemble clubhouse sessions of a football team in first place," and John M. Bailey "gloried in it all."[5] It was there the party's political chief and the Ribicoff brain trust (Ella Grasso, Jon Newman, C. Perrie Phillips, and George Conkling) worked together with the legislative leadership to develop the Democratic stance on upcoming legislation. Ella's role in these discussions was crucial because she frequently reminded the party leaders of their Democratic platform promises and public commitment to abolishing county government and supporting court reform — issues she had long backed during her tenure in the legislature. The Ribicoff

team pushed for and achieved legislative approval of court reform, abol-
ishment of county governments, reorganization of the Department of
Health and the creation of both a Department of Mental Health and a
Department of Consumer Protection, as well as a law banning discrimination in housing on the basis of race, religion, or nationality.[6] The bill
to ban discrimination in housing, which had been pushed by a coalition
of "blacks, labor, and liberal groups," was not favored initially by John
Bailey.[7] Jon Newman (later a federal judge) and Ella prodded him, and
Bailey eventually supported the bill. As a result, "Connecticut became
one of the first states to have a statute prohibiting discrimination on the
basis of race, religion, or nationality in dwellings of five or more con-
tiguous units.[8]

Bailey's politically skillful handling of Democratic legislators and
Grasso's riding herd on them, as well, were important components in
building the Ribicoff legislative record as progressive and forward looking. Bailey's approach to the legislators was that he did "not demand that
the bill be accepted," noted former legislator Duane Lockard. "But he is
a convincing advocate. By patient explanation of the circumstances surrounding a bill, and probable loss or gain for the party, he can inveigle
support where none seemed possible."[9] The Democrats trumpeted all of
these actions as having been undertaken without raising taxes or imposing the political poison of an income tax.

In the months following the 1959 legislative session, Ella Grasso embarked on a concerted effort to enhance her own image and public recognition by moving around Connecticut, meeting local government
leaders, and also making contacts with Democratic Party officials and
non-political people, as well. One of her most skillful political decisions
was to announce that "she and her elections division attorney Molly Toro,
would make personal visits" to each town to meet with the town clerks
and registrars of voters throughout the state.[10] This announcement was
news to the local officials, who were accustomed to meeting the Secretary of the State twice yearly at the statewide Secretary's Town Clerks

Conference. Ella's decision was also a surprise to Molly Toro, Elections Attorney in Grasso's office, who had not been informed of Ella's decision prior to the Secretary's announcement. Molly recalled that she "couldn't believe it. I said to her, 'Ella, why didn't you tell me before so we could at least talk about it.'" Toro remembered Ella replied, "because I thought of it at 2 o'clock in the morning."[11] As a consequence of her early morning brainstorm, Ella would take herself and Molly Toro to each city hall and town hall in the State of Connecticut to discuss election laws, legislative changes that had been mandated by the General Assembly, and other business pertaining to voting, election procedures, and related matters. Her intention, she emphasized, was "to make Connecticut's election officials the most closely knit group in the country."[12] In Toro's opinion, "It was a very constructive thing to do because local officials really appreciated it."[13]

Ella's interpersonal skills and working relations with Molly Toro, Elections Attorney in the Secretary's office, and with other staff in her office (she hired and dismissed numerous deputies during her tenure as Secretary of the State), as well as with legislative leaders around the State Capitol, proved to be stormy. Her feisty temperament and, often, domineering intellectual attitude was often on display behind the scenes in meetings and discussions. Molly Toro remembered numerous heated arguments with Grasso, often so loud that staffer "Mary Romano would go around closing doors and windows," so others would not hear the screaming and yelling between the two. One time, the elections attorney recalled that she was asked to pick up Ella Grasso at home and the two were going to drive to an evening appointment. Toro was late having been detained at the office by a visit from the City Attorney from Bridgeport. Upon arriving in Windsor Locks, Ella berated Toro "What were you doing? What were you thinking not being here on time?" Toro, not easily intimidated replied, "Do you think I was playing games? I had to talk to the city attorney who raised some issues that I had to answer." While these arguments were often lively and fiery, the two remained long-time friends, and Ella later appointed Molly Toro to a judgeship on the Superior Court. But these kinds of outbursts, verbal barrages, and quick tempered reactions usually aimed at staff or associates, were indicative of a tough and often uncompromising attitude of a politician determined to always get her way in the political arena.[14]

Ella's motives for undertaking the statewide travels, however, also had political implications. Her local visits would enable her to meet not only the town clerks and registrars of voters — many of whom were women — but also to pay calls on mayors and first selectmen on their home turf. Obviously, many of those officials, "probably at least half," were members of the Republican party, and those courtesy visits helped build a reservoir of good will across party lines, particularly in small towns throughout the state.[15] These visits also provided her the chance to renew acquaintances with local Democrats including Democratic Town committee members and Democratic State Central Committee people. So this endeavor was an energetic, multi-purpose effort to reach out in a seemingly non-partisan way, which gained Ella Grasso significant political and public good will at the local level.

"She went everywhere," a close aide observed, "and she made a name for herself."[16] As a result, "through intense personal contact," she built up a statewide following, becoming the "main link many people had with state government."[17] The strategy of intense personal contact would become a hallmark of Ella Grasso's political life. At every level of her political career, as Secretary of the State, and, later as Congresswoman in the early 1970s, as well as during her terms as Governor in the mid-1970s, Ella made weekly and monthly visits to each town and city in her Congressional district and, as Governor, throughout the state. That style of reaching out to ordinary citizens, by holding office hours for people to meet personally with her, was key to her political success.

These visits also enabled her to secure press coverage and media attention. In fact, the local and state press closely followed her visits, and as a result newspapers periodically reported on her travels. One account in late September 1959 noted that the Secretary of the State reported she had visited sixty-four towns in Middlesex, New London, and Windham counties. In that report, Grasso explained that the response of the local officials was "excellent" and the "civic interest of many individual citizens who appeared at the meetings was . . . also heartening."[18]

One of the concerns that local officials expressed to the Secretary of the State focused on election moderators. She began to realize after visiting various municipalities that polling place moderators were frequently not "fully instructed regarding the import and the technique of their duties." As a result of those concerns, Ella announced that before "each major election day in the state" she would hold an "instructional session for polling place moderators."[19] Another concern she encountered was the frequent breakdown of voting machines in towns and cities across Connecticut. Ella eventually urged the creation of a statewide "Voting Machine Force" that would be available on Election Day to help eliminate machine breakdowns throughout the state.[20] Another reform, which she favored in the 1958 election campaign, and which eventually became law, was to make voter registration permanent in the state, eliminating the need to re-register each time a voter moved from one town to another.[21]

These modest proposals and reforms often trumpeted in the press and media, reinforced the public's perception that Mrs. Grasso was an activist, conscientious guardian of the state's electoral process, and ever watchful and protective of the voting public's rights and duties under the state's election laws. In sum, she was perceived as ably fulfilling her sworn duties as the chief elections official for all Connecticut elections. And she was putting into practice a lesson learned from the League of Women Voters — the importance of using the media to secure a positive public image for a statewide officeholder.

It was her attention to those good government efforts that enabled Ella Grasso to become well known in virtually every part of the state. "Everyone knows Ella, from one end of the state to the other — they know she's smart and they know they can trust her," said a Democrat who had known her for many years.[22] To many people, she was known simply as "Ella," and she became one of the most familiar political personalities on Connecticut's political scene.

There is little doubt that those contacts made during her statewide travels were not only helpful in building up her personal stature at the local level but they provided a favorable, positive public perception of the Office of the Secretary of the State and the person who occupied that seat. Her continuous public activity brought stature to the office, which had not been traditionally in the public spotlight.

She was urged by the Chief Executive (Governor) to "become involved in agencies and organizations as the governor's liaison to various organizations and non-profit groups," observed Robert Killian a future state Attorney General and Lieutenant Governor.[23] In moving about the state, Ella Grasso also championed the causes of various nonprofit, charitable groups—particularly Cystic Fibrosis (State General Chairman in 1960),[24] Mental Retardation, and Mental Health, which in turn closely identified her with those human service and humanitarian efforts throughout Connecticut. These links connected her with organizations composed of citizen volunteers who would come to feel admiration and respect for the long-term commitments she made to their personal causes. Ella remained closely identified with those charitable efforts throughout her entire public life.

As a result, the regional and statewide associations provided Ella with another network of people who closely identified with her in her official capacity while also recognizing her personal efforts to further their social service program. In turn "she acquired a reputation as a concerned public advocate"[25] at the highest political levels, often hounding the state's chief executive to insure sufficient budgets for state institutions for the retarded.[26] At the same time she worked to advance legislation and the state government's commitment to embracing and expanding programs for the handicapped, disabled, and people with special needs.

One way the Secretary worked to bring the "cause of mental retardation to the forefront was through lobbying the legislature." In 1953, she noted that, "lobbying at the state capitol consisted of a few parents and friends of retarded children. By 1955, the lobbying forces had grown substantially because people became conscious of the fact that mentally retarded people can lead healthy, useful lives." The "consciousness of the legislature had been aroused," in large measure because of her consistent efforts on behalf of these advocacy groups.[27]

Lobbying for the humanitarian causes she espoused became a vital part of what Ella Grasso, a "very compassionate and kind person" continued to do as an elected official. [28]One of her earliest and most enduring achievements was to lead the public effort to require mandatory public education for retarded children.[29] That progressive step placed the Secretary of the State in the public's mind as a compassionate leader, committed to programs and policies, which furthered the state's role in expanding social services but which also engendered enormous public sympathy, grass roots support, and political benefits for Ella Grasso. She became so closely identified with public efforts on behalf of Connecticut's mentally challenged people that, in the minds of parents of these children, Ella Grasso was "almost synonymous with much that has been achieved for their children.[30]

Another result of her personal commitment and dedication to the growing public awareness of Mental Retardation was the 1959 General Assembly approval of legislation creating the Office of Mental Retardation within the Department of Health. That action provided Connecticut with one of the first agencies of state government, anywhere in the United States, supporting humane programs and care for the state's children and adults. Once asked where her interest in the physically disabled and mentally challenged came from, she replied that it emanated from "our gratitude for our own blessings and our firm belief in the principle of sharing of responsibility with those who have problems."[31]

Ella's dedication to these humanitarian causes also emanated from her deeply held, religiously grounded, morally based concern for the less fortunate in society. It was at the core of her moral principles and political commitment to expand the government's role and provide services ameliorating the worries people and families burdened with mental and emotional suffering faced every day.

At the same time, the scope of her responsibilities took on greater breadth and importance as the 1960 presidential election loomed on the national horizon. Governor Ribicoff and John Bailey were early supporters of John F. Kennedy's presidential aspirations, just as they had pushed and sponsored his earlier unsuccessful bid for the Vice Presidential nomination in 1956. Ribicoff, Bailey, and the Connecticut Democratic organization were among the early, most vocal, influential, and politically significant supporters of Kennedy's quest for the presidential nomination in 1960. In fact, many politicians were convinced that Kennedy's Presidential bandwagon really originated in Connecticut.[32]

After the Massachusetts Senator's close election victory in November 1960, Connecticut's political landscape was altered significantly when both Abraham Ribicoff and John Bailey took on national responsibilities in Washington, D.C., Ribicoff was one of the first prominent Democrats Kennedy invited to his Palm Beach, Florida, home shortly after his election. There the Connecticut Governor was given his choice of any Cabinet position he desired (the Attorney General's spot was to go to Robert Kennedy) and he chose to become President Kennedy's Secretary of Health, Education, and Welfare, and John Bailey was designated the Democratic National Committee Chairman. Bailey, however, did retain his state party chairmanship, while handing over day-to-day operation of the Connecticut party to his long-time assistant Katherine Quinn. As a consequence of the President's decisions, Ella Grasso took on day-to-day coordination of the party's legislative agenda, monitoring, cajoling, and strategizing in Bailey's absence. "Her responsibility would be as grand strategist, consultant on content in the Governor's program, and public relations manager." Her counterparts in this responsibility were

C. Perrie Phillips, Deputy Commissioner of Finance (later appointed by Governor Ella Grasso as State Personnel Commissioner, and later a state judge), who was responsible for drafting the administration's programs and helping Democratic legislators with their legislation, and State Senator Arthur Healey (who was also later appointed a state judge, and eventually became a Justice of the Supreme Court of Connecticut), who was the "political captain" of the three member team.[33]

Governor Ribicoff's Lieutenant Governor was John Dempsey, from the town of Putnam in eastern Connecticut. He succeeded Ribicoff in early 1961when Ribicoff joined the Kennedy Cabinet. Even more than his predecessor, Dempsey was totally dependent on the same team of advisors. Dempsey, an Irish Catholic immigrant, had served as legislative floor leader in the General Assembly alongside Ella Grasso in the 1950s and then became Ribicoff's Lieutenant Governor in 1959. He was admired as a genial glad-hander and popular figure, but in large measure, he relied on the "brain trust" for providing legislative initiatives and political guidance during his gubernatorial terms. In fact, Dempsey, years later, frequently referred to one of that inner circle of advisers—Ella Grasso—as his "right hand when I was in office."[34] But Ella's relationship with Governor Dempsey never reached the same level of cordiality as that maintained between herself and Abraham Ribicoff. Ella's superior intellect, political acuity, and outstanding speaking and writing skills were often demonstrated in attitudes and ways that Dempsey and others resented.[35]

The perception developed among many political insiders that Ella was condescending, intolerant of less able and talented people, and displayed little patience for individuals with inferior political skills. These traits of her character would become more unmistakable as she became more prominent and politically known. At the same time, she cultivated a public image of thriftiness, both in her own personal appearance and with public monies. For example, she declined to attend the annual Secretary of the State national conference, saying it would be a waste of public funds to attend. This impression, generated in large part by Ella's unforgettable recollection of the Depression and the necessity to conserve and spend sparingly, was a particularly appealing quality and characteristic, which appealed to the conservative, frugal, old-line Connecticut Yankee mind-set, as well as to other voters in the state.[36]

During the Dempsey years, one Republican lawmaker, Gerald Stevens of Milford, Connecticut, remembered seeing Ella walking through the halls of the Capitol in the company of two men. "She would walk through the halls in sneakers, a skirt, and glasses up on her head and in the company always of two men—John Bailey and John Dempsey." Stevens added that he was told, "these were the three people . . . that made all the decisions and ran the state of Connecticut." Furthermore, the freshman legislator noted, "You had the political boss in the person of John Bailey, you had the brains in the person of Ella Grasso, and you had the personality, the very loveable governor in the person of John Dempsey. A very interesting combination."[37]

Ella's political duties and varied roles also expanded to include writing speeches for John Bailey in his capacity as Chairman of the Democratic National Committee.[38] Moreover, her activities advising Governor Dempsey, strategizing with the legislative leadership, and serving as public relations manager for the party did not diminish. It became obvious that all of these responsibilities, however, "cut the time she gave to the General Assembly."[39] One result was legislative inertia, and the team momentum so successful under former Governor Ribicoff and John Bailey was absent. Dempsey's lack of experience in the Executive Office, his lack of clout within his party's legislative ranks, and the absence of Bailey took its toll on the legislative achievement ledger of the 1961 General Assembly. And it would pick up only upon Bailey's return in late May before the General Assembly adjourned on June 7, 1961. The hand picked "troika" was not successful in achieving any important legislative victories in a General Assembly in which one house was in the control of one party and the other chamber by the party opposite. Once Bailey returned and exerted his experienced hand at the "art of the deal" with his Republican counterpart Ed May, the legislative logjam was broken, and legislative compromises on the budget, on highway construction, school aid and urban renewal assistance were approved.[40]

Despite wearing many hats and her sometimes tempestuous personal relationships with legislators and staff, Ella's role as the Secretary of the State seems not to have suffered in the eyes of the voting public. In her reelection bid in 1962, she led the entire Democratic ticket garnering an 82,972-vote margin over Helen Loy (Newington), a well-known Republican activist, even surpassing the popular Dempsey's 66,000 margin over John Alsop in his bid for a full four-year term.[41] It was a sweet victory for Ella Grasso to savor as she led her party to its third consecutive statewide electoral win.

She would repeat that reelection victory in 1966, outpolling Governor Dempsey, who won his second term with a 115,000-vote margin over E. Clayton Gengras. Ella decisively defeated her opponent Phyllis Shulman (R) of New Haven, a party insider with little statewide recognition, by a plurality of 148,848 votes.[42] So in the eyes of Connecticut voters, Ella Grasso was a winner with decisive margins each time she ran as well as being the leading statewide vote getter for the Democratic Party in 1962 and 1966.

In retrospect, one reason for her electoral success was that "she was not perceived by voters as a mere politician . . . but as a concerned public advocate." Another factor was her "unbroken ties to small town Connecticut and her folksy, open style of campaigning."[43] Both of these perceptions stemmed from her vigorous public activism and her travels throughout Connecticut as an advocate for election and voting reforms and as a leading spokeswoman for human service organizations. Her standing among Democratic Party leaders, enrolled Democrats, and unaffiliated or independent voters was unchallenged.

Ella Grasso's unbridled success at the polls also spurred her to champion issues and causes that were not popular among party leaders in the state. Those efforts, in the 1960s, focused on urging campaign finance reform. In her own campaigns she had always publicly disclosed all her campaign contributions and expenditures and also fully disclosed her income and assets and those of her husband. She followed that procedure in every campaign waged.[44] Her stance put her at odds with Bailey and other party stalwarts, pointing to a political position with popular appeal but disappointing party insiders.

Campaign finance laws in Connecticut had been adopted in 1895, and only minor revisions had been put in place in the twentieth century. In 1959, she headed a Commission to Revise Election Laws, which recommended changes in reporting requirements, but the legislature failed to approve them.

One Connecticut campaign law that had been on the books required the state to keep campaign records, including a list of campaign contributors, for fifteen months after an election—after that, the records were destroyed. Long after the 1964 U.S. Senate election, A. Searle Pinney, the Republican State Chairman, was unable to review the financial records of Senator Thomas A. Dodd because the fifteen-month deadline had passed. Dodd, accused of using campaign funds for personal purposes, was eventually censured by the U.S. Senate. Unable to acquire Dodd's records, Pinney joined the chorus of complainants that Connecticut needed a "complete overhaul" of its Corrupt Practices Act, as the campaign laws were called.[45]

In response, the Secretary of the State proposed major revisions including several campaign disclosure reforms, which she submitted not only to the respective Democratic and Republican State Chairmen but also to the president of the Connecticut League of Women Voters and to the president of the Connecticut Bar Association. In each instance, she asked them to study her proposals and respond to them.

The proposals, which Ella had previously discussed with her staff, included full disclosure of all political contributions and expenditures not just during the campaign periods but year round, before and after elections.[46] "Full accounting of political testimonials and fund raising dinners, noting how much money was raised and how it would be spent by individuals or political parties" was another reform she included in her package of recommendations. [47] And to answer Pinney's concerns, the Secretary of the State proposed that campaign finance records be filed in her office—with full public access—and kept on file for the length of the term of office of the candidate.

She used as a guide for these proposals a model drafted by the National Municipal League, some of which the State of Florida had adopted.[48] Interestingly, she proposed a maximum be established on campaign expenditures, though no dollar amount was suggested. Following that, she urged a prohibition on cash contributions and proposed instead the filing of all cancelled checks for campaign expenditures in the Secretary's office within thirty days of the election.

While these proposals were seen as quite drastic by the party leaders and not supported by the legislature, they served to develop a dialogue among the political and legislative leadership and the public and once again firmly established the Secretary of the State as the "Conscience of the Democratic Party" and her motivation as "always in the public interest."[49] What is also noteworthy is that she sought the support of her trusted good government ally the League of Women Voters, and in an obvious gesture to the legal community, she sought input from the Connecticut Bar Association. Obtaining their response and possible support from a broader constituency other than simply the political parties made good sense. It sent a signal—one more—to the citizens of the state that the Secretary of the State advocated election and campaign reforms that party leaders did not support but which had broad public appeal, and it further strengthened her image as one who worked continuously "to improve . . . campaign finance laws" and to see "that they were administered strictly and fairly."[50] It was an image that would not easily be erased from the minds of the Connecticut electorate.

One of Ella's most noteworthy and enduring contributions to the public good occurred in 1965 during her second term as Secretary of the State. It revolved around her role in organizing, planning, and managing the State Constitutional Convention of 1965. In February of the previous year, a three-judge federal court ruled that voting districts of both houses of the General Assembly were imbalanced in violation of the Fourteenth Amendment of the United States Constitution. Eventually, both political parties reached an agreement to hold a Constitutional Convention in 1965 to address the issue of balanced representation and to adopt other resolutions to revise the Connecticut Constitution.

When the Court ordered reapportionment, the legislature eventually sent out a call to cities and towns throughout the state to elect delegates — fourteen delegates from each of the six Congressional Districts. No more than seven individuals in a district could be chosen from one party.[51] Ella Grasso tallied the highest vote in the Sixth Congressional District, which included her hometown of Windsor Locks. Sadly, only 5 percent of Connecticut's eligible voters bothered to vote for Convention delegates. That was an extremely low turnout.[52] She had also been chosen by Governor Dempsey to be on the Planning Committee, which was set up to organize the Convention, scheduled to open July 1, 1965. Eventually, she was also selected chairman of the Planning Committee, a key position in the pre-Convention maneuvering.

During a Planning Committee session on June 30, 1965, Meade Alcorn, a committee member and a former Republican National Committee Chairman, commented that when Ella Grasso was "elected as chairman of this Planning Committee, she was elected because of her competence, and because of her demonstrated knowledge in this particular field."[53] This statement, voiced by one whom some people called Connecticut's Mr. Republican, reflected clear affirmation of the esteem and respect the other political party held for the state's Secretary of the State. His comment sent a signal of mutual trust, which would characterize the Grasso-Alcorn relationship in the planning stages prior to the convention itself. That sentiment would subsequently typify their actions when they were both elected floor leaders of their respective parties during the convention, which commenced on July 1, 1965, at the Old State House in Hartford.

The Constitutional Convention was presided over by former Governor Raymond E. Baldwin (R), with retired Connecticut Supreme Court Justice Patrick B. O'Sullivan as Vice-Chairman. Also in attendance as delegates were former Governor John D. Lodge and widely respected Judge Abraham Borden. All of them remembered as "giants" by one awe-struck young delegate Chad McCollam from Bethel, Connecticut.[54] Meade Alcorn and Ella Grasso were the floor leaders of the convention, responsible for shepherding legislation and directing debates of the convention in a positive and productive direction. Moreover, while both political parties State Chairmen, John Bailey and A. Searle Pinney, were designated official advisors, they were realistically the men who called the shots from behind the scenes. Both men were closely consulted about all of the convention's eventual proposals and resolutions. Indeed it had been at the Chairmen's insistence that a two-thirds vote would be required to pass any resolution on the floor of the convention.[55] And it was their sagacious monitoring of the debates and discussions that proved to be meritorious in moving the delegates along to an eventual successful completion of their tasks. But it was the skill and political agility of Ella Grasso and Meade Alcorn, their daily presence and influence on the floor of the convention during daily floor debates, verbal skirmishes, and public posturing, that kept the Convention moving forward toward eventually adopting twelve resolutions and several proposed Constitutional Amendments.

There seems little doubt that the spirit of bi-partisanship demonstrated by the two floor leaders carried over to the delegates as well. It was a "co-operative affair, fifty-fifty party wise."[56] And in the end, while the Convention generated few headlines, it constituted real progress in bringing the Connecticut Constitution of 1818 into conformity with the court mandate and modern constitutional requirements. Included among the delegates' decisions was an addition to Connecticut's Bill of Rights (Article 1), affirming that segregation and discrimination based on religion, race, color, ancestry, or national origins was prohibited. Further, the Convention proposed a decennial census, which would redefine the Senate and House districts to better reflect population changes based on a one-man, one-vote basis, leaving the party levers as an option for voters, and requiring the election of the Governor and Lieutenant Governor as one unit.

After weeks and months of public hearings around the state and sessions of the full convention in Hartford, the delegates voted to place before the Connecticut electorate on December 14, 1965, the suggested Constitutional changes approved by the convention delegates. Connecticut voters accepted the revised Constitution with the final vote 178,432 in favor, 84,129 opposed.[57] Barely 20.2 percent of the state's eligible voters turned out for that important decision.

Clearly one individual who emerged from the Convention with enhanced political stature was Ella Grasso. In one observer's opinion her political standing was raised considerably among the convention's Democratic Party delegates—of whom many were long-time Democratic leaders from towns and cities across the state.[58] Ella earned their respect and confidence by her hard work, political acumen, and careful attention to detail. And she was viewed as John Bailey's "alter ego" on the Convention floor.[59] Among those party leaders brought together at the convention were veteran Democrats, such as Mrs. Chase Going Woodhouse of Sprague who had been the first female Democrat elected to Congress in 1944, and young "awe-struck" Chad McCollam,[60] a skillful political operative who would later become Ella Grasso's Chief of Staff during her tenure as Governor.

Several statements recorded in the convention minutes reveal a profusion of admiration that emerged for the Democratic floor leader Ella Grasso. Much of that praise came from the Republican side of the aisle. Ella's counterpart, floor leader Meade Alcorn noted, "We have been impressed with the tact and fairness with which she has discharged an exceedingly difficult role in this convention. She is an exceedingly capable adversary when it has been necessary for her to be an adversary. She is a welcome and tremendous and effective ally when she is with you. I think her party should be proud of the qualities of her fine service and . . . we recognize these fine qualities too, and salute her for the fine contributions she has made to the work of this convention."[61]

In retrospect, while plaudits flowed from many sources in a spirit of bipartisanship, they seemed particularly effusive toward Ella Grasso, floor leader, the first woman in Connecticut history to hold that position—one that she regarded then as "the greatest challenge of my career."[62] Her public persona was perceived, among the state's political leaders, as hard working, trusting, and admirable as a result of her leadership role during the Constitutional Convention. "She was never a fall on your sword Democrat," noted one convention delegate, "in that she understood . . . sometimes you had to make compromises with members of the other party."[63] She had displayed consummate political skills in directing the often tendentious and obtuse legal and constitutional debates that took place on the floor of the convention and during the voting process of the convention. Republican sentiment, as expressed so warmly by Alcorn, praised Ella Grasso in the following way. "I think we need to recognize that the lady is not only a scholarly woman and a woman of great intellectual attainment but she is a woman who has shown, at least in my work with her, an uncommon dedication to the good of the people of this state."[64]

There is little doubt that her political star gleamed very brightly as a result of her leadership role at the convention. In James Grasso's opinion, his mother always believed that her service in the Constitutional Convention was "one of the highlights of her career."[65]

While working diligently for the good of the people of Connecticut in her position as Secretary of the State and enhancing her reputation statewide among her own party leadership and rank and file, as well as among the political opposition, Ella began to appear on the national political stage. One of the earliest occasions occurred in early 1959, when Ella spoke at a national $100-a-plate Democratic Victory Dinner in Washington, D.C. She spoke about the huge Ribicoff re-election victory sweep in November 1958, which she called "phenomenal," and she spelled out for the audience what she saw as the key to Connecticut's back-to-back Democratic party victories. Connecticut's Secretary of State emphasized in her remarks, that the Democratic Party "must not be content with good candidates but they must have better candidates, supported by better organizations that will attract capable and devoted citizens and encourage better candidates." Connecticut's election results were, she said, a "testament of faith in Governor Ribicoff," and the "climate of opinion Ribicoff created" was the turning point for the Democratic Party in Connecticut.[66] It was a clear, unmistakable message to the national Democratic leadership as to why Connecticut, which had not reelected a Democratic Governor since Wilbur Cross in the 1930s, was now turning the corner and electing and reelecting Democrats to statewide office.

Ella also paid tribute to the leadership of the state party organization led by John Bailey. She reminded the audience of his successful string of electoral victories and his astute political skills just as the national party was gearing up for the Presidential election contest of 1960. Bailey, who was deeply involved in lining up support for Kennedy's bid for the Presidential nomination, clearly relished the fact that his victorious record was now being recognized and touted on the national political stage. In fact, Ella's comments summed up the tried-and-true Bailey formula for electoral success: Good candidates, good issues, good organization.[67]

That Bailey formula would work out successfully on the national scene with John F. Kennedy's election victory over Richard Nixon in the 1960 campaign. With Kennedy's successful campaign and subsequent designation of Bailey as national party chairman, Bailey's star shone brilliantly on the national level, and he brought Ella Grasso to national attention as well. He was instrumental in President Kennedy's appointment of Ella Grasso to the national Board of Foreign Scholarships, which monitored the Fulbright scholarship program. She was subsequently reappointed by President Lyndon B. Johnson and served until 1966.

Among Bailey's myriad duties as Chairman of the national party was planning, organizing, overseeing, and running the party's quadrennial national convention, which was to be held in Atlantic City, New Jersey, in August 1964. Knowing Ella's abilities and longstanding work as platform committee chairman in Connecticut, he appointed her Co-Chairman of the national party's Platform and Resolution Committee — a task she shared with Congressman Carl Albert of Oklahoma. As Co-Chairman, one of her duties was to preside over committee hearings that the party convened prior to the opening of the Convention. One day, when she was presiding, Alabama Governor George C. Wallace appeared to "condemn the proposed civil rights plank." Ella recalled that "I sat there and listened and watched and never have I seen the face of evil as it was personified by this man. The threats, the boasting, the innuendoes — all of these were completely repugnant to me."[68]

Despite Wallace's protests, the 1964 Convention later adopted the civil rights plank that the platform committee presented. The dispute was overshadowed, however, by the controversy concerning the seating of the Mississippi delegation. The official delegation did not include any black delegates, and that prompted Fannie Lou Hamer and her black Mississippi Freedom Party colleagues to challenge the seating of the official, all-white Mississippi delegates. Eventually Hamer's group was recognized, and two Freedom Party members were seated — the all-white Mississippi delegates had to pledge loyalty to the national ticket.

Nevertheless, as it turned out, the 1964 Democratic National Convention afforded Ella Grasso the opportunity to speak before the convention audience. In her role as Co-Chairman of the Platform and Resolutions Committee, she presented a portion of the Committee's report to the delegates, and she did so though she said she was "petrified," likening it to "being prepared for surgery.[69]

The Committee's recommendations to the full convention, however, reflected what Lyndon Johnson desired—a civil rights platform that "reconciled differences, to bind (the delegates) and hold them together," and which reflected a theme the President had consistently pursued in his speeches, One Nation—One Party.[70]

The 1964 Atlantic City Democratic Convention has been described as having been staged with the ultimate control exercised by the President from the White House. Theodore H. White, a widely respected and keen observer of the political scene, asserts that even the platform proposals had been prepared at "LBJ's direction by Willard Wirtz" (Secretary of Labor) and that the committee's role was "almost entirely editorial, adjusting minor points."[71]

Ella's role, however, as Platform Co-Chairman in 1964, which she would repeat in 1968 in Chicago, enabled her to establish a working relationship with Congressman Carl Albert who would eventually become Speaker of the United States House of Representatives at the time Ella became a member of Congress in 1971. Albert, who in 1964 was the Democratic Majority Leader of the House and Co-Chairman with Ella of the Platform Committee, was high in his praise of the way Connecticut's Secretary of the State carried out her convention responsibilities. "Mrs. Grasso has been my very able and strong right arm," he said, and she "has brought to the rostrum a charm which has made the hearings a pleasure."[72] It was a friendly, cordial relationship, which would endure for many years and be of particular use to Ella when she sought Albert's help with committee assignments in the 92nd Congress.

In the 1968 Democratic National Convention Ella Grasso gained the national spotlight once again as Co-Chairman of the Convention's Platform and Resolutions Committee, this time, sharing duties with Congressman Hale Boggs of Louisiana. At a committee session, Ella acting in the absence of her co-chairman broke a 9–9 tie vote of the committee members. The stalemate concerned the Kerner Report on Civil Disobedience, which Democratic Party leaders did not want mentioned in the civil rights plank of the party platform. That report had concluded that America was racially divided into two societies—one white, suburban and prosperous, and one non-white, inner city, and struggling near the edge of poverty.[73] The conclusion was something neither President Johnson nor the White House wanted included in the party's platform. It was believed it would only exacerbate the alienation minorities felt in a racially divided society. And the Democrats realized they needed the huge number of urban black voters to win in the November election. Later, recalling that what she did essentially placed the Report's conclusions in the Democratic Platform, Ella said "I accept it [the Kerner Report], lock, stock, and barrel. It [the platform resolution] makes the Administration acknowledge the existence of the Kerner Report—finally."[74]

However, it was the war in Vietnam that was uppermost in the minds of the convention delegates that summer, and it deeply divided them, including the Connecticut delegation. That division, combined with the violent street protests in Chicago and the ensuing clashes that occurred between the police and demonstrators, created an atmosphere in the Windy City that Ella characterized as "macabre."[75] She walked out of the convention, along with hundreds of other delegates, protesting the tactics of Chicago's police force against the street protesters.

The convention's Platform Committee adopted a plan, which President Johnson and the national party leadership wanted the full convention to support. It promised a conditional bombing halt, provided North Vietnam did not further endanger the lives of American troops in the field. Ella, along with others, supported an alternative plank, which offered an "unconditional end to all the bombing, a mutual withdrawal of U.S. and North Vietnamese troops from South Vietnam," and encouraged "negotiations of a political reconciliation."[76] She prevailed on John Bailey to seek an audience for her with Congressman Carl Albert, Chairman of the Convention. "I thought John was going to throw me out of the window that day. He was talking about the vote and I told him I'm not going to support the President,"[77] she recalled telling her mentor. Bailey managed to get her to see Congressman Albert, who agreed to give Ella one minute to present her position on the proposed bombing plank. Bailey's reluctant willingness to help his longtime protégé illustrated the "kind of guy he was. He held power lightly."[78] But the balloting on the opposing proposals eventually occurred after endless hours of floor debate from proponents of both resolutions. The minority resolution was defeated 1,567¾ to 1,041¾.[79]

Ella Grasso's support for the minority report reflected her personal opposition to the war — "the wrong war in the wrong place"[80] — which in her view had become such a quagmire for the President of the United States and his administration's foreign policy. It also emanated from her realization that a continuing war might involve her own son James, who was now age seventeen — one year shy of being eligible for the draft. Her opposition to the war would continue in the years ahead when Ella became a member of Congress.

Ella's appearances on the national convention stage were primarily a consequence of her longtime partnership with John M. Bailey. Each time she appeared in the national spotlight, it was the result of Bailey's direction or entreaties on her behalf. He could have blocked her effort to speak at the 1968 convention regarding the minority report on the bombing halt resolution. He could have short-circuited her appointment as Co-Chairman of the Platform Committee at both national conventions. But Bailey's political instincts reassured him that, while Ella Grasso's political positions and liberal outlook might momentarily demonstrate a split in Connecticut's Democratic delegation and be seen in 1968 by the Johnson-Humphrey forces as a sign of his inability to corral his own delegation, his decision to ensure that Ella Grasso spoke on behalf of the minority plan was a skillful political maneuver. In effect, it was designed to placate the liberal, anti-war faction of his party, and principally those among the Connecticut delegates. He realized how deeply divided the convention delegates were, and to not allow the minority report to be presented, which was supported by some Connecticut delegates, would have opened up an even deeper divide among the state's Democratic convention contingent, wounding more deeply the presidential candidacy of Vice President Hubert H. Humphrey. Ella, John Bailey, and Governor John Dempsey, like the majority of the Connecticut delegates, were committed to supporting Humphrey for President. If Bailey had prevented Ella from speaking out, it would have pushed many of the pro-Humphrey, anti-war supporters into the arms of Senator Eugene McCarthy (D-Minnesota) or even Senator George McGovern (D-South Dakota), whom Senator Abraham Ribicoff backed. Ribicoff, who split from the Connecticut delegation's pro-Humphrey stance, did not support the Vice President's nomination. He went so far as to nominate Senator McGovern and recalled that he was "with the people that the organization looked down upon—this bunch of radicals."[81]

As it turned out, the Democratic delegates left Chicago deeply divided over the Vietnam War situation, and as a consequence the national party's chances of defeating Republican Richard Nixon's presidential bid deteriorated significantly. Connecticut's Democrats were likewise deeply divided, and those divisions, it was feared, might hurt the party's chances to deliver the state for Humphrey in 1968. (Humphrey won Connecticut's 8 electoral votes by a margin of 92,000 votes).[82] Part of the fallout of that convention split also included an anti-Bailey insurgency, which would deeply affect the Connecticut political scene between 1968 and 1970. One consequence would be that Ella Grasso, who had set her ambitions and personal drive toward a bid for the governor's chair, shifted her political horizons toward a congressional run. And that decision would prove to be another leap forward for Connecticut's most successful female politician.

❧ 6 ❧

I CAN BE A GADFLY HERE

Washington, D.C., the political epicenter of the nation, has been derisively described as a one-shop town, a place where politics is the only game in town, and where politics is frequently the principal topic of conversation among people who live there.

Often the political dialogue that takes place in the capitol city is fueled in part by rumor, gossip, and hearsay. But it is often given sufficient credibility to stoke the fires of suspicion, wariness, mistrust, and discord, which frequently envelop the relationship between two branches of the federal government.

In 1970, Republican President Richard M. Nixon occupied the Oval Office in the White House, while at the opposite end of Pennsylvania Avenue 535 members, the majority Democrats, comprised the Congress. The usual tense relationship between the two branches grew increasingly contentious during the spring and summer of that year. Part of the reason was the President's decision to expand the war in Southeast Asia by ordering air attacks on the nation of Cambodia.

In late April 1970, President Nixon issued a directive to the armed forces to commence bombing Cambodia. His decision was perceived by many as widening the scope of the nation's military involvement in Southeast Asia rather than reducing American entanglement as Nixon had vowed to do. The resulting outbreak of anti-war demonstrations and virulent anti-Nixon, anti-administration outbursts on many of the nation's college campuses were accompanied by protests and violence in

Washington and throughout America during that spring. In one tragic incident, which took place on May 4, 1970, a demonstration resulted in armed confrontation on the campus of Kent State University in Ohio. There, four students lost their lives as a consequence of protests and strife between students, demonstrators, and the Ohio National Guard.

That tragedy brought home to the American people the state of discord, tension, and frustration felt in many quarters about the Commander in Chief's bombing decision. It seemed to many Americans that the President's actions broke his campaign promise of the 1968 election campaign in which he assured the American electorate he would greatly reduce American military involvement in Vietnam. However, the escalation and widening military action in Cambodia that spring, taken without congressional consultation, sent a contrary message to the Democratic majority in Congress and to the nation. It was a pivotal moment in the Nixon presidency because it exacerbated political tensions and turmoil in the nation, and it sundered political good will in Washington, D.C., among congressional lawmakers and the White House. Furthermore, it seemed to deepen the distrust and suspicion between the American public and their political leaders in the White House. It was obvious that the nation's capital was not awash in cordiality that summer, and as the future would demonstrate, two of America's political institutions — the Executive and Legislative branches — became mired in what some called the worst political crisis since World War II.

Even without the political tensions that gripped Washington in the spring and summer of 1970, the District of Columbia's environment can be a "difficult place" for politicians to live and work.[1] It is so particularly for the men and women elected to Congress whose family ties are deeply rooted in their home states. It is especially challenging for a new congressman, who, the late House Speaker Sam Rayburn (D-Texas) said, "always feels so unalterably lonely and useless."[2] Congressional life is hectic, sometimes frenetic, with long hours, and it is nearly always disruptive of normal family life. Frequently, the lawmakers uproot themselves, their spouses, and children and relocate to the nation's capital, and that can be quite an upheaval for any family. Some members of Congress choose not to move their families to Washington's hectic whirlwind and its occasionally poisonous atmosphere. Thus, they create domestic situations not always conducive to a stable family life: one spouse and the children remain at home while the other—the elected official—goes off to Washington, D.C., and returns home on weekends, holidays, and during Congressional breaks and summer recess to visit loved ones and meet with constituents. It is not a life for the faint-of-heart, nor one for those with strong family roots whose hearts are firmly planted in the soil of their native state and congressional district.

There is little doubt that the Congress of the United States in the early 1970s was still largely an unwelcoming, difficult, and even isolating place for female members. Between 1917 and 1973, the number of women elected to Congress totaled only eleven in the Senate and seventy in the House. About half of the women who served during that fifty-six-year period succeeded their husbands in office after their spouse's death. And the number of women would increase minimally in the years after 1973, so that by 1987, only one hundred and twenty women were among the twelve thousand persons who had served in the United States Congress.[3] (Currently 17 women serve in the Senate and 73 in the House of Representatives.)[4]

Jeanette Rankin (R-Montana), was the first woman elected to serve in the House of Representatives, and she arrived in Washington in 1917. Rebecca Felton (D-Georgia), the first female to become a member of the United States Senate, served for only one day, November 21, 1922. She declared in her maiden speech on the Senate floor that while she might be the first, she would not be the last of her gender in Congress and that with women in Congress "you will get ability . . . integrity of purpose . . . exalted patriotism, and you will get unstinted usefulness."[5]

It was not until the 1940s that Connecticut voters saw fit to send women to Congress. The first was Clare Booth Luce (R) elected in 1942 and reelected in 1944, followed by Chase Going Woodhouse (D) elected in 1944 and again in 1948. Both were talented, able, successful women, and they more than lived up to Senator Felton's promise that there would be able women forthcoming to serve in the male-dominated Congress.

Clare Booth Luce served as a Republican Congresswoman from the lower Fairfield County region of Connecticut. She had a distinguished career as a writer, journalist, and playwright prior to running for Congress. As the wife of Henry Luce, owner-publisher of the Time-Life magazine empire, Mrs. Luce had been an ardent critic of President Franklin D. Roosevelt and his policies before she entered the Congress and continued that spirited opposition while in the House of Representatives. Several years later, in 1952, she was touted (in some quarters) as a possible Vice Presidential candidate on the Republican ticket.[6] Later, President Eisenhower appointed her Ambassador to Italy where she served from 1953 to 1957.

Chase Going Woodhouse, elected to represent the sprawling Second Congressional District in eastern Connecticut in 1944, was the first woman to graduate with honors in economics from McGill University in Montreal, Canada.[7] Over the years, she had been a member of the faculty at Smith College in Massachusetts and Connecticut College for Women in New London, Connecticut. The Canadian native compiled an outstanding reputation as an advocate for women's issues particularly in the area of consumerism, and she had been elected Connecticut Secretary of the State in 1940, serving one two-year term. Mrs. Woodhouse also had the distinction of serving in the House of Representatives with a former Smith College student, Jessie Sumner, who was enrolled at Smith when Mrs. Woodhouse was on the faculty. Sumner (R-Ill.) became a member of Congress and went on to serve four terms in the House of Representatives (1937–1947).[8]

By 1970, Mrs. Luce and Mrs. Woodhouse were the only women who had been elected to Congress from the Nutmeg State. Connecticut, however, was poised in that election year to send a third, in the person of Ella Grasso. Ella's eventual two terms in Washington as a member of the 92nd and 93rd Congresses would not be the happiest time in her political career; in fact, it would end up being a four-year stint that was characterized by a Washington friend as being "lonely and isolated."[9] Her decision to run for Congress was considered a "real mistake" by her son.[10] And in the eyes of one critic it was not the "most luminous . . . nor the most productive" time in her career.[11] It also placed a strain on her marriage to Tom Grasso, who described her four years in Congress as "the toughest years" of their marriage because she spent "most of her time in Washington and I remained in Connecticut."[12]

Her decision to seek the Democratic nomination for Congress in 1970 was not the first time she toyed with the idea of running for a seat in the House of Representatives. In 1964, several people had urged her to run for the newly created Sixth Congressional District seat in the northwest corner of the state. "I am not a candidate for Congress at this time," she announced in April 1964, "but I can't tell you anything about the future."[13]

While closing the door on speculation she might run in 1964, she coyly left it slightly ajar for the future. She turned her attention to the work that would occupy her over the next year — the work involved in the planning and management of the State Constitutional Convention. Following that significant event, she won her bid for a third term as Secretary of the State in 1966, leading the Democratic ticket to victory once again. As a result of that huge win, she was immediately catapulted into the spotlight as a possible candidate in 1968, a candidate who would take on the Republican incumbent Congressman Thomas J. Meskill in the Sixth District congressional race. There seems little doubt that John M. Bailey wanted her to run, believing her to be "the best candidate, if not the only one who could defeat the Republican incumbent."[14] Ella, however, closed the door on seeking the nomination. Instead she indicated she would not run, primarily due to family considerations.

Actually, it was a decision that occurred against a backdrop of a number of events—some personal, some political. The pressing family concerns revolved around Tom Grasso's health. While he was improving after two heart attacks, his condition was still worrisome. Her daughter Susane's continuing recovery from a near fatal car accident in 1965 required Ella's frequent monitoring. Ella also had concerns about her parents, both of whom required more attention now that they were close to eighty years of age.[15] Those family matters took precedence over a political run in 1968, which as it turned out was a victorious election year for the Republicans. By 1970, however, Tom and Susane were recovering well enough, although Ella's parents still required a great deal of attention. As a dutiful daughter and only child, Ella had always been attentive to her parents, and the thought of leaving Windsor Locks to serve in Washington tugged at her close familial ties to home and family. But decisive political shifts, almost as momentous as those in 1960, altered the fortunes of the Connecticut Democratic Party, and those changes directly affected Ella Grasso's decision to run for Congress.

At the outset of 1970, Governor John Dempsey let it be known privately that he was not going to seek a third four-year term. While that decision in and of itself was not earth shattering, it was a choice he made in large measure because of a series of events that transpired during the previous two years.

First, the state legislature's leaders Senate Majority Leader Edward Marcus (D-New Haven) and Speaker of the House William Ratchford (D-Danbury) made several bold moves that began "the demise of John Bailey as a strong political leader" of the state Democratic Party. "Marcus and Ratchford began to raise their own money" for legislative candidates "outside of the Democratic State Central Committee," observed Chad McCollam. And he added that this effort "diffused the money away from the State Central Committee treasury which Bailey controlled."[16] Some of the antipathy toward Bailey, particularly that of Marcus, rested on the premise that he had served long enough and it was time to let younger leaders move up and exercise leadership within the party ranks. And it was Marcus who coveted Bailey's chairmanship and hoped he could take control of the state party apparatus. (Many years later Edward Marcus served as the Connecticut Democratic State Party Chairman).

Added to these concerns, in 1969, both houses of the General Assembly approved legislation calling for annual legislative sessions (which required a constitutional change by the voters in 1970) and created a Office of Legislative Management with a professional staff, which effectively removed the patronage that State Chairman John Bailey had traditionally utilized to appoint faithful, loyal supporters to various salaried staff and committee positions within the legislative branch of state government. Bailey had often held out the promise of a job for a friend or relative of a legislator in turn for that legislator's support for bills that Bailey wanted passed. It was the time-honored way Bailey operated within the parameters of Connecticut's political structure. "Marcus and Ratchford did make their moves for more power for the legislature," asserts Jay Jackson a former Democratic State Senator from West Hartford. "I think it did crimp Mr. Bailey's wings but did not cut them off." [17]

Governor Dempsey opposed the Legislative Management legislation and vetoed it only to have both chambers, in a "fervent show of self-assertion" unanimously override his veto. [18] The legislative and executive jousting continued, and, eventually, the Governor vetoed the legislature's budget vote, necessitating a special session in late June 1969. The wrangling and legislative infighting convinced a frustrated Governor Dempsey that his third term would be his last.

With this new legislative management and oversight power, including hiring professional staff to manage and operate the General Assembly and its committees year round, the legislature effectively shut the door on Bailey's traditional patronage system. By creating an independent, bi-partisan, legislatively supported management office, the legislative body felt it was not only bringing itself into the modern age by removing patronage for professionalism, but it was relegating Bailey's traditional approach to the scrap heap of politics. Though no one believed Bailey could be dethroned, or that patronage was dead, legislative leaders believed that by these moves, political power and patronage at the State Capitol would be more equitably shared.

One legislator, William A. O'Neill (D-East Hampton), who would many years later succeed Ella Grasso as Governor, remembered that by instituting legislative management the General Assembly "took the powers of all the jobs at the Capitol away . . . and gave them to the Legislature — all the political jobs. So there was a definite demise of the party bosses already in motion."[19] Furthermore, Bailey's frequent absences from Connecticut to attend to his Democratic National Committee duties provided the legislative leaders with enough determination and independent muscle of their own to set the legislative agenda on their terms. As a result, they undermined Governor Dempsey's legislative initiatives and budget priorities, which had been largely ignored by the upstart legislative leadership.

Also, the time-honored tradition of allowing John Bailey to attend and participate in the legislative caucuses came to an abrupt halt. The Democratic House members actually barred Bailey from attending their caucuses, and that effectively shut Bailey out of the Democratic House caucus deliberations on legislation and legislative priorities. And it was clear that Marcus and his allies in the Senate did not hold out the welcome mat either.

Finally, the General Assembly's leaders and Hartford's political organization promoted their choice of candidate for governor they believed could win in 1970. With Dempsey's decision not to seek another term, attention shifted to Hartford Congressman Emilio Q. Daddario, a respected veteran Congressman from the state's First Congressional District.

Mim Daddario was not particularly close to John Bailey. However, he had built up a solid reputation in Congress, though he had never run for statewide office. He was a member of the House Committee on Science and Astronautics and served as Chairman of the subcommittee on Science, Research, and Development, and he had earned plaudits as a respected legislator, particularly watchful of Connecticut's aviation and space-technology interests.

Bailey, who had never run an Italian-American for governor, seemed less than enthusiastic about Daddario's chances of winning the November 1970 election. John Bailey "did not feel comfortable at all with the Daddario campaign," noted a Bailey associate. "Hardly anyone would speak to him at Daddario's headquarters . . . he had been pretty much eliminated from the campaign."[20]

The relationship between the two had not been particularly close. After announcing his candidacy, Daddario, in response to reporters' questions, reminded them that, "John Bailey and I have not always seen eye to eye . . . he originally did not support me in 1958 but I see no antagonism to him at all." While those comments were hardly tactful, Daddario went one step further and commented that he sensed "a need in the party to expand and be more flexible . . . I think there should be greater participation of small towns now . . . I think he will be flexible and adapt himself to these changes."[21]

Moreover, the Republicans were poised to nominate Sixth District Congressman, Thomas J. Meskill, an Irish-Catholic from New Britain. He had compiled a solid, moderate-conservative record as a two-term Congressman and was a popular former mayor of New Britain, one of the state's largest urban centers. The prospect of the Republicans nominating an Irish-Catholic from a large industrial city—normally a Democratic stronghold—emulated the traditional Bailey strategy of running an Irishman for Governor or U.S. Senator (Ribicoff was the exception) and assembling a statewide ticket with careful attention to ethnic makeup, urban representation, and geographic balance. The GOP strategy of running an Irishman against a largely untested Italian would, in Bailey's mind, undermine any hopes the divided Democrats had of retaining control of the Executive Branch of Connecticut's government.

Adding to the Democratic Party woes that year was the three-way, in-traparty challenge to U.S. Senator Thomas J. Dodd. Dodd, who had been investigated and censured by the Senate in 1967 for illegal, personal use of campaign funds, was being challenged for the nomination by three other Democrats: Alphonsus Donahue a millionaire businessman from Stamford (whom Bailey favored), the State Senate Majority leader Edward Marcus of New Haven (who would not only lose the U.S. Senate primary but also lose his State Senate seat in a primary to Joseph Lieberman, today a U.S. Senator and, in 2000, Vice Presidential nominee), and Reverend Joseph Duffy, a Protestant minister from Hartford who would eventually become the Democratic Senate nominee. It was a troubling scenario for John Bailey to see the party and the political organization, which he had carefully crafted over two decades, become mired in the first statewide Democratic primary that ultimately would not benefit the Democratic Party at the polls that fall. To make matters worse, Senator Dodd eventually decided to withdraw from the Democratic Party nomination contest and announced he would run as an independent.

For Ella Grasso, these political machinations narrowed her options. One likely course would have been to move up to the Governor's chair. It seemed like a logical next step. Once again it was John Bailey who dissuaded Ella from pursuing that path as it would have engendered a primary between herself and Congressman Daddario. As they both sur-veyed the Democratic Party turmoil, the more promising option for her would be to seek the open Congressional seat in the Sixth District, which Congressman Meskill was vacating to run for Governor. Bailey was not convinced that a woman—even a popular Italian-American woman—could run and win the governor's race, particularly in a year in which Democratic prospects looked so dismal. Once more, Ella was receptive to his advice and "chose the comparative security of a run" for the con-gressional nomination in Connecticut's sprawling Sixth District.[22]

Going after the Congressional seat seemed like "the most logical thing for her since she did not want to serve as Secretary of the State under a Republican Governor," commented her son James Grasso. And since both of her children were "out of the house" it seemed like "a good time to run."[23] In early March 1970, at the state party's annual Jefferson-Jackson Dinner in Hartford, two thousand cheering Democrats gave Ella Grasso a rousing ovation "that rivaled the one given to Representative Daddario," as the party's eventual gubernatorial candidate.[24] Noting that she was "impressed and affected by the demonstration," the *Hartford Courant* account reported that "the ovation for Mrs. Grasso was the talk of the crowd after the dinner . . . and the talk continued on Sunday in important places."[25] Her decision to seek the nomination became known to the public shortly after the ovation when the Hartford *Courant* headlined a story two days later that the "Sixth District Run Appears to Be Luring Mrs. Grasso."[26]

Shortly thereafter, on March 17, 1970, Ella announced her candidacy in a letter to each of the Democratic Town Chairmen within the forty-seven-town congressional district. She wrote to the party leaders noting, "This is a year of unique challenge and opportunity for service to the Democratic Party. More than ever, we need candidates who will reflect the concern of the people" and "provide a strong voice of Democratic principles which the citizens of our district should have in Washington."[27] Following her announcement, an editorial in the *New Britain Herald*, mentioned that Ella Grasso was a "formidable candidate . . . well known as an aggressive, progressive leader willing to innovate, to make politically bold moves." And further, the editorial stated that she is "a persuasive orator, with a flashing sense of humor, and a strong sense of ideals."[28] It was the kind of praise that would hearten any candidate so early in a campaign.

Two other contenders had previously announced their intention to seek the Democratic congressional nomination: attorney Anthony De-Nuzze of New Britain and Arthur Powers, a popular mayor of Berlin, Connecticut, a Hartford suburb. Powers' initial reaction to the Secretary of the State's decision to enter the congressional race emphasized that,

"Mrs. Grasso is a fine person and I don't question her qualifications," but he linked her with the party bosses (Bailey and the Hartford leaders) who he said "had apparently urged Mrs. Grasso to run," and he was critical of them for attempting to hand pick the candidate. "They've got to realize that the small towns must be represented. She is from Windsor Locks but is Hartford oriented."[29]

By early summer, however, Ella Grasso had lined up enough support among the delegates to the congressional convention enabling her to clinch the nomination on the first ballot. The final first ballot tally was Grasso 136, Powers 28, and DeNuzze 25.[30]

During the ensuing campaign, Ella campaigned hard and went everywhere: to the picturesque, rolling hills and far corners of Litchfield County and to the drab, aging factories and machine shops of the district's urban areas of Torrington, Bristol, and New Britain. But she ran a campaign that "very much" distanced her from the party's gubernatorial and senatorial candidates. [31]It was a calculated strategy to avoid being too closely identified with Congressman Daddario's bumbling, lackluster, and ultimately losing campaign, as well as that of senatorial candidate Rev. Joseph Duffy, whose campaign was unable to keep the Democrat's moderate-conservative voters from defecting to the Dodd camp.

Ultimately, Ella's strategy worked, and she bucked the Republican tide "to squeak through to a 4,063 vote victory in the Sixth District," over Richard Kilborn her Republican opponent.[32] Ella received 96,969 votes to her opponent's 92,906. As it turned out, her victory was one of the few Democratic bright spots in that fall election of 1970. In fact, the Democratic Party's internal squabbles resulted in the election (for the first time since 1950) of a Republican Governor, Thomas J. Meskill, and a Republican U. S. Senator, Lowell P. Weicker, Jr., who took Dodd's seat, as well as a pickup of two congressional seats for the Republicans.

Ella achieved her win with campaign expenditures of less than $60,000, the bulk of which came from AFL-CIO coffers.[33] Ella's close association with the unions (especially the UAW), which she had cultivated over many years, was vital to her electoral success on November 3, 1970. She had personally campaigned at factory gates and made appearances in the plants that manufactured machinery, equipment, and textiles in the urban, union-dominated centers of the congressional district. Labor, in turn, provided assistance with volunteers, drivers, and phone solicitation efforts as a way to assist in the campaign.[34] Employing the campaign tactics she had successfully used in her previous campaigns, she concentrated on personally meeting and greeting as many voters as possible and attending the inevitable political outings, dinners, and town committee functions as time permitted. Her folksy campaign style fit in well, whether she was campaigning in the wealthy towns nestled in the bucolic hills of Litchfield County, home to writers, playwrights, and actors, or in the more densely populated blue-collar areas of the district.

Ella, ever the worrier, spent a "straining night" on that election evening November 3, 1970. As the results began to show a Republican trend for Governor and U.S. Senator, she told a reporter, "I don't expect to win . . . I'm going to take a bath." And noting that she did not have much money to spend in the campaign, she pessimistically complained that, "I figure I've been outspent 3–1 in media," and "I didn't plan to win. What can I say?"[35] After forty-five of forty-six towns had reported their returns "Ella was 2,000 votes behind," recalled Frank Mancuso of Enfield, Connecticut.[36] Once the final tally came in from Enfield, Ella squeaked through and won by 4,063 votes. Her father, who was 83 and still a registered Republican, noted happily that, "today I voted straight Democratic," as he basked in the joy of seeing his daughter elected to the Congress of the United States.[37]

Ella Grasso's ability to pull through a victory in a Republican year is testimony to her standing among Democrats, Independents, and Republicans in a district that two years before had given a 50,000 vote margin to the Republican incumbent Meskill. Her impressive turn around was proof positive that all the years Ella spent as a popular, well-respected, and well-known Secretary of the State had earned her the plaudits and support from voters across the political spectrum in the Sixth District. It was truly a personal triumph for Ella, especially when one considers that the Republican candidate for Governor (Meskill) trounced his opponent (Daddario) by over 34,000 votes in that district.[38]

Historically, the Sixth Congressional District was viewed as a swing district, electing Congressmen from both political parties at different election cycles. And in 1970, political registration statistics revealed nearly an even split among the party registrants: 38 percent Democrats, 34 percent Republicans, and the balance being unaffiliated voters.[39] It was clear her victory in 1970 reflected once again Ella Grasso's ability to reach out to voters regardless of party affiliation, to garner support across gender and socio-economic lines while also earning diverse ethnic support, all of which enabled her to achieve electoral victory. Her unmistakable political prowess at the polls would bode well for her in campaigns she would undertake in the future.

The dominant issue in that first campaign for Congress had been the economic problems that plagued the district, particularly affecting the ball bearing industry, one of the largest employers in the Sixth District. The city of Bristol, Connecticut, the center of ball bearing manufacturing in the state, was in severe straits because of the fierce competition brought on by the challenge of cheap Japanese imports.[40] As a result, the city's unemployment rate of 24.1 percent was higher than the national average.[41] Ella realized her number one Congressional priority would be to focus on unemployment. Her major goal, she said, would be "to get something done about the unemployment situation, to provide training and retraining for more jobs in the public sector."[42]

In order to be positioned to help her constituents, Ella decided what congressional committees would be most helpful in reaching her goal. In a letter written a few weeks after her election, she informed Congressman James A. Burke (D-Mass.), whose responsibility encompassed assigning committee slots to new House members from New England, which committee assignments she desired. Ella told Burke that the

"Committee on Education and Labor is my first choice with Interstate and Foreign Commerce my second."[43] It was clear she realized those committees would have direct impact in the areas of employment, commerce, and international trade, all of which directly affected the main industrial and manufacturing interests in her district, as well as the needs of labor and the unemployed. She also requested appointment to the Veterans Affairs Committee since this is "an area of particular concern to me and the people of my district."[44] As if to underscore her interest in veteran's issues, she attempted to meet with the Veterans Affairs Committee Chairman Olin Teague (D-Texas) during a visit she made to Washington after the November election. Unable to see him personally because he was ill, she followed up by writing to him. She expressed hope that he would be "restored to good health," reiterated that veteran's issues were "an area of particular concern to me," and she mentioned how she had found "most helpful" Teague's remarks on veterans' issues, which had been forwarded to her by Congressman (soon to be Speaker) Carl Albert (D-Okla.) and which she had used during her congressional campaign.[45]

Fortunately, Ella received assignment to both committees — Education and Labor and Veterans Affairs. One reporter noted that she "got two plum appointments. Both assignments she sought — a distinction that isn't achieved by many freshmen." While "election pluralities are taken into consideration for important committee assignments, privileges, and favors," Ella's long-standing friendship and association with House Speaker Carl Albert and Majority Whip Hale Boggs (D-La.) with whom she had worked closely at the 1964 and 1968 national conventions undoubtedly helped her obtain those choice committee assignments.[46]

The freshmen class that entered House of Representatives in January 1971 included Bella Abzug (D-N.Y.), Louise Day Hicks (D-Mass.), and Ella Grasso. They joined seven other women colleagues who had been reelected to the House in the fall of 1970. Ella struck up an immediate friendship with her freshmen colleague Bella Abzug, who was described as the flamboyant, "rough talking, liberal with a salty streets of New York vocabulary."[47] While it was predictable that the two "women will attract more attention and make more waves than the average fresh-man,"[48] Ella's approach would turn out to be more "low profile" in order to "get the job done."[49] "Bella and I have great rapport. She's earthy and there's a goodness about her," Ella explained. "I don't go around making waves, I just try to find a way through them. While Bella's rocking the boat, I might get to shore."[50]

Early on in their congressional service, both women agreed that Congress was a slow-moving deliberative body. In fact, at the first Democratic caucus, when the House rules were being debated, Ella and Bella joined with a number of their colleagues to urge that steps be taken to reform the way the House conducted its business—principally, elimi-nating the seniority rules, which enabled committee chairmen to retain their posts based on their years of service in Congress. The reform ef-forts, however, failed to chip away the powers of seniority, and Ella was resigned to failure, admitting, "It looks as though the changes will be minimal, miniscule."[51] These early "meanderings" of the Democratic caucus sent a clear message to the Congresswoman from Connecticut's Sixth District about how "frustratingly slow" Congress worked com-pared to state government.[52] Despite that realization, she resolved to do the job well all the while grumbling about the slow moving ways of Congress.[53]

In her tenure as Congresswoman, she made a solid, favorable impres-sion on the House leadership, particularly on Congressman Tip O'Neill (D-Mass.). O'Neill, who was the deputy Majority Whip of the House of Representatives when Ella first arrived in Washington, and then Major-ity Whip succeeding Congressman Hale Boggs, "adored" her and she "loved" him. It was strictly a political "romance" and he became a strong admirer of Ella Grasso and "praised her to the hilt."[54] And virtually every Tuesday and Thursday afternoon she would visit O'Neills's office and have tea. Sometimes Congressman William Cotter from Connecticut's First Congressional District accompanied Ella and other times she arrived alone. What drew her there was Linda Malconian, a member of Congressman O'Neill's staff, whom Ella had befriended, and who in turn came to perceive Ella as her political mentor.

Malconian, a native of the Springfield area of western Massachusetts was, like Ella, a Mount Holyoke College graduate, Class of 1971. She had interned in Representative Edward Boland's (D-Mass.) office while a senior and then joined the staff of Congressman Tip O'Neill after her graduation. Malconian recalled having tea with Ella Grasso at 4:00 P.M., which reminded them of the tradition of late afternoon tea that they remembered from their days at Mount Holyoke. However, their friendship went deeper. "We were both women from the Connecticut River Valley area," noted Malconian, "the first from our families to attend college, both of us had a lot of the same skills and background and educational experiences, and held similar values."[55] Those ties brought them together.

In Malconian's view, Ella Grasso "radiated sunshine" and lit up any room she entered. The way "she smiled" and displayed "charm, genuine and sincere interest in ordinary working people" is what the vibrant Massachusetts native recalls most vividly of her time with Ella Grasso. While acknowledging that Ella "could be tough" and uncompromising on issues that she believed in, the young woman (eventually a State Senator in Massachusetts) remembers Ella as being "lonely" away from Connecticut and one whose "heart was in Connecticut" and who did not "socialize with her colleagues" while in Congress.[56]

One person she did socialize with while a member of Congress, however, was Sally Maycock Johnston, her former Mount Holyoke College roommate, who lived in nearby McLean, Virginia. Johnston, who taught at Montgomery County Community College in Maryland, had expected Ella "to become an economics professor at a New England college."[57] But she provided a relaxing and steady presence for Ella during their frequent get-togethers in the nation's capital.

Being a female member of Congress in the early 1970s, according to Senator Malconian, was a "difficult time" and the Congress was "not a pleasant, warm place," particularly as tensions heated up over the country's increasingly contentious international and domestic problems (Vietnam, Koreagate, Watergate).[58] Those problems tainted the political atmosphere in Washington, D.C., and increased the isolation women in Congress felt about the impact they had on the direction of the nation's affairs and its policies. Resigned to the reality of women not being included in the key decision making of the congressional leadership (something she had been a part of in Connecticut), and unable to break through the seniority system as it pertained to committee chairmen, Ella vowed to concentrate her energy on issues important to her and the congressional district.

Ella initially focused her congressional legislative efforts on several principal areas in order to build a record that people in the district would identify as pocketbook issues of great concern to them. Those issues were: the economy (jobs, unemployment, job retraining), consumer advocacy issues, veterans affairs, senior citizen issues, education, children and early childhood concerns, child daycare, and labor problems. In addition, she would also focus on the overriding foreign policy issues relating to Vietnam and the widening war in Southeast Asia, as well as on the contentious debate over the adoption of the Equal Rights Amendment (ERA).

She worked on these issues determined to make an impact by trying to garner support for them amongst her colleagues. Ella was realistic about the need for the New England state's congressional delegations to work in a bi-partisan manner in order to "effectively focus on common problems . . . and cooperate in trying to solve them on a non-partisan basis."[59] Ella participated actively in the New England caucus early in her term[60] and worked closely with not only the Connecticut congressional delegation but also the Massachusetts contingent, and she remained committed to the idea of regional cooperation throughout her time in Washington.

Two issues that galvanized the New England congressional caucus were the escalating prices of oil and gas and the diminishing supplies of those resources so vital to the economic livelihood of the northeast region of the country. Indeed the energy problems would continue to escalate during the 1970s as the war continued in Southeast Asia and the domestic needs of the American economy put pressure on the suppliers and refineries to produce enough for the war, for industry, and consumers.

Ella also understood that she would "never acquire any real power in the House" at the age of fifty because of the rules of seniority and male domination of the legislative branch.[61] She quickly realized that several women in the House of Representatives who had been in Congress for many years (Leonor Sullivan D-Mo., for example) still did not hold leadership positions on any key congressional committees. What Ella could do was to try to move some of her bills and legislative proposals forward successfully by garnering the support of the New England caucus.

By crafting legislative proposals in the areas with which she felt comfortable and which took into account her freshman status, she would attempt to build a consensus among the Connecticut delegation and among members from the other five New England states. "I can be a gadfly here,"[62] she said, and in essence select the issues that she believed were important to the people of her district and that might gain wider support from colleagues from throughout New England. Indeed her legislative accomplishments should not be minimized but should be seen as reflecting her focus on consumer issues, economic problems, and unemployment—issues of major concern to constituents in her district, and, in one instance, an issue that attracted national media attention.

Her focus on consumer issues included a Fair Packaging and Labeling Act, which she introduced and co-sponsored.[63] The act required retailers to display in a prominent place the cost per weight measure, as well as the cost of the product as packaged. And it included a requirement of a "last date" or pull date for perishable goods, for consumption without a high risk of spoiling. She also supported a Truth in Food Labeling Act because "each citizen has the right to know the ingredients a food product contains and to have assurance that these ingredients are fit for human consumption."[64]

Furthermore, she supported a bill establishing a federal office of Consumer Protection, which was similar to the Consumer Protection Department she had advocated in Connecticut, and which came to fruition during Governor Ribicoff's second term. Ella urged passage of the bill, which would, with some adjustments, eventually become law. She received plaudits for her efforts from the first presidential appointee to administer the agency, consumer advocate Virginia Knauer. Noting that Ella had supported establishing an agency for consumer advocacy when she first became a member of the House, Mrs. Knauer wrote that, "Such House passage would not have been possible without your help."[65] It would prove to be a positive development that Ella Grasso was proud to see become a vital part of the federal government's ongoing efforts to protect the consuming public.

Her consumer advocacy also included keeping a close eye on meat importation by cosponsoring legislation to amend the Meat Inspection Act, in order to provide for more effective inspection of imported meat to prevent diseased, contaminated, or unwholesome products being brought into the country.[66]

All those early efforts to safeguard consumers did not go unnoticed by another well-known and widely respected consumer advocate, Esther Peterson. Mrs. Peterson had been involved in worker's education, consumer issues, and women's activities, and in earlier years was associated with the Hudson Shore Labor School, where she had first come to know Ella. She had also served as Assistant Secretary of Labor and head of the Women's Bureau of the Labor Department under President Kennedy. In a warm and friendly note to Ella when she entered Congress, Peterson emphasized that, "No one could be more pleased that you are here [in Washington] at last."[67]

It became obvious over time that a great deal of Ella's time in Washington was engaged in "action on many levels to create and safeguard jobs, and give Connecticut's business and industry a needed stimulus."[68] In a letter to Secretary of Labor James D. Hodgson, Ella "bitterly complained about the high unemployment rate in her district," which averaged 12.4 percent in mid-January 1971.[69] She urged the administration to "provide more federal assistance for Connecticut's unemployed."[70] And as a member of the Select Committee on Labor, she helped draft the Emergency Employment Act of 1971 and the Comprehensive Employment and Training Act (CETA), which eventually provided over 8,000 public service jobs for Connecticut.[71] Of signal importance was her continuous effort to obtain additional funding for the Neighborhood Youth Corps program, which put young people to work during the summer.[72] She was a "most active supporter" of the Youth Conservation Corps, which provided environmentally related summer employment for young adults.[73] Her amendment mandated, as part of that legislation, that 30 percent of the funds be used for a state's YCC program, even though that state (that is, Connecticut) had no national parks within its borders.

In the fall of Ella's first year in Congress, she was featured on the NBC network show *First Tuesday*, hosted by correspondent Garrick Utley. The news program provided her an opportunity to discuss, in front of a national audience, the grim economic picture in Connecticut's Sixth Congressional District. The September 7, 1971, program entitled "The Psychology of Unemployment" analyzed the destitute condition of unemployed workers in Bristol, Connecticut, one of the major manufacturing cities in her district.[74]

Out of work, unable to meet their family's needs, many people were facing the end of their eligibility for unemployment benefits. Moreover, the tragic story of Bristol's 24.1 percent unemployed was dramatically presented against a backdrop of the sober realization that the city's historic role as an industrial powerhouse was gone forever. Bristol had been the center of clock manufacturing, machine tool production, and the ball bearing industry in Connecticut boasting a proud tradition of skilled labor working in the many diverse industries located in the urban city. But Bristol, in 1971, was facing the future without the prospect of ever regaining its position as a major industrial and manufacturing center. Many of the businesses, particularly the ball bearing industry, had lost their competitive edge, to foreign manufacturers, particularly in Japan.

The show's narrative detailed the emotional and psychological effects long-term unemployment engendered among individuals and families in Bristol. Interviews with white and minority workers emphasized the hopelessness and despair many of them felt about ever returning to the industrial and manufacturing workforce. Sadly, many individuals expressed their concerns about the growing dysfunction and disharmony that families experienced. Exacerbated by long-term unemployment, hostilities engendered between parents and children often resulted in the increased use of drugs and alcohol. Most tragic was the startling number of suicides that were a direct result of the effects that long-term unemployment created among individuals, families, and the community.[75]

This broadcast not only provided evidence of the serious economic problems plaguing Ella Grasso's district, but it placed emphasis on the bitterness and frustration felt by the workers and their Congresswoman about the federal government's inaction to relieve their suffering. Challenging President Nixon to come to Bristol, Connecticut, Ella urged him to "walk down the street and meet some of the people who are desperate and hurting." Taking particular note that the city and region was in the midst of an "economic recession without parallel in the country," she spoke forcefully about the "long drought" of unemployment and added that the "situation here has been serious for a very long time" and that the "people want action." Further, she argued that Bristol, facing an unemployment rate of 24.1 percent "has perhaps the highest unemployment rate" in the United States. Where it once had a workforce of 25,000 working in defense-related industries, clock and ball-bearing manufacturing, and machine tool production, Bristol's unemployed had reached 6,000 people by September 1971 with little hope for a return to gainful employment. The plants had either closed because of foreign competition or moved to other regions of the country where manufacturing costs were far less.[76]

In one key segment of the interview, Ella sternly reminded viewers that during World War II, Bristol's ball bearing industry manufactured 88 percent of the ball bearings in the United States. "Now it produces only 26 percent" with the bulk of production coming from outside the country.[77]

It was the plight of that industry that would occupy much of Ella Grasso's attention from that time forward. In the fall of 1971, she learned that seventeen Japanese citizens were permitted to work at a Japanese-owned Chicago ball bearing plant. She asked the U.S. State Department for an explanation as to why the United States allowed Japanese citizens to work in the ball bearing plant in the United States while 4,600 Connecticut citizens in the ball bearing plants of Connecticut's Sixth district lost their jobs because of the steady growth of foreign imports from Japan. One result of her persistent efforts on Capitol Hill regarding the hard-pressed industry was the President's decision to increase duties on some of the imported ball bearings, which provided some relief to the domestic ball bearing manufacturers in Connecticut's Sixth District.

The opportunity for Ella Grasso to focus national attention through the lens of the television camera on an important segment of the manufacturing economy brought much needed attention to a national problem of the increasing loss of manufacturing production and jobs to foreign competition. The network program provided her with national exposure on an issue that the American public could easily understand, one with which she would become identified in the foreseeable future.

Further, in late November 1971, Mrs. Grasso released a scathing statement criticizing the Republican administration's decision to allocate $115 million dollars to study the use of federal funds in areas of high unemployment. Connecticut, however, was not to be included in the study. "I am appalled and outraged," she said bluntly. "How can a state with the second highest unemployment rate in the nation not get its fair share of any and every government program."[78] Yet her protestations fell on deaf ears.

One of Ella's most significant efforts early in her first term was to engage in challenging the White House over the President's refusal to release some $11 billion that the Congress had authorized for spending on social welfare programs throughout the country. Ella and Congressman William Cotter from Connecticut's First District joined with Democratic leaders to force a showdown floor-debate in the House of Representatives over the President's actions. Their efforts to have the House override President Nixon's vetoes of bills challenging his impoundment policy were not successful. Still, it showed their strong determination in the struggle with the White House. Tip O'Neill noticed Mrs. Grasso's role and wrote a note to Ella thanking her for her work and "very fine efforts."[79]

Ella also invested considerable time, energy, and muscle in trying to obtain the release of Connecticut native John Downey, who was imprisoned in solitary confinement in a Chinese jail. Hailing from New Britain, Connecticut, the largest city in Mrs. Grasso's Congressional District, Downey had been recruited by the CIA after his graduation from Yale in 1951.

He had been shot down over Mainland China in 1952 and languished there for nearly twenty years. During her time in Congress, Ella met with State Department officials repeatedly and bombarded the department with letters urging that his release be moved to the top of their agenda.[80] As part of President Nixon's diplomatic overtures to the Communist regime in 1972, Grasso urged the administration to press for Downey's release in light of the détente in relations between the two powers. Eventually Chinese Premier Chou En-Lai ordered Downey's release, and he returned to Connecticut to a hero's welcome in March

1973. Subsequently, he embarked on a public career in state government. Ella eventually appointed him to a key position in her future gubernatorial administration. In 1987, Governor William A. O'Neill appointed Downey a judge of the Superior Court of Connecticut. He has served with distinction on the Connecticut bench since his initial appointment.

Ever diligent in fostering efficient and effective constituent service, Ella introduced an "Ella Phone" as an innovative way to expand ways she and her staff could remain in close communications with people in the congressional district. Believing, as she did, that superb constituent service was one of the "most important areas of activity for a member of Congress," Ella had installed a twenty-four hour, toll free telephone service for people to use to phone her district office in New Britain.[81] It was to be a convenient way in which people could express their concerns and communicate their problems and needs to Ella through her office staff. "It was my way of bringing government closer to the people and the people closer to government," she explained.[82] It was the first time a Member of Congress had provided the toll free service, and it served as an example for her congressional colleagues, many of whom quickly adopted the service for their constituents.

Another initiative she undertook was to institute monthly public office hours in her New Britain Congressional District office, as well as similar monthly visits to one of the forty-seven towns that made up the Sixth District. These regular appearances provided Ella with a conspicuous presence, offering voters and her constituents easy accessibility to her. Those efforts established Ella Grasso's congressional office as one that emphasized efficient and effective constituent services. Indeed by the time she left Congress, "excellent constituent services" was the hallmark of the Sixth District office and set a standard for her successors in that particular district.[83]

Several other areas of legislative interest became the focal point of her attention during her two Congressional terms. One issue was the fractious and contentious debate over adopting the Equal Rights

Amendment. Ella's position regarding adoption of the ERA was firmly in support of the proposed Amendment. In letters, interviews, and in her remarks on the floor of the House of Representatives, there was no doubt where she stood on the issue.

Ella Grasso was a successful, achieving woman long before the modern feminist movement emerged in the mid-1960s. Having been a student at Mount Holyoke College in the late 1930s and early 1940s, she was imbued with and "instilled in a very real way [with] a powerful and attractive sense of concern and responsibility" for service to others, to society, and to her fellowman.[84] This principle was exemplified by the lives and careers of Sister DeChantal and Professor Amy Hewes, Ella's early role models and mentors, as well as by the examples of Secretary of Labor Frances Perkins and Mount Holyoke's President Mary Wooley, who clearly demonstrated the "continuous thread of relationships which seems so much a feature of Mount Holyoke."[85] As advocates for women's rights and equality of sexes, by their careers and activist public and professional lives, they revealed a commitment to working to improve society in ways that transcended women's traditional social welfare and suffrage activism, which had focused initially on child labor reforms and voting rights. Mary Wooley, Frances Perkins, and Amy Hewes were uncommon women — path-breaking pioneers who led the way for women into the public and political sphere both at home and abroad, areas where women seldom ventured. It was to that legacy, that commitment to service in the public sector, outside the home, seeking the same rights men had, to "achieve changes in laws and public policy" that Ella Grasso committed herself in the years prior to the emerging women's liberation movement in the 1960s.[86] While Congresswoman Grasso would unquestionably benefit from the consciousness-raising women's movement unleashed by author Betty Friedan in her 1963 landmark study *The Feminine Mystique*, she had been a precursor to that movement running and winning elective public office years before the movement emerged in the 1960s. While the movement gained recognition, momentum, and evoked public awareness of the gender inequities in American society, it also sought to motivate more women to seek public office, a career path Ella Grasso had already taken.

Interestingly, Ella achieved her success in the public sector by sheer will — by her own abilities, talents, determination, and luck. She broke through barriers, working first through the League of Women Voters, and then in the political vineyards, long before the wave of the modern women's liberation movement took hold and "shaped in the dissent and violence of the 1960s."[87] Ella had already "landed on the shore" before the waves of change brought the modern women's liberation movement closer to the center of the nation's attention. The women's liberation movement of the 1960s, however, did not limit itself to simply achieving changes in public policy as did the earlier women's rights advocates. The '60s feminists "embraced a transformation in private, domestic life as well. They sought liberation from ways of thinking and behaving that they believed stunted or distorted women's growth and kept them subordinate to men."[88]

In contrast, Ella Grasso did not think of herself as an ardent advocate of the women's movement.[89] "She had not operated as a woman in politics," but "as a person who is also a woman."[90] And this same sentiment is echoed in other studies of successful women politicians who won high public office prior to the mid-1960s. Janann Sherman, in a biography of U.S. Senator Margaret Chase Smith (R-Maine), argues that for women, "The difficulty was in conveying a sort of gender neutrality. Most women then in public life . . . repeatedly referred to themselves as human beings not just women."[91] In Ella's case, she "probably felt she could be more effective just by doing her thing as a person without emphasizing the woman's part," noted attorney Jay Jackson legal counsel to Ella when she became governor. "If she became too closely involved (in the women's movement) it would hamper her bridge building which is a very necessary part of being a governor, or congresswoman," added Jackson.[92] Indeed no female politician, as Sherman suggests, "could afford to align herself with one half of her constituency when the powerful half was threatened by that allegiance."[93]

Ella Grasso's successful career demonstrates the persuasiveness of Sherman's compelling observation. She did not identify herself with the feminist movement of the 1960s but rather moved early and successfully in her career into the male-dominated sphere of politics, subsuming her gender while simultaneously developing a style that worked for her and did not alienate the "powerful half" in the process.

As a result, Ella supported the drive for adding an equal rights constitutional amendment, which she said would "provide the constitutional framework upon which to build a body of law to achieve the goal of equal rights." Indeed her remarks on the floor of the House of Representative October 12, 1971, are among the clearest statements she ever uttered about women's rights. Citing numerous examples of inequities in the nation's legal system, she reminded her colleagues that "our legal system . . . looks well into the past. In fact, it clings to some vestiges of English common law under which a woman was not a legal entity but a chattel." She mentioned that in some states at that time criminal statutes require women to be given longer sentences than men for the same crime; that twenty states had different provisions for qualifying women for jury duty; and that some states even prohibit a wife from establishing a business without court sanction. Citing a figure of 70 million women in the United States of whom 43 percent adult women were part of America's working labor force, Mrs. Grasso noted that, "for too many, discrimination in some form is a part of daily life." Finally, she reminded her House colleagues that "women cannot rely on the courts to achieve their rights," nor could they depend on "the fifth and fourteenth amendments to accord equal rights to women." In her view, therefore, Congress had the "opportunity to correct this situation by passing the amendment."[94]

When the ERA vote took place on the floor of the House of Representatives October 12, 1971, Ella voted in the affirmative. The final tally was 354–23. The United States Senate followed suit on March 22, 1972, approving the ERA 84–8.[95] Then, Congresswoman Grasso moved to push the effort for Connecticut's ratification of the ERA amendment, advising women lobbyists on matters of "tactical strategy, intimating that she would also use some influence of her own regarding the issue."[96] And one tactic that she strongly urged the ERA advocates to adopt was to "lower the pitch of their message, in the hope of reducing some of the hostility that they had built up."[97] Connecticut eventually ratified the ERA amendment, and Ella Grasso used her considerable influence to help secure its passage.

Two other contentious issues, Vietnam and impeachment, were front and center for Ella Grasso during the remaining months of her congressional tenure. Both were topics that were addressed by Ella, either by sponsoring or cosponsoring key legislation

Her opposition to the war in Vietnam was of long-standing. Having stood in opposition to the war in 1968 at the Democratic National Convention, she maintained a consistent position opposing it throughout her tenure in Congress. She opposed the war because it became evident as the war dragged on that it was unwinnable and that the United States had no business being there.[98] Questioned by reporters about the war in early June 1970 during her quest for the Democratic congressional nomination, she replied that, "the war has profoundly affected our lives. It has dragged on from generation to generation. It has given rise to concerns and tensions here at home . . . Our people are polarized," Ella noted, and as a result, "it is difficult to communicate with young people."[99] Ella also had concerns about the war because her son, James, who was of draft age, could be sent off to fight—a nightmare most parents dreaded. Simultaneously, she supported legislation to maintain the nation's defense commitments to protect its vital interests and security arrangements, and to end U.S. military efforts in Indochina. She voiced vigorous protest against U.S. bombing raids over North Vietnam and voted for the Boland Amendment, which threatened to withhold financial support for the military effort in Southeast Asia.

Her consistent stance against the war was coupled with a persistent plea to get North Vietnam to release American POWs, along with an accounting of men missing in action. In fact, she joined others in Congress in opposing a plan to help North Vietnam until the communist north gave an accounting of the missing soldiers.[100] In 1973, she cosponsored war powers legislation, which became law, limiting the President's power to commit American troops overseas in the absence of a declaration of war or specific authorization by Congress.[101] When President Nixon renewed the bombing raids over North Vietnam, Ella joined many of her colleagues in sending a strongly worded telegram to the President opposing such action.

While she was not a loud, vociferous, outspoken opponent of the war, she was publicly opposed to it and coupled that opposition with urging North Vietnam to provide an accounting of the prisoners of war and the missing in action as a gesture to veterans groups and families of men missing in action. Veterans and veterans' organizations and families of men missing in action were important, vocal, and comprised large groups of citizen voters in the Sixth Congressional District, and Ella was acutely aware of their political weight. Her stand on the issue was something voters were well aware of and had come to terms with long before.

In keeping with her concern for veterans, Ella actively sponsored legislation to bolster benefits for former POWs—a 13.6 percent increase in all GI educational benefits. And she consistently supported programs to establish drug treatment programs for every needy veteran.[102] When the Pentagon froze expansion of Veterans Administration Treatment Centers, she characterized the Nixon administration's decision as "very disturbing."[103] And she led a successful fight to have the proposal withdrawn.[104]

The year 1972 was a presidential election year, and President Nixon's bid for a second term was perceived as an easy road despite the contentious relations with the Democratic majority in Congress. John Farrell, of the *Boston Globe*, observed that in the fall of 1972 the "prognosis for

Democratic candidates was grim."[105] The major factor was that the Democratic Party's nominee Senator George McGovern (D-South Dakota) was seen as an ultra-liberal, anti-war Democrat, and his "presence at the top of the ticket was wreaking havoc" in a number of states.[106] As a result Congressman Tip O'Neill (D-Mass.), who was the controlling authority of the Democratic Congressional Campaign Committee, allocated committee funds to "sixty Democratic incumbents judged vulnerable" in that fall election.[107] Ella Grasso's reelection bid was placed on O'Neill's "vulnerable" list in an effort to bolster her reelection campaign fight. He "doled out money like a field commander," and Ella's campaign received $10,300 from the congressional campaign committee.[108] In Ella's mind, however, Nixon's anticipated reelection had created "grave misgivings" about her own ability to win a second Congressional term.[109] Nevertheless, working night and day over the course of a long campaign, Ella's campaign strategy was, as always, predicated on meeting and greeting voters "on a person to person basis."[110] It was a campaign energized and activated by Ella's own vigorous, dynamic campaign style, conducted with her usual high degree of intensity and tireless effort.

Typically, Ella frequently scheduled campaign stops in factories like Fafnir Ball Bearing in New Britain and the Torrington Company plant in Torrington, followed by a luncheon with local service clubs such as the Kiwanis Club and Rotary, and afterward would make an appearance on a radio call-in show at the local station. Nancy Lewinsohn, Ella's Washington Chief of Staff, who took time out from campaign headquarters to spend a grueling day with Ella on the campaign trail, recalls being inspired by her style of meeting and greeting everyone, no matter what their station in life, from the lathe operator in the bearing plant to the white collar manager and executives of the large factory. The lathe operators feverishly "cleaned their hand of the grease and dirt" in order to shake the Congresswoman's hand, recalls Lewinsohn. They truly "adored her" and conveyed that adulation and admiration as she moved quickly and easily through the noisy, dirty, oil-soaked factory floors. The trill in her voice at once charming and friendly conveyed a sense of genuine warmth and pleasure at meeting the workers, who in turn reciprocated by the cordial, friendly welcome extended to their familiar Congressional Representative.[111]

In that reelection bid in 1972, Ella's Republican opponent, John Walsh, criticized her on two major issues — school prayer and the rights of newsmen to protect their sources. On school prayer, Walsh noted that the Congress, including Ella, had voted against a measure to allow prayer in public schools. Ella responded that she was not anti-prayer but supported an alternative bill that included "proper language" in school prayer.[112] Ella's mother reportedly broke down in tears when she confronted her daughter about her vote. Not aware of all the implications of the legislation, she could not understand how her daughter, a faithful and devout Catholic, could vote against prayer. It took some effort on Ella's part to calm her mother down and explain her position on that particular legislation.[113]

On the measure regarding news reporters' rights, Mrs. Grasso indicated she would vote for a measure protecting the rights of newsmen, "who have historically used their power honestly and scrupulously."[114] In the final analysis, the Republican challenger did not seriously or effectively diminish Ella's standing among the Sixth District voters. Her untiring efforts were duly recognized by the size of the mandate given to the Congresswoman in that election battle. She won handily 140,290 to 92,783, a comfortable margin even in light of President Nixon's victory in Connecticut. Her plurality was a solid 47,507 votes. It was a remarkable personal triumph in view of the President's plurality of nearly 50,000 votes in the Sixth District. Fortunately for Ella, all her hard work in Washington, D.C., and effective constituent service paid off. Certainly, her attention to the economic issues affecting the congressional district helped boost her public image, and her attention to consumer-oriented issues bolstered her support among a good cross section of the district's voters.

Her victory brought an outpouring of congratulatory letters recognizing the importance of her reelection. Two of those letters, from quite different political operatives, are noteworthy. Wilma Scott Heide, a resident of Vernon, Connecticut, and President of the National Organization for Women (NOW), wrote Ella offering congratulations and adding, "I think it's good for Connecticut." And as if to prod the Congresswoman-elect, Heide urged Ella to join NOW saying, "other members of Congress belong to NOW, you should know we would welcome you."[115] Ella's reply was silence and she never joined NOW. Her decision was predicated on her belief that a woman needed to work hard as an individual person without relying on women's organizations for success in seeking public office. She never became closely associated with women's groups except for the non-partisan League of Women Voters, although she participated actively in the Congressional Women's Caucus during her time in Congress.

The second letter written right after the November election came from Malcolm Baldrige, a well-known corporate leader and longtime Connecticut Republican who would later serve as Secretary of Commerce under President Ronald Reagan. Baldridge, in his congratulatory letter, noted that, "I have not heard of such ticket splitting. Your constituents like you even this one who has to stay on the other side of the fence."[116] His letter serves as an unmistakable example of the admiring sentiment Ella Grasso frequently generated among voters — including prominent party leaders from the opposite political party.

Ella's electoral drawing-power, not only from her fellow Democrats but significantly from Republicans and Independents as well, was obvious in those 1972 results. While Connecticut Democrats lost the Presidential election, the party also lost two Congressional District seats in the state, leaving only Ella from the Sixth District, William Cotter from the First District, and Robert Giaimo from the Third District as Democratic members of Connecticut's Congressional delegation. One perceptive observer concluded that Ella's reelection victory in

1972 "clearly strengthened" any claim she might have for future "state office."[117]

Once back on Capitol Hill, Ella and her colleagues had to come to grips with the most volatile political issue that vexed the 93rd Congress in 1973 and 1974. It was the issue surrounding the Watergate break-in and the subsequent debate regarding impeachment of President Nixon. On both topics, Ella was outspoken and was consistently opposed to letting those issues fade into the background.

On June 17, 1972, five men broke into the Democratic Party national headquarters at the Watergate office complex in Washington, D.C. John Bailey had moved the party's offices there prior to his stepping down from the party chairmanship. An alert security guard thwarted the burglary attempt, and most people did not pay too much attention to the incident until after President Nixon's November reelection. In mid-March 1973, a few months into Nixon's second term, one of the accused burglars disclosed to federal Judge John Sirica that high Republican officials knew of the burglary in advance and had paid money to the defendants to keep the connection secret. Subsequent revelations uncovered the fact that the trail of suspicion and connection led to the White House staff and to dismissals and resignations of Nixon's closest advisers.

The President's ongoing refusal to allow investigators to examine White House documents on the grounds of executive privilege exacerbated the mounting tensions between the legislative branch and the executive branch of the federal government. As the disturbing evidence multiplied, compounded by the release of taped conversations from the White House Oval Office indicating President Nixon knew in advance of the Watergate break-in, a call went out for an investigation by the House Judiciary Committee. Eventually there were hearings followed by a committee vote for three articles of impeachment against the President. Shortly thereafter, on August 8, 1974, Nixon resigned the Office of the President effective the following day.

Early in this scenario of events, Ella had cosponsored a resolution in October 1973 directing the Judiciary Committee "to investigate the situation and to report its findings to the House."[118] On October 22, 1973, she publicly supported the appointment of a special prosecutor to "follow up all the loose ends of the unfinished Watergate investigation."[119] However, at that time, she was reluctant to join or contribute to the growing talk of an impeachment attempt against Nixon. "I certainly hope we don't come to that," she explained.[120] In fact she chose to refrain from publicly expressing her own views on the Watergate matter until the Committee reported to the full House. However, her reluctance to discuss the question of impeachment was jettisoned when in late summer 1974 President Nixon admitted, "he deliberately obstructed justice," and also by the "attitudes he demonstrated in the tapes," to which she was entitled to listen as a member of Congress.[121] It was at that juncture she announced, "I will vote for impeachment," if it is brought to the floor of the House of Representatives.[122]

President Richard Nixon resigned on August 8, 1974, and the nation's long nightmare over Watergate began to recede slowly from the nation's obsessive focus. But the fallout from that scandal would work to the benefit of the party of Jefferson and Jackson.

At that moment, Ella Grasso was deep into her election run for higher office back in Connecticut. Her four years in Congress had been marked by the loss of both her parents within eight months of each other. In June 1971, her father died at age 84, and her mother died shortly thereafter in March 1972, just shy of her eightieth birthday. The personal loss of both parents only deepened Ella's determination to return to Connecticut to be closer to her husband and children. She told Fourth District Congressman Stewart McKinney (R-Conn.), "I like Connecticut." And she indicated to McKinney that she, "wanted to get back to Tom" and what she called "normalcy."[123] Most observers sensed she did not like Washington, particularly "the distance from family . . . and the constant travel between the two."[124] Initially she "hated" flying, noted her Washington aide Nancy Lewinsohn.[125] To her credit, she learned to take it in stride, even though early on she incurred a middle ear infection, which affected her sense of balance. Over time she became physically acclimated to flying, and the ear problem slowly dissipated. For a brief time Ella considered not running for reelection in 1972 because of her husband's constant nagging about her absence from Connecticut.[126] But that notion did not persist very long. Tom Grasso was "spoiled" and was frequently on the phone in late afternoon "moaning about her absence," noted Nancy Lewinsohn.[127] That view of Tom's demeanor is confirmed, in part, by Tom Grasso who bemoaned the fact that Ella was in Washington and unable to be "the typical Italian wife . . . [formerly] whenever I needed something she was there for me."[128]

Ella Grasso's own comments to a *Detroit News* reporter summed up her basic reason for not seeking a third term in Congress. "I feel a strong attraction to my state. I think my roots are so deep it would be difficult for me to go anywhere else. I found my four years in Washington most instructive . . . but would have been happier if they moved the capitol to Hartford."[129] She went on to say, "It was difficult for me to be away from Connecticut, my roots are so deeply entwined. I think it was really a pulling up process to go to Washington every week."[130]

Ironically, during the last year and a half of her second term, Ella confided to Nancy Lewinsohn that she had come to "feel comfortable in Washington and was enjoying many aspects of her life there." Lewinsohn noted that Ella was taking advantage of music and theater offerings at the Kennedy Center, not far from Ella's apartment on Virginia Avenue in the Foggy Bottom section of the District of Columbia.[131]

A family view, offered by Ella's daughter Susane, suggests Ella was "very uncomfortable in D.C." She disliked being separated from her family and felt that Congress "did not move fast enough" on legislation and congressional committee reforms.[132]

As the 1974 election year approached, however, there was little doubt Ella would return to Connecticut and seek the statewide office she had long desired. Her frustration in Washington was twofold: first, she found the wheels of Congress moved very slowly; second, as a two-term representative, in an institution built on seniority, Ella's chances to truly wield influence and clout were severely constrained.

A great deal of Ella's success had been her close political relationship with the party leadership in Connecticut and their reliance on her intellectual skills, political know how, and leadership abilities. She was especially valued as a politician with an exemplary reputation for integrity and knowledge of state government operations.

Above all she had a wealth of good will among Connecticut voters, which made her desirous of returning to Connecticut where she could make a difference—and where her considerable talents could have an impact on the lives of the state's citizens.

On January 19, 1974 she made her history-making announcement that she would seek the Democratic nomination for Governor of the State of Connecticut.

❧ 7 ❧

I BELIEVE WORKING FOR PEOPLE IS
THE NOBLEST PROFESSION

January 19, 1974, unfolded as a stormy, wintry New England day in Connecticut. Snow, ice, and sleet blanketed the roads and highways throughout the state. For Ella Grasso, however, it was the day of her long anticipated announcement that she was running as a candidate for the Democratic nomination for Governor of Connecticut.

It was a day she had long hoped would come. The idea of running for Governor "was there for a long time but it didn't seem possible," she said, "women weren't candidates. You remember John Bailey's famous statement that he'd run a woman when he thought he'd lose. He would say that and chortle ho-ho-ho."[1] Molly Toro remembers from her time with Ella in the Secretary of the State's Office that running for Governor "was in her mind . . . she knew she was going to be Governor some day."[2] Susane Grasso recalls that her mother "definitely wanted to be Governor and she was focused . . . she was just waiting for the door to open."[3]

After months of speculation, rumor, and private discussions, Ella made her official announcement January 19, 1974, before an excited and happy throng of family, hometown friends, neighbors, and political supporters. Not surprisingly, Ella selected Windsor Locks as the location for her declaration, which took place at the local Ramada Inn. Making the announcement in her hometown seemed especially appropriate for this woman who reminded the crowd what Windsor Locks meant to her. "This is the town in which I was born. I learned here about the meaning of neighbor, my personal responsibility to state and country, and the wisdom of a proper respect for the opinion of others." It was a gentle reminder to all of her deep hometown roots, the lessons she earned early in her life and of that which prepared her for "a long and hard and difficult undertaking."[4]

In her announcement address she promised to offer Connecticut's citizens "new confidence in government and positive leadership." She emphasized that, "The time is NOW to restore government, CONNECTI-CUT STYLE, the diligence, the dialogue and direction that means once more — people, all of the people — working together in the service of our beloved State." She put forth what would become a major theme of her campaign: openness in government. "The time is NOW," she said, "to establish the principle that in order to serve the people, government must be open, direct and available. The governor must seek the voices of people in each of our cities and towns and the counsel of their elected officials in a new PARTNERSHIP of citizens and government for a better Connecticut."[5]

Ella also reminded the gathering of "dedicated party workers, old and new friends, and associates in other causes without party labels," that there had been one principle that motivated and guided her public career, "to work for people and to serve them with all my heart and mind and spirit."[6]

Ella's announcement on that cold, stormy morning conveyed to the excited crowd of friends and supporters her sincere commitment to public service. And it demonstrated clearly her skillful use of a rhythmic, cadenced flow of words intended to inspire and engage people in her most ambitious and challenging political endeavor.

Ella's decision to run for Governor had been rumored for several months in stories she neither confirmed nor denied. Prior to her January announcement, a front-page story in the *Hartford Times* in early November 1973 quoted personal friends of Ella as saying that she told them she was going to make the run.[7] In fact, her campaign chairman Bill O'Neill, Democratic state representative from East Hampton, recalls being called by Ella in late November or early December 1973 and asked, "if I would help her."[8] O'Neill, who did not know Ella well, conferred with John Bailey before acceding to Ella's request. O'Neill explained that, "it made great sense if you were an Italian running for Governor in the State of Connecticut" to select an Irishman as the campaign chairman. "I was Irish and I had not made any enemies in the legislature."[9] Indeed the careful ethnic equilibrium between the Irish and Italians so critical to political success in Connecticut politics was secured by Grasso's designation of O'Neill.

That Ella was running for the nomination did not surprise a lot of Connecticut voters because she had emerged in public opinion polls "as the strongest contender for the nomination and the general election."[10] "Thanks to her own efforts," wrote columnist David Broder, "she has lined up enough votes to guarantee her nomination for Governor."[11] John Bailey did not immediately voice his support for Grasso's candidacy. In fact, Ella told veteran *Hartford Courant* reporter Jack Zaiman that, "Bailey was for Killian."[12] Publicly he was "neutral," since there were other Democrats interested in seeking the nomination, and Bailey could not afford to alienate them or their supporters.[13] The other major contender, Attorney General Robert Killian, was an Irish politician from Hartford who also happened to be a close friend and associate of John Bailey. One longtime Bailey admirer, who saw John Bailey frequently at lunch at the Parma restaurant in Hartford, recalls that Bailey favored Killian. He remembers he told Bailey, "you elected the first Jewish Governor, you elected the first Catholic President, now you are going to elect the first woman governor in her own right." And "he would listen and say I want Killian."[14]

There were several reasons Bailey favored Killian. One was that the Attorney General was of Irish ancestry (his mother was Jewish). And Bailey believed "the Irish favorite" at the top of the ticket spelled victory.[15] Second Bob Killian was a longtime key member of the Hartford Democratic political organization (although he had recently been ousted as the Chairman of the Hartford Town Committee), which Bailey had controlled, and they had been political and personal friends for decades. Further, his reluctance to support Ella Grasso for Governor was grounded in his belief that an Italian-American at the head of the Democratic ticket would not be a winning proposition. (Mim Daddario's defeat in 1970 was a constant reminder of that fact). Ella's gender was a factor in his thinking as well. No woman had ever been nominated or made a run for Governor in either party in Connecticut, ever. Thus, there was no doubt that Bailey's traditional male chauvinistic belief that running a woman spelled defeat was enough to make Ella's efforts seem less than hopeful in his political calculations. However, it seems plausible to also suggest that Bailey's reluctance about her candidacy also stemmed from the fact that while he admired Ella's talents, among his concerns was her forceful, erratic temperament, which sometimes led to an uneasy relationship with her staff and colleagues. Bob Killian's calmer more considerate personality, Bailey felt, would make a more suitable candidate and governor.[16]

Bob Killian, who had been appointed to fill a vacancy as Attorney General in 1967, ran for a full term as Attorney General in 1970. He squeaked through to victory that year by a margin of 1,763 votes.[17] He had not been particularly forceful or aggressive in that visible state office, though he was well liked, admired, and trusted, particularly by John Bailey. The public's perception, however, was that he was reserved and laid back, and hardly a household name to many Connecticut voters. But Killian had been attentive to Democratic Party leaders and political organizations around the state and felt confident he could count on that grass roots support in vying for the nomination. In early 1973, despite the efforts of two other interested contenders, Homer Babbidge, former President of the University of Connecticut, and Frank Zullo, former Mayor of Norwalk, Killian was thought to be the frontrunner.

In the spring of 1973, the *Hartford Times* published the results of a poll, which showed Bob Killian "trailing Governor Meskill, but revealed Ella

Grasso far ahead of the incumbent governor."[18] Another poll showed Killian losing to a Republican Congressman Robert Steele (the eventual GOP candidate) 36 percent to 34 percent.[19] At that point, Bailey urged the contenders to "go around and see people" and urged key local and statewide political leaders to remain "loose" and not commit to anyone.[20] However, by mid-summer 1973, a poll of 906 people conducted by *Connecticut Magazine* revealed that Congresswoman Grasso would defeat the sitting Governor Thomas Meskill 44 percent to 34 percent.[21]

In mid-1973, Bailey's political and personal problems increased. He was confronted with serious health problems and underwent surgery for lip cancer. At that time, the disease had not spread, but it was a serious personal setback for the long-time Democratic leader. He also encountered one of the thorniest political problems that he ever faced as State Chairman. It became obvious that both Ella Grasso and Bob Killian were the two strongest rivals for the nomination—and both were close friends and political associates of the veteran party chief. Yet for John Bailey, the bottom line, the prime-motivating factor in backing political candidates throughout his long and successful political career was winning elections—"to get a candidate who could win."[22] Many political observers believe Bailey would have "even run his mother."[23] Or, "he would run the devil—a good devil," if he felt that individual could win.[24] But his early neutrality and "hands off" approach actually served Ella Grasso's interests better because she could campaign around the state as her own person without being perceived as the candidate of the party boss. Bailey's position mirrored that of Abraham Ribicoff who announced, "I have no intention of telling the people of this state who they shall nominate for governor. That's up to them."[25] Ella was "never able to budge her old allies Bailey, Ribicoff, and John Dempsey from their cautious neutrality," until she soundly defeated Killian in his hometown delegate primary in Hartford.[26]

In the ensuing months of 1974, the shifting tides of the political waters of Connecticut moved in Ella Grasso's direction. A poll taken by the respected Washington, D.C., pollster Peter Hart, released March 24, 1974, showed Ella Grasso beating her expected GOP rival Congressman Robert Steele 55 percent to 23 percent.[27] In addition, she was moving about the state lining up delegate support and endorsements, especially among key political leaders. She managed to persuade the New Haven Democratic Town Committee Chairman Arthur Barbieri to back her, and she received the support of Stamford's entire convention delegation.[28] The Windsor Locks native also benefited from an ascending sentiment in the state that "it was time for a woman."[29] The results of municipal elections in November 1973 in three traditionally Republican towns of Clinton, Westport, and West Hartford affirmed this judgment. For the first time three Democratic women were elected to the post of First Selectman or Mayor. It was "proof of strength" that women candidates "had drawn substantial support from Republicans and independent voters," something Ella Grasso had been able to do throughout her political career.[30]

Washington Post columnist David Broder described 1974 as a "year of mobilization by women for political power," in the United States.[31] It was a time of escalating sentiment of support for women candidates, combined with "strong—very strong ethnic support for her" among Italian-American voters in Connecticut.[32] All of these factors gave impetus to Ella Grasso's quest for significant pre-convention delegate support.

Another plus was Ella's high recognition among the electorate, which was bound to play a very important role in the pre-convention weeks. "Mrs. Grasso is greeted wherever she goes," noted newspaper reporter Bob Conrad, "with much adulation. It is genuine, because she is enormously popular. These outpourings of warmth also enable the people around her to tell critics, just look—they all love Ella."[33] Even the Republican Governor Thomas Meskill, who had decided not to seek a second term, speaking about Ella, opined that, "She's always been popular and I don't think she has many enemies . . . I think she can win."[34] Thus, the momentum of a Grasso bandwagon appeared unstoppable and reached a climax on May 23, 1974, when a Democratic state convention delegate primary occurred in the city of Hartford. The rival delegate slates, committed to either Robert Killian or Ella Grasso, mounted a spirited and, as it turned out, pivotal campaign. Nicholas Carbone, who had spearheaded the ouster of Killian as Hartford Democratic Town Committee Chairman, and who had become an early Grasso supporter, masterminded the Grasso effort in Hartford against the Killian forces. It put Carbone on a "collision course with . . . Killian," once again, and resulted in "one of the most bitter political fights" in Hartford's storied political history.[35] The battle resulted in a stunning triumph for Ella Grasso in Killian's hometown. The final tally was 6,481 to 4,562.[36] At that point, realizing Bob Killian was mortally wounded as a result of his Hartford defeat, John Bailey stepped forward in his capacity as State Democratic Party Chairman. He moved to strike a deal that would put together a Grasso-Killian ticket, which he was convinced would be a winner in November.

Several weeks went by during which Bailey sought to bring Ella Grasso and Bob Killian together. Eventually two meetings were held at Bailey's home in Hartford. It was obvious that Ella Grasso had the upper hand in the negotiations because she had commitments from a majority of the delegates to the upcoming state convention. Killian, for his part, "resentful" and bitterly disappointed with his Hartford defeat, warned that he would have to "take a good hard look at the whole situation," eventually agreed to Bailey's entreaties and accepted second place on the Democratic ticket on July 3, 1974.[37] Killian, putting his best face on the situation, told a press conference that, "This is the first step toward the unification of the Democratic Party. It is not a phony patch up." And Ella Grasso noted that she came to the conclusion "it would be very good if we could serve together as a team." After all, she added, "Isn't that what politics is all about."[38]

Killian, who was "never close" to Ella Grasso, believed that John Bailey would rather have had him as the candidate. Bailey was convinced, however, that Ella's "enormous popularity" made it likely she could win the November election. Killian emphasized there was no quid-pro-quo between John Bailey, Ella Grasso, and himself that if victorious Ella would serve only one term. Rather he emphasized that Ella Grasso "would not sell herself short like that" and agree to a deal limiting her service to only one term.[39]

From the start "it was an uncomfortable relationship" between Grasso and Killian recalls Bob Conrad, a veteran State Capitol reporter. Conrad goes so far as to characterize the former rivals political marriage as being like the "odd couple."[40] Larrye DeBear, an experienced state Capitol television reporter and later Ella's gubernatorial press secretary, remembers that Grasso "did not want him" and that they barely "tolerated each other."[41] Most observers agreed that Bailey's ability to mend fences and bring the two opposing candidates together was one of his most amazing political achievements. Seen by some as a master stroke, it clearly reflected Bailey's keen political skills and his special talent for patching up party wounds in order to win elections. The state party Chairman, for his part, publicly stated, "It was an agreement made by old friends interested in the success of the Democratic Party. Their agreement makes sure the Democratic Party will be successful in the election."[42] For Bailey, winning was everything. The Republican side, led by Governor Thomas Meskill, saw the Grasso-Killian "political marriage" in a quite different light. In a pointed and acerbic comment, Meskill brusquely pushed aside the Grasso-Killian merger as the announcement "that the over the hill mob is back together for a re-run of the tragedies of the sixties."[43] It would be a theme the Republicans would revisit frequently in the months leading up to the November election.

John Bailey's physical health began to deteriorate noticeably as the pre-convention activities gained momentum. The chairman, facing ongoing medical problems related to cancer, continued to direct the party organization as it prepared for its biennial convention at the Bushnell Hall Auditorium in Hartford. As fate would have it, it would be the last convention Bailey presided over in his almost thirty-year career as

Connecticut's Democratic State Chairman. From a historical perspective, Bailey's "reign as state chairman" was the "longest of any statewide political leader in history," and it remains a record no one has come close to breaking in the State of Connecticut.[44]

The Democratic Convention was held July 19–20, 1974. Amid the hoopla of flags and signs a cheering crowd of excited Democratic delegates mingled on the floor of the cavernous hall. The air was stifling on that hot, humid mid-summer weekend, but the atmosphere was upbeat, and the expectations of a November victory wafted through the auditorium. Nearby at the Hilton Hotel the mood was anything but boisterous. There the Grasso and Killian families were together, acting friendly but hardly able to disguise their personal discomfort as they waited the long roll-call process of nominations taking place one block away. There was little speculation about the top of the ticket since the convention delegates were all aware of the Bailey deal, which placed the two former rivals on the ticket as running mates. Former Norwalk Mayor Frank Zullo, Ella's only remaining rival for the gubernatorial nomination, withdrew since he did not have the necessary 20 percent delegate support to force a primary. As it turned out, in almost an anti-climax, the convention delegates selected Ella Grasso for Governor and Robert Killian for Lieutenant Governor without opposition. The rest of the Democratic slate included Gloria Schaffer, Secretary of the State; Henry Parker, State Treasurer; J. Edward Caldwell, State Comptroller; and Carl Ajello, Attorney General. The list of endorsed candidates reflects John Bailey's long-standing, successful practice of assembling a geographic and ethnically balanced ticket: a minority (Parker), a Jew (Schaffer), an urban representative (Caldwell), an Irishman (Killian), and two Italians (Grasso and Ajello).

On Saturday July 20, 1974, Ella Grasso delivered her acceptance speech to the twelve hundred assembled delegates. It was a history making moment with "two hundred sets of press credentials" issued to national and international press organizations covering the event, doubling the number issued at the previous gubernatorial nominating convention. "Those figures indicate the interest Ella Grasso's candidacy stirred," commented *New York Times* reporter Linda Greenhouse, a Connecticut native.[45]

In her remarks, Congresswoman Grasso pledged to "restore good government and . . . respect for government and those who serve." Calling on her best political instincts, she laid out what would become a theme of the 1974 campaign emphasizing that the "people are tired of a state government that hides its acts behind a curtain of secrecy." She promised "a government that is open, honest, vital, concerned." Government secrecy, a legacy of Watergate, had become a concern of many people in the state and Ella Graso would eventually propose legislation (Freedom of Information Act), which would deal with that concern head on. Next, she promised "tough-minded economic policies" along with a continuation of the "needed range of humane services . . . within the limits of our resources." Thirdly, Ella promised to "bring economic growth" to the state along with "quality education."[46]

In her acceptance speech, she laid out rather broadly what she viewed as the issues for the campaign-open government, sound financial management, education, transportation, and human service programs. It was vintage Ella Grasso speaking in generalities but touching all appropriate political chords of determination, optimism, and hope, and she reminded the audience of the guiding principle that motivated her public career: the "sounds of the people . . . the voices that have guided me in all my public life . . . will continue to be my strength and inspiration."[47] Ella's heartfelt remarks reflect a theme that she often expressed throughout her career and provides affirmation not only of her strength of character but also the trust she engendered among Connecticut's citizens.

Ella Grasso's nomination by the Connecticut Democratic Party, the first woman that the party of Jefferson and Jackson ever nominated for Governor in the state, represents in a very real way the culmination of a long career in Connecticut elective politics. Since her first run for office in 1952, Ella Tambussi Grasso had dedicated her entire career to public service and elective office, and she was, at that point, a "proven vote getter" with "top political backing," who became the favorite to win the November election.[48] Alan Olmstead, an experienced journalist and veteran observer of the Connecticut political scene explained, "Ella is a candidate whose time has come," and, he added, that it was as if her nomination were the "natural and proper moment for which all her previous activities and experience had been preparing her."[49]

What Ella Grasso's long political experience and public persona brought to the political playing field in 1974 was a smart, gutsy, political warrior, a "complete political professional."[50] She could boast of a wellspring of good will, she was popular across party lines, and she had strong voter recognition among the voting public in Connecticut. Another important factor in her successful quest for the nomination in 1974 was that with all of the political turmoil and strident political rhetoric and revelations swirling around the Watergate investigations in Washington, D.C., the voters "highest priorities are honesty and integrity: virtues which have long been a part of Ella's profile."[51] In large measure, Ella's strengths would prove to be too formidable a winning combination against her eventual opponent, popular two-term Republican Congressman Robert Steele, Jr., of Vernon, Connecticut.

Exactly one week later, on July 27, in the same auditorium where the Democrats had met, the Connecticut Grand Old Party gave the son of a well-known Hartford radio talk show host Bob Steele Jr. the nod to run for Governor. Steele, a young, photogenic, thirty-five-year-old had "worked as a Soviet specialist for the CIA" earlier in his career.[52] And he was touted as a new breed Republican, not tied to the GOP Old Guard faction that had long dominated Connecticut's Republican party. He had been elected twice to the United States House of Representatives from the sprawling Second Congressional District east of the Connecticut River, and had developed a reputation as a hard-working, dedicated, energetic Congressman who would present a sharp contrast to his plain, folksy, unpretentious, older opponent Ella Grasso.

Baby Photograph, 1919.
Courtesy of Susane Oliva Grasso.

Ella on the Beach,
Old Lyme, Connecticut.
*Courtesy of Susane
Oliva Grasso.*

ELLA T. GRASSO
FOR SECRETARY OF THE STATE

Ella Tambussi Grasso is a housewife and mother, an educator and an experienced state legislator, well informed on the affairs of Connecticut. She is equipped to understand Connecticut's problems and to act wisely for her state.

Campaign Brochure, 1958. *Courtesy of Susane Oliva Grasso.*

State Representative Ella Grasso of Windsor Locks, 1953–1957. *Photograph by Bachrach.*

The Tambussi family. *Upper row, far right* Ella's mother Maria; *middle row, far right*, Ella's father James; Ella, *center*, with Susane and James, *first row, right. Courtesy of the* Hartford Courant.

The Grasso family. Tom, James, Ella, and Susane.
Courtesy of Susane Oliva Grasso.

Ella with Democratic State Chairman John Bailey, 1970.
Courtesy of the New Haven Register.

Ella with Christopher Dodd,
candidate for Congress, and Betty
Hudson, candidate for State Senate, 1974.
All three were victorious. *Courtesy of
Betty Hudson.*

Ella receives phone call from
Lieutenant Governor Robert Killian
conceding the Democratic gubernatorial
primary, September 12, 1978. *(AP Photo/
Bob Child) (7809121176)*

Governor Grasso signs Urban Jobs Bill, 1978.
Photograph courtesy of Riley D. Johnson, Jr.

Ella speaks at a groundbreaking ceremony, April 1979. *Photograph by Al Coutoure.*

Ella with Dick Cavett, May 1978. *Record Group 005, Governor Ella T. Grasso, State Archives, Connecticut State Library.*

Ella on Connecticut Valley Line, Essex Steam Railroad Engine. *Record Group 005, Governor Ella T. Grasso, State Archives, Connecticut State Library.*

Senator Abraham Ribicoff and Ella Grasso celebrate Carter-Mondale election, 1976. *Record Group 005, Governor Ella T. Grasso, State Archives, Connecticut State Library.*

Ella campaigning with Vice President Walter Mondale 1980. *Record Group 005, Governor Ella T. Grasso, State Archives, Connecticut State Library.*

Ella Grasso and First Lady Rosalynn Carter campaigning in April 1980. *Record Group 005, Governor Ella T. Grasso, State Archives, Connecticut State Library.*

Ella greets President Jimmy Carter at the White House. *Courtesy: Jimmy Carter Library.*

Medal of Freedom awarded posthumously to Ella Grasso, October 1981. *Courtesy of Susane Oliva Grasso.*

Steele, in his acceptance speech, fired an opening salvo tying Ella Grasso into the ongoing debate over the income tax that he believed the Democrats would impose in order to keep the "promises of the Democratic platform." He contrasted what in his view was an "unparalleled record of fiscal achievement and fiscal management by the Republican Meskill administration" to the "inept record of fiscal management of the last Democratic administration" of which Ella Grasso had been a part. And Congressman Steele also promised campaign reforms as one of his major campaign issues "because it's right to try to drive big money and special influence out of politics." But it was not a speech that truly inspired his supporters or set a tone to introduce Steele adequately to the electorate, so important because his statewide exposure had been limited.[53]

However, this was to be Ella Grasso's year. It would be the year of a breakthrough for women in an election contest that drew charges by Steele that Ella was "hand picked by her boss, John Bailey," which was totally untrue. But knowing that Bailey initially had not favored her candidacy, she responded, "I am not a handpicked candidate," and added, "I had to fight for the nomination. I am Ella Grasso."[54] Her deep-rooted popularity among the electorate, however, would not be swayed, diminished, or tainted by those types of charges. Rather, Ella's long-time bond with Connecticut voters, established over several decades of public service, would go a long way to insure victory that November.

The issues separating the Democrats and Republicans became clear in the days following the two conventions. Taxes, government secrecy, utility costs, and the future of the state's economy topped the list of issues in the ensuing campaign.

Ella's Washington Administrative Aide, Nancy Lewinsohn, took a "leave of absence from her regular chores" and was brought up to Connecticut to manage the Grasso campaign.[55] And as the campaign unfolded in the summer of 1974, Ella Grasso focused on several key themes and issues, many of which aimed to revitalize the state's sagging economy.

Highlighting the fact that one in five production jobs in Connecticut factories had disappeared between 1967 and 1972, she continuously re-emphasized her commitment to improving job training programs and retraining production workers for new jobs in the changing economy.[56] A proposal for a seven-point program that signaled her determination to reinvigorate and revitalize Connecticut's distressed economy was made.[57] While she was well aware of the obvious need for such a program, her placement of economic issues on the front burner of the heated political battlefront stemmed from a conviction, burnished in the Depression years, that an economy on the skids brought great economic and emotional harm to people, families, and indeed the whole community. Thus, Ella's introduction of the Seven Point Package containing her economic program had principally one aim — job creation. It remained the focus throughout her campaign and during the administration when she became Governor.[58] It included: an Early Monitoring Support and Action team to spot failing industries and provide assistance to stave off closure; tax incentives and exemptions to business and industry for expanded research and development of new products; encouragement for Connecticut firms with their national headquarters in the state to open operational units here; expanded major opportunities for venture capital to invest in Connecticut; a task force on Emergency Employment Programs to focus on weak areas in the job market in regions around the state; placing the Council of Economic Advisors under the Governor's Office; and lastly, revitalizing and reinvigorating the Commerce Department.[59]

Those seven components became the core of Ella Grasso's economic proposals throughout the election campaign. Then, a few days later, after introducing the Seven Point Package, she reiterated her stand on the general campaign issues by outlining what she believed were the central issues of the 1974 campaign: jobs, an aggressive Commerce Department, expansion of the efforts to protect consumers (posting unit prices for food and drugs, truth-in-lending disclosure, control of utility rates), and restoring confidence in government. Also she noted her determination to restore humane programs, develop an integrated public transportation system, develop better partnerships with local government (through the use of revenue sharing money to lessen the property tax burden), and, finally, to keep the tax structure with no income tax.[60]

Those pledges contained the essence of Ella's stance on the campaign issues as she saw them. It would presage an aggressive "pro-jobs, pro-business" approach, which would make jobs and expanding Connecticut's economic base a major cornerstone of her future gubernatorial administration.

Steele, for his part, attempted to tag Ella as a tax and spend liberal and referred to her sarcastically as "Spenderella."[61] Tying her in with the budget deficits of the previous Democratic administration of Governor John Dempsey, Steele also commented that if Ella were elected and stuck to all the "far-fetched promises" of the Democratic platform, then the income tax was going to be imposed.[62] In response, she noted that an income tax "is not a good idea for Connecticut because the people of the state have said time and time again that this is a tax program that is not acceptable to them."[63] In a campaign statement in August 1974, she responded to Steele's taunts portraying her as supporting an income tax, by announcing again "I am opposed to a state income tax and as Governor would design the budget within the framework of our present tax structure. I stand by this statement today and in the future."[64]

The Republican standard bearer, by pressing Ella on the issue of a state income tax, repeated his theme that the Democratic platform of 1974 would require expenditures of "$375 million to $400 million beyond the present budget levels." His "campaign blitzkrieg" conveyed the idea that Ella would need an income tax to bail her out of the "spending jag" that the Democratic platform required.[65]

Bristling under the Steele salvos and placed "on the defensive" immediately by the "pressure cooker push" of the Republican attack, Ella found herself fending off the offensive in several ways.[66] First, she and her running mates held a joint news conference and went on record opposing a state personal income tax.[67] Second, she reacted by placing herself firmly against the income tax, saying on the public record that she would "veto such a measure if it came before me as Governor."[68] Third, coyly and adroitly she sidestepped the issue of whether the Democratic pledge to increase spending would force her to impose an income tax. Instead Ella emphasized that the "platform is a set of goals and aims and that they will be realized only within the framework we have before us tax-wise."[69]

In effect, the income tax debate and the requisite Grasso pledge to veto such an initiative forced her into an "economic position without regard to the conditions that may prevail in several years . . . it set a precondition for the full term she hopes to win."[70] Despite that incisive observation by one observer of the Connecticut political landscape, Ella remembered the Chester Bowles debacle of the late 1940s, when his proposal of an income tax led directly to Bowles' reelection defeat in 1950. Ella Grasso was not going to be caught in the same political trap. As a result, she reiterated the pledge not to impose a personal income tax on Connecticut taxpayers.

It was the issue concerning utilities and energy matters that ignited the most attention and discussion during the 1974 campaign. In that year, Connecticut citizens were facing increasing energy costs that were in large measure due to what was called the fuel cost adjustment charge levied on customers of the state's three largest utility companies. Utilities burned fuel oil to produce electricity, and as fuel costs rose and the utilities expenditures for oil increased, the companies passed on those expenses to their customers. Also, the utilities were allowed to pass on those charges without a public hearing conducted by the Public Utility Commission. Further, the utility companies continued to charge that expense even though they now burned less oil to produce electricity. By 1974, they were still allowed to pocket the difference between their costs and what they charged customers.

Ella latched onto this issue and pounded away at it for the duration of the campaign. It was, perhaps, the most successful campaign issue she raised and it captured the attention of the voters as few other issues did in the race for governor.

Her basic position was that the utilities, which had been allowed to levy the fuel cost adjustment charge for the previous twelve months, overcharged the public by eleven million dollars. Second, she pointed out that the situation was allowed to continue without oversight by the state's Public Utilities Commission, which was "not protecting the public." Third, if the utilities had "legitimate extra expenses," those costs were supposed to be handled in a regular rate case public hearing before the Commission not through the fuel cost adjustment charge.[71]

Those overcharges, affirmed by a study undertaken by a research firm authorized to study the issue by the Grasso campaign, led Ella to say, "It is clear that this agency (the PUC) does not serve the purpose for which it was created. There is no course but to abolish the Public Utilities Commission and establish a new Commission that will protect the public interest." The utility companies responded to the Democratic candidate's charges and "confirmed that the formula used to charge customers for fuel may have been outdated and that overcharges may have occurred." In fact, the United Illuminating Company, one of the three utilities supplying electricity to various areas of Connecticut, revealed it had overcharged consumers $5.7 million dollars over a three-year period.[72]

That startling admission by the public utility companies, called a "campaign coup" for the Democratic candidate by a *Washington Post* reporter, resulted in an outcry of public indignation and outrage.[73] The public's reaction provided additional and substantial momentum to the Grasso campaign, fueled in part by widespread press and media coverage for the Democratic candidate. As a result of the overcharge revelations, Ella Grasso moved quickly to capitalize on public reaction and called for the abolition of the Public Utilities Commission replacing it with "a new Utilities Control Authority with power to regulate the utilities, to begin proper energy planning, and to streamline the regulatory process bringing it into the twentieth century and to protect against special interests."[74] Her proposal for reform suggested a new authority with five commission members to be appointed by the Governor with consent of both houses of the General Assembly. The proposal she put forward deviated from the previous appointment process, which had provided the Governor with complete authority to appoint commission members without Assembly approval. Under Ella Grasso's proposal, members of the commission would serve fulltime for six-year terms, disclose financial holdings, and have expertise in areas vital to utility regulation. Key to her reform proposal was the provision that the new authority have sufficient staff and experts, so that it could compete equally, or at least not be disadvantaged by the staff and resources of the utilities. The revitalized commission would be required to hold public hearings on all changes in the fuel cost adjustment clause. And her proposal called for establishing an Office of Consumer Advocate appointed by the Legislature and responsible to that branch of government rather than the executive.[75]

In the weeks that followed, two of the utilities rate hike requests were granted by the Public Utilities Commission, leading Ella Grasso to threaten court action to stop the implementation of the hike.[76] She joined with Ralph Nader's consumer watchdog group and a Hartford Consumers Activist Association to seek a court injunction.[77] A few days later, Judge Maurice Sponzo announced a temporary injunction against the PUC until a fall hearing in December after the election.[78]

For his part, Ella's opponent Congressman Steele seemed unable and unwilling to enter the fray, fearful of taking on the electric utility companies and the PUC, whose five-member commission included the Republican Party's former State Chairman Howard Hausman. Ella's daily, hard-hitting, headline grabbing statements and comments energized her and resonated with the public and effectively boxed Steele into a defense that was marked initially by silence.

In one of her most dynamic, assertive, and attention getting campaign actions, Ella took "the battle to the doorstep of the opposition." Armed with a copy of the research firm's report on utility overcharges and trailed by a large contingent of radio, television and print media, she "stormed into the state office building to present the Public Utility Commission Chairman Howard Hausman with a copy of the report." When confronted by a commission official who asked if state officials could "cross examine" the individuals who wrote the report, "Mrs. Grasso boomed, 'My dear, I would hope you would feel it was not cross examination but sharing information. As a matter of fact, most of the information came from your own files.'" She turned "on her heel, [and] left with as much authority as she entered."[79]

Congressman Steele, on the defensive, eventually offered his own set of proposals including retention of the PUC, annual confirmation of the members by the General Assembly, and a proposal to build an oil refinery off the southeast coast of Connecticut. The refinery proposal was a ludicrous suggestion that neither addressed consumer's outrage regarding overcharges nor considered environmental concerns about potential damage to Long Island Sound.

By taking on disclosure of utility overcharges "Mrs Grasso pulled off a campaign coup" wrote a *Washington Post* reporter dispatched to cover her campaign.[80] And she emerged as a populist champion protecting consumers while at the same time proposing a reform of the system that would restore people's confidence in government. That very objective Ella had promised the voters when she announced her run for Governor.

Consequently, it is not surprising the first piece of legislation that Connecticut's future governor would submit to the General Assembly was the Public Utility Control Authority reform proposal similar to that put forward during the campaign.[81] While campaigns are not won on one issue, surely Ella Grasso's public success with the fuel cost adjustment charge persuaded many voters that she was a fighter for them, and it lent credence to her long-held belief that "the political process has a very direct impact on the lives of everyone . . . and I have a profound respect for people and hope to use the machinery of the law in the service of people."[82]

Another commitment that Ella Grasso made and continually advocated was an updating of Connecticut's Right-To-Know law. Sensing a strong public sentiment to have the government conduct the "public's business . . . in public," in reaction to the climate perpetrated by Watergate in Washington, Ella proposed conducting the state's business like leases or contracts, with insurance policies and major public policy issues out in the open, and making them accessible to press and public scrutiny.[83] To refuse access or to prohibit releasing that information would create a climate that would produce an environment similar to what occurred in the Nixon Watergate cover-up controversy.

Seeing it as a keystone of her promise of openness in government and convinced that the old laws needed "tightening and closing of the loopholes," she announced that she would insure public access and open government at all levels of Connecticut government. And pledging that there would be no more secrecy in government, her concept included the idea that there would be no closed meetings by any town, administrative, legislative, or executive agency of government. Her proposal included a requirement that the public meetings law be applied to the General Assembly committees (which were exempt under then current law). Further, it provided stiff penalties of up to a year in jail for public officials who violated the open meeting statute.[84] She also promised that all of her commissioners appointed to Cabinet-level posts, as well as individuals appointed to key positions on the Governor's staff, would be required to publicly disclose their finances at the time of their appointment. By requiring full disclosure of their assets, she continued a practice, which had always been followed in every campaign she ever waged. It would not be a requirement some of her appointees relished, but in the post-Watergate environment it would prove to be a popular decision among the Connecticut electorate.

Ella's idea of openness extended to the promise of holding public budget hearings around the state, providing "all the people an opportunity to be heard" on the governor's proposed budget.[85] This proposal, welcomed by many individuals, groups, and organizations, would eventually become a reality. It served as a vital, direct link between the Governor and Connecticut's citizens on formulating budget priorities, budget suggestions, and budget requests.

As the campaign ensued, Ella's non-stop, indefatigable style of campaigning and her continuous discussion of issues that appealed to a broad spectrum of voters sparked an outpouring of volunteer support for her candidacy. Throngs of volunteers descended on campaign headquarters all around the state, including the operations center of Ella's campaign located in modest offices at the Bishops Corner shopping center in West Hartford, Connecticut.

Campaign manager Nancy Lewinsohn remembers the frenetic, fast-paced activity that emanated daily from that unpretentious office complex. She recalls that large groups of students, senior citizens, party loyalists, and newcomers to political campaigns were among the backbone of the campaign volunteer force.[86] These groups brought additional energy, excitement, and dynamism to the campaign, which was already caught up in the spirited and vigorous campaign Ella was waging throughout the state. Volunteers distributed bumper stickers, buttons, lapel pins, and brochures emblazoned with the familiar green color that became immediately and widely identified with Ella and her candidacy.

On the campaign trail the "usual barrage of handouts" that blanketed the Connecticut terrain was in part entrusted to this nucleus of campaign volunteers.[87] The commitment and dedication of volunteers, along with the local organizational grass-roots work to get out the vote, facilitated by members of the Democratic Town Committees and labor unions, provided extra drive, enthusiasm, and momentum to the state-wide campaign.

The 1974 Connecticut gubernatorial contest was unique: for the first time in American history a woman was running for governor — not tied to the political fortunes of her husband's previous service as an officeholder or public official. Ella Grasso's tireless, high-energy style of campaigning generated additional widespread public interest in the governor's race.

Typically, Ella believed it was essential to meet, greet, and talk to as many voters as she could. For example, by the end of September 1974, she had held town meetings in each of the eight counties of the state. Another part of that strategy was Ella's personal campaigning with Democratic Party candidates. Betty Hudson, a Democratic candidate for the State Senate from Madison, remembers campaigning with Ella Grasso that fall. "The first thing I remember is how down to earth she was . . . we campaigned on the beaches at Hammonasset (a state park on the shore of Long Island Sound) and of course I should have known . . . how fluent she was in Italian. She was going along the beaches and talking with people . . . and she was speaking Italian with people." Hudson, who would go on to win in November becoming the first Democrat elected in the 33rd District and one of only four women elected to the Senate that year, recalls that "she (Ella) was a wonderful campaigner . . . just to be with her made me feel good."[88] Ella's campaigning in the sprawling district, which encompassed three different congressional regions, provided Hudson's campaign with a big lift in a State Senate district that contained heavy Republican voter advantage and had never elected a Democrat to the upper house of the state legislature.

A large contingent of reporters from national and international media frequently accompanied Ella on her daily campaign stops. A *Washington Post* news reporter described the frenetic pace while campaigning with her in New Haven. There her fast-paced, high-energy effort, characteristic of her campaign style, was duly reported. After filming an interview with a television crew from Sweden, she proceeded to give back-to-back speeches to mostly "male audiences" of union members.

Taking note of Ella's "breezy, self-assured campaign style" and forceful verbal attacks on retiring Governor Thomas Meskill, the *Post* journalist describes a boisterous and rousing scene at a New Haven hotel: She brought "400 unionists to their feet, cheering her repeated attacks on Governor Meskill." Not waiting for their leaders to commence the formal endorsement procedure, the crowd simply shouted out their "unanimous endorsement of Mrs. Grasso."[89]

Her combative campaign style often employed rhetoric aimed at energizing and invigorating audiences. And Ella's speaking manner often included altering her diction to suit the audience, "incorporating conversational Italian to finishing school French" and interjecting the "vivid language of backroom politics," capturing the attention and approbation of onlookers. Vivid language was evident in her speeches that day in New Haven, where she spoke at a luncheon of the state employees union and later at a Joint Labor Council afternoon meeting in the Elm City. Her strategy, repeated often throughout the campaign, was to go on the offensive against the Meskill administration, forcing "her opponent to either defend the unpopular Governor or remain silent." And she often cited the Meskill administration's "deficiencies."[90] In particular, she emphasized the governor's veto of the Martin Luther King, Jr. holiday bill; his ill-timed, irresponsible, and expensive outlay of funds to construct a monorail at Bradley Field airport (Tommy's Trolley as it was derisively called); and the Republican Governor's Vermont vacation, which occurred during a severe and paralyzing December ice storm. Those three topics resonated to Ella Grasso's advantage each time she emphasized them to an audience.

Congressman Steele "cautiously avoided identifying himself with Meskill," and stressed that the previous Democratic administration of which Ella was a part "took the state to the brink of financial disaster." The embattled Republican candidate never gained traction in his effort to defuse his Democratic opponent's campaign offensive. Her forceful and contentious verbal barbs on the unpopular Meskill administration's failings "caught the attention of the voters," leaving Steele unwilling and frequently unable to persuasively or convincingly respond.[91]

From Ella Grasso's perspective, she believed her energetic style of campaigning would "bring the campaign closer to the people."[92] But Steele, on the other hand, seemed tentative and unable to mount an active campaign. He "operated alone, making his own plans and decisions. It was entirely his campaign."[93] The Second District Congressman refused to have the retiring and unpopular Republican Governor Thomas Meskill or maverick Republican United States Senator Lowell Weicker campaign for him. Both of those Republican office holders represented different factions in the party from which Steele distanced himself as he tried to project a "new face on the statewide level."[94]

The contrasting styles of the two gubernatorial candidates were obvious to reporters, who followed them on a daily basis. For example, on September 16, 1974, Ella spent the day in New Britain celebrating German Day activities in that very ethnic oriented city. She involved herself most of the day in German Day festivities and even participated in German figure dancing, after which she went on to a Veterans of Foreign Wars dinner in the evening, and later extended greetings to the Jewish community celebrating Rosh Hashanah. In contrast to her whirlwind day, Steele was reported to have spoken to fifty people, with no other events on his calendar.[95]

Throughout the campaign Ella actively reached out to Republican and independent voters. One pollster described as "nothing less than astounding" Ella's appeal to Republicans and independents, as well as Democrats. And an example of that effort was her evening meeting with a group of one hundred Republicans and independent voters in Simsbury in early September. A local doctor and his wife who had never met Ella Grasso prior to that evening organized the session. Dr. James V. Magrini said he had "lost confidence in Republicans and the Meskill administration" and that "Mrs. Grasso offers the type of leadership the state needs." Furthermore, he commented, "Mrs. Grasso was a candidate above reproach in the way she has conducted herself in public office."[96] In many respects, that statement echoed Connecticut voters' sentiments about Ella Grasso as a candidate with whom they were so well acquainted after more than twenty years in public life.

One issue that emerged during the fall campaign was would Connecticut voters elect a woman governor? Ella's pollster, Peter Hart, found that there was skepticism and doubt among some voters about a woman's ability to govern Connecticut. To counter the sentiments, Hart advised the Grasso campaign to run television advertisements showing Ella Grasso "running a meeting, calling on different people asserting the sort of sense of command that people wanted."[97]

Some Democratic strategists warned that the gender issue would emerge, and it did so in a particularly disparaging and derogatory way. Bumper stickers emblazoned with the slogan "Connecticut doesn't need a governess" were displayed on cars around the state. Many observers speculated that individuals in the Republican Party were behind the effort, and consequently the GOP received blame. Women voters resented the chauvinistic and demeaning tactic aimed at Connecticut's most popular and recognized woman politician. Ella publicly stated it was a non-issue for her, saying "I thought this might be a factor because I had been told that it would be . . . I've talked with thousands of people since I started my campaign and I have not yet seen any indication of rejection because I am a woman."[98]

Yet concerns existed among key staffers in the Grasso camp. Campaign manager Nancy Lewinsohn recalls that the campaign staff worried about the impact the issue was having on the public's perception of Ella's candidacy. Anxiety and doubts also emerged from the candidate herself, but only in private conversations. Lewinsohn describes one Saturday afternoon when Ella, virtually in tears, telephoned her at campaign headquarters. She had been at a shooting range and was asked to fire a gun at a target. She reported that she did not hit the bull's-eye despite several attempts. Lewinsohn's reassurances notwithstanding, Ella was despairing because her opponent had been able to hit the target in his appearance prior to Ella's arrival. Would voters see this as an example of her inadequacy? Would her opponent cite this as proof that she lacked ability to "take command" or "lead?" Despite this revealing example of her insecurity, Lewinsohn recalls calming Ella down, explaining that perhaps Congressman Steele was a hunter and had experience with guns and that voters would not think less of her or her ability to govern because of this incident.[99]

Publicly Ella maintained her positive outlook on the issue. In an interview with a Swedish television interviewer several questions were asked about women's roles in politics. She "responded almost mechanically to several cliché questions about women's roles in politics" and reminded the questioner that, "she was campaigning as Ella Grasso a person with a lifetime of political and public service behind her, and not as a woman."[100] She explained, "I think that one of the reasons is that I've been around a long time. People know me, they know my capacity for work and my involvement and my interests."[101] Indeed after more than two decades in public life, voters were well acquainted with her. In a noteworthy column published in the *Waterbury Republican* columnist Alan Olmstead summarized it well. "Mrs. Grasso," he wrote, "has worked and stored and saved a political lifetime to amass that beautiful nest egg of popular esteem and reputation . . . this nest egg of esteem and popular appeal was the supremely important asset she was bringing to her effort to get elected Governor of Connecticut."[102]

More than any other factor, Ella's widespread recognition among the electorate helped make her the frontrunner, a position she never lost throughout the campaign. Clearly, though, the Grasso run for governor also drew attention because she was a woman seeking the state's highest elective office, and if elected she would become the first elected Governor in the history of the United States who did not succeed her husband in that office. In 1974, there were no women Governors in the fifty states, no female U.S. Senators, and only sixteen women in the United States

House of Representatives. As a result, Ella's candidacy drew national and international media and press attention throughout the summer and fall of that campaign year.

Newsweek magazine, which placed a photograph of Ella Grasso on the cover of its November 4, 1974, issue (the weekend prior to the election), placed a reporter on the campaign trail who followed Ella around at various campaign stops and reported that at a state NAACP convention meeting in Hartford, "she greeted many of the delegates by name," and she reminded them that, "You and I have been friends in many projects." Then in a pointed jab aimed at the Meskill administration she told the audience that blacks had been "locked out of government" and promised "that will end this January." Her opponent, according to *Newsweek*, was also at the event and he "droned on about his concerns over unemployment" and was visibly dismayed when several delegates addressed her as "Governor Grasso." The article characterized Ella as a "tough, tenacious professional" and emphasized Ella's political capabilities noting that she could "plot, coerce, compromise, and charm with the best of her masculine peers."[103]

The *Washington Post* dispatched news reporter William Claiborne and columnist David Broder, who had met Ella Grasso when she was Secretary of the State, to cover the gubernatorial campaign. Broder wrote that in his judgment Ella was "a complete political professional."[104] He noted that in his opinion Ella Grasso had several major qualities: one "is brainpower-native intelligence" and another was that she became the "master of her trade." Reminding his readers of her long rise in the political echelons of Connecticut politics, he recalled that, "Abraham Ribicoff and John Dempsey when each was governor . . . used her talents to draft platforms and budget messages," and she handled "the toughest policy problems."[105]

Other well-known journalists and reporters covered the campaign, providing nationwide and worldwide coverage of the Connecticut gubernatorial election campaign. It was just the kind of national and international attention that would energize any candidate's campaign, and it certainly provided Ella and her campaign supporters with a surge of pride that would generate momentum for that last push over the top that makes a winning campaign even more exciting.

The long campaign climaxed on a rainy Election Day Tuesday November 5, 1974. Forecasters had said inclement weather would hold down the number of voters going to the polls that day. Low voter turnout was thought to be detrimental to the Democratic candidate's anticipated victory. Republicans, so the pundits argued, would come out to vote despite the weather. On the other hand, others argued, inclement weather would keep Democrats away from the polls, lessening Ella's chances in her election bid. But the results proved the political "weather forecasters" dead wrong. Ella trounced Congressman Steele 643,490 to 440,169.[106]

It was a margin of 203,321 votes in a turnout of 69 percent of the state's 1,581,037 registered voters. Ella Grasso's victory margin was the second largest in the state's gubernatorial history, "topped only by Abraham Ribicoff whose margin was 246,000" in 1958 and remained the greatest in Connecticut history for four decades.[107] (A gubernatorial election victory by former Governor John Rowland [R] in 1998 topped Ribicoff's margin. Rowland's margin was 274,420 votes.)[108]

In a perceptive post-campaign analysis, *Hartford Courant* political reporter Jack Zaiman concluded that Republican Steele's campaign was knocked off its stride by several national issues that negatively affected the Republican Congressman's campaign. The devastating and negative effect that the Watergate controversy had on Republican candidates across the country, along with the sharp rise in prices around the nation was blamed on Republicans. And President Gerald Ford's pardon of Richard Nixon "pulled the rug from under the Steele campaign." Almost in desperation, three weeks before the election, "Steele decided he had better talk to the Meskill and Weicker people." That decision was too late, noted the *Hartford Courant*'s Zaiman, who wrote, "you don't do things this way in top level politics: none of this last minute stuff. These deals should have been made in July." And he concluded that Steele had "peaked at the GOP state convention in July and his course from then on was down."[109]

While the major national issues were out of the control of the Republican and Democratic state campaigns, most voters took out their wrath on the party in power—and that was the Republican Party under President Gerald Ford. As happened in other parts of the country, the Democratic Party benefited from that anti-Republican sentiment. Indeed the Congressional results showed a Democratic gain of 3 seats in the U.S. Senate to 61 seats, along side 39 Republicans. And in the House of Representatives Democrats gained forty-three seats for a majority of 291 to 141 Republicans.

In Connecticut Ella received the election returns at her home in Windsor Locks alongside her husband and children. They were joined by a large contingent of print, radio, and television media who were there to record the historic event.

Afterward, she and her family and a few campaign staffers drove to Hartford to savor her victory with supporters at the Democratic Party State Central Committee Headquarters and at the Polish-American Home in the downtown capital city. As the evening wore on the Grasso's moved on to John M. Bailey's gracious home on Scarborough Street in the western part of the city for a late night evening victory celebration.

In Connecticut, it was Ella Grasso and the Democratic Party that rode the wave of anti-Republican, anti-Watergate sentiment into an election year landslide victory. She became the first woman Governor of Connecticut and the first in the history of America to win a Governorship not succeeding her husband in that office.

8

THE DAUGHTER OF A TORTONESE
GOVERNS CONNECTICUT

La Stampa one of Italy's largest newspapers proudly proclaimed the news headline "The Daughter of a Tortonese Governs Connecticut" after Ella Grasso's historic gubernatorial victory. And it reported "wide rejoicing in Tortona and nearby villages" from which her parents had emigrated decades ago. The sense of pride and joy in Ella's electoral win reached her father's birthplace of Perleto (population 200) where 50 percent of the villagers were members of the Tambussi family.[1]

Besides being the first woman elected Governor in her own right, Ella Tambussi Grasso became the first woman of Italian ancestry to reach a Governor's chair in the history of the United States. Italian-Americans in Connecticut, throughout America, and in Italy savored her political victory. It also helped to remove several stumbling blocks that hindered women's political advancement: the inability of a woman to be elected governor who did not follow her husband into elective office, and the failure of an ethnic Italian first generation child of Italian immigrants to succeed to the highest elective office in Connecticut state government.

Ella noted "I don't think there are any more barriers" for Italians to face in the world of American politics, "and if there are, you have helped put them there by thinking they exist." She noted with some humor that with her electoral breakthrough "its wonderful" that Americans have learned "there is something more to Italian cooking . . . than pasta."[2]

While Ella's pride in her ethnicity was reflected in her comments, her victory also thrust her into the national spotlight as the nation's only woman Governor. The three major national television networks and two major weekly news magazines devoted coverage on Election Day and were present at her victory celebration that evening. Ella was clearly cognizant of the historic and national implications of her victory. "I am aware," she said, "this is an historic occasion. I hope I have been a credit to women, and to all persons."[3] Indeed her victory was seen as a "very important breakthrough" for women nationally because "it will certainly encourage others" to run for major state office.[4] Frances Farenthold, chairman of the National Women's Political Caucus echoed that same sentiment. She commented that, "Ella Grasso's victory in Connecticut raises the hopes and expectations of all women considering political careers. In the past, women have been forced to set their sights lower than men. But that, thank heavens, is now in the past."[5]

Two years later in 1976, in the state of Washington, Dixie Lee Ray, would run for Governor successfully, and several other women in other states would follow in subsequent years: Ann Richards (D) Texas, Kay Orr (R) Nebraska, Madeline Kunin (D) Vermont, and Martha Layne Collins (D) Kentucky.

Ella's election also signaled her emergence as a potential candidate for national office. *New York Times* columnist Tom Wicker, four days after her Connecticut triumph, mentioned the Governor-elect as someone who might be considered by the Democratic Party for the 1976 Vice Presidential nomination. "Against a Ford-Rockefeller ticket," Wicker wrote, "the Democrats could do a lot worse than to run say Tom Bradley (Mayor of Los Angeles) or Ella Grasso the new governor of Connecticut for vice president."[6] Speculation among political reporters and commentators would continue despite Ella's repeated denials of any national political ambitions.

Evidence of media interest came quickly with an invitation for the new governor to speak at the annual all-male Gridiron Club dinner in Washington, D.C., on March 21, 1975. The dinner marked the induction of the first woman journalist, White House correspondent Helen Thomas, into the Gridiron Club. Ella Grasso's appearance at the white-tie event attended by hundreds of Washington journalists, media representatives, members of the United States Senate and House of Representatives, Supreme Court Justices, and President and Mrs. Ford, underscored the national press corps' recognition of her path-breaking electoral breakthrough. The Governor's remarks, delivered to a large audience gathered in a Washington, D.C., hotel, poked fun at members of the Fourth Estate and Washington politicians. She reminded the audience that she was often asked by reporters, "How I made it in a man's world." Pausing momentarily, she answered, "everyway I could." It was a light-hearted opening line, which demonstrated a sense of humor more often noticeable when she spoke off the cuff than in her formal public speeches. She tweaked the humor level of the predominantly male audience further by commenting, "It feels a bit strange being a female in this former male bastion. It's rather like finding Henry Kissinger all of a sudden here in the United States . . . like finding Phyllis Schlafly at a Bella Abzug testimonial or on the Board of *Ms.*" And she added "I've been to livelier parties at Leisure World and met younger and more beautiful people."[7]

Her speech was partly prepared with the help of several Washington hands, including Liz Carpenter former press secretary to Lady Bird Johnson, Fran Lewine, Associated Press reporter, and Isabelle Shelton of the now defunct *Washington Star* newspaper whom Ella later acknowledged, "took the time to help make me funny on that splendid evening."[8] It was a moment in the Washington limelight that she savored immensely.

The significance of the invitation and her appearance at the glittering Washington gala was not lost on Ella. Her electoral success placed her in the national media spotlight, and it occurred as speculation mounted about potential candidates for the Presidential nomination, which loomed on the horizon for the following year's election. Despite repeated denials, Ella never tired of the flattering press attention she continued to receive.

Back in Connecticut, Ella's landslide victory also brought with it Democratic majorities in both houses of the Connecticut General Assembly. In the House of Representatives, the lineup was 118 Democrats and 33 Republicans, and likewise a majority of 29 Democrats in the State Senate alongside a minority of 7 Republicans.[9] Women increased their representation in the House from 20 to 25, while 4 women were elected to the upper chamber, 1 more than in the previous legislative session. Many freshmen Democratic legislators, elected from traditional Republican districts, were swept in on the tidal wave of Ella's victory. One newcomer, elected to the Senate was Betty Hudson (D-Madison) with whom Ella had campaigned at Hammonasset Beach. Another was Wilda Hamerman (D-Orange), the first Democrat elected in the 114th House District. Hamerman remembers that "we were drawn together as members of the Democratic Party and the goal of the General Assembly was to pass her (the Governor) legislation and legislation we had in the General Assembly. I don't recall a great deal of opposition between the two agendas."[10]

Several days after the election, however, the *New York Times* reported that Mrs. Grasso faced "a mixed blessing of Democratic majorities in the General Assembly that she may have trouble coping with." Reflecting back on former Governor John Dempsey's last term when an "independent Democratic faction" created problems by establishing their own leadership in defiance of the Governor and State Chairman John Bailey, *Times* reporter Lawrence Fellows predicted, "There will be pressure on Mrs. Grasso from legislators who will want to spend on favorite projects and from voters who will resist new taxes . . . needed to pay for the projects."[11]

While Fellows was virtually predicting challenging days ahead, another experienced Capitol reporter, Jack Zaiman of the *Hartford Courant*, reminded readers that Ella Grasso "knows well that gubernatorial administrations can quickly rise or fall on its initial impact on the public."[12] Both reporters would be quite prescient in their judgments of the Connecticut political scene, which would focus mainly on Connecticut's first woman Governor and how she handled responsibilities particularly her initial budget and legislative proposals.

One of the Governor-elect's main worries, in the immediate aftermath of the November election, was the deteriorating health of her mentor John Bailey. He was periodically confined to a bed at Hartford Hospital. However, Ella consulted him frequently about the composition of her administration team. She sent potential commissioners and other high level appointees to see Bailey seeking his approval or disapproval of the individual for a particular post in her administration.[13]

One future commissioner remembers receiving a phone call from John Bailey urging him to come to see him in his hospital room the next afternoon. Edward Stockton, who would become Ella's respected Commissioner of the Department of Commerce (later renamed the Department of Economic Development), remembers being asked several questions by Bailey. "Stockton, what do you want?" was the Chairman's initial question despite his deteriorating physical condition.[14] Another Grasso appointee, Finance Commissioner Jay Tepper, remembers meeting Bailey when he arrived in Hartford from Ohio. Bailey quizzed him about why Tepper's previous employer, Governor John Gilligan (D-Ohio) lost his reelection bid for Governor in 1974.[15]

Ella Grasso learned "politics at Bailey's knee" and she was considered "his most successful pupil."[16] He was clearly someone Ella trusted and relied on to provide sound political advice and direction for her new administration. "He wanted to get Ella started off well" . . . He summoned politicians to his bedside to get patronage straightened out."[17] But as Ella's inauguration day, January 8, 1975, approached, it became clear that her friend and political mentor's physical strength and mental focus could not continue to be centered on substantive matters pertaining to the incoming Grasso administration. Despite his failing health, "looking pale and wan but smiling," John Bailey would leave his hospital bed to attend Ella's swearing-in and Inaugural Ball saying, "I wouldn't have missed this day for all the world."[18]

Amidst the pomp and circumstance at the inaugural swearing in, Ella Grasso arrived wearing a blue dress fashioned by Bice Clemow a veteran journalist/columnist and press personality associated with the *West Hartford News*. In keeping with her frugal ways, Clemow's offer to make Ella's dress for that special occasion was readily agreed to by the Governor-elect. While some thought it unusual for a woman governor to appear in a home-sewn dress, it was in keeping with Ella's minimal interest in fashion or expensive clothes. It demonstrated once more her plain, ordinary, unpretentious attitude about her attire that was associated with Ella's image throughout her career. In the view of her chief aide Nancy Lewinsohn, the dress did not "fit well" nor did it "seem fashionable for the occasion."[19]

The Inaugural Ball took place the evening of January 8, 1975, and was a joyous celebration for the Democratic Party and the state's new leader. Dressed formally in a long gown, escorted by the Commandant of the Governor's Foot Guard on one side and her husband on the other, Ella led the procession of state officials in the Grand March at the State Armory. It was festooned with patriotic bunting, flags, and balloons — and a jubilant throng of supporters, excited not only by the occasion, but also delighted with the presence of John M. Bailey.

Bailey's strength and stamina had been deteriorating as a result of the regimen of cancer medication and treatments and the prolonged hospitalization he had been undergoing. His presence that evening was one of his last public appearances, and that realization by the party faithful added to the poignancy of the gala event.

The realization also set in that Bailey's crucial role as the political middleman, or "interceder,"[20] between the Governor and the legislature (something Abraham Ribicoff freely admitted helped him immensely),[21] would not be available to the Governor much longer. And it placed a major hurdle in her path as she prepared to take the reins of office. While John Bailey had been a brilliant strategist with many attributes and positive characteristics, one weakness had been apparent for a very long time: He had not entrusted anyone who might fill his shoes as State Democratic Chairman with enough clout or stature to do so. Finding a potential successor to Bailey would prove to be a signal challenge to Ella Grasso's considerable political leadership skills.

Those talents would also be measured by her ability to work cooperatively with the General Assembly leaders. In 1975, upon Ella's accession to the executive office, the leadership of the legislative branch took on a new look with State Representative James Kennelly (D-Hartford), Bailey's son-in-law, as the new Speaker of the House of Representatives, along with State Representative Bill O'Neill (D-East Hampton) as the new House Majority Leader. In the other legislative branch Senator Joseph Fauliso (D-Hartford) was chosen Senate President Pro Tempore, and New Haven Senator Joseph I. Lieberman (D-New Haven) was elected the Majority Leader in the Upper Chamber. Representative O'Neill had been Ella's campaign chairman and Senator Lieberman had been "one of Ella's top policy advisers and traveled around the state with and for her" during the 1974 campaign.[22] All were men she knew fairly well (she had known Senator Fauliso since the 1950s), and all were men with whom the Governor was expected to work cooperatively. But the road ahead would not be trouble free, especially after April 1975 when John Bailey's death left the Governor without the presence of the man who could build bridges to the legislative leadership. As particular issues emerged, they spawned serious differences and tensions between the executive and legislative branches of Connecticut's government.

In the days leading up to her inauguration in January, Ella worked with George Conkling, her special advisor on finance and budgetary matters. He had served in previous Democratic administrations and was respected for his strong grasp of the intricacies of the state budget. What he quickly discovered and conveyed to the Governor-elect was a projected budget deficit ranging between $80 and $100 million dollars — a major contradiction from what the outgoing Governor Thomas Meskill said his administration was leaving for the next administration.

In a strongly worded letter to the outgoing Governor, a few days after her election victory, Ella emphasized that Horace Brown, Director of Planning and Budgeting in the Finance Department, projected "a budget gap of at least $200 million and that the 1974–75 budget, balanced by the use of almost $125 million in one year, non-recurring windfall revenues would not be available next year." And as a result, "revenues to date and inflationary demands have thrown the 1974–75 budget balance into serious question."[23]

Unfortunately her fiscal chief uncovered a huge backlog of unpaid bills that the Meskill administration did not pay in order to announce a budget surplus during the course of the fall campaign. At that time Ella insisted that the Meskill administration was "juggling the books."[24] The Republican administration repeatedly denied the accusation. Conkling discovered that the so-called surplus was in reality a budget deficit, which would require herculean efforts to balance in the years ahead.

The sobering reality was that the new Governor would face several major challenges as she began her first term as Connecticut's 83rd Chief Executive, and she would need all of her talents, political instincts, and patience (a skill she said she learned from John Bailey) to steer the ship of state successfully on a positive course.

As Ella's Inauguration Day approached, it became obvious to her that the economic challenges—rising inflation, recessionary factors like joblessness and layoffs, and a resultant gap between revenues and expenditures would prove to be the most serious problem facing her administration.

The Connecticut economy, like that of the other forty-nine states, was staggering through a period of economic slowdown as a result of a decade-long cycle of inflation, high energy costs, and economic dislocation brought on, in large measure, by the war in Vietnam. The "guns and butter" policy of President Lyndon Johnson, which had torn apart the social and political fabric of the nation had at the same time wreaked havoc on the economic health of Connecticut's economy.

Connecticut's large military and defense related industrial complex produced significant material for the war effort. But the economic stress left behind in the war's wake—galloping inflation, increased costs of living, escalating energy costs for fuel and power supplies, which generated the manufacturing, industrial, and civilian needs of businesses and industry—all served to bring added strains to the state's economic well-being. President Richard Nixon instituted a policy of gradually turning the war over to the South Vietnamese. And in 1975, following President Gerald Ford's directives ending military involvement in Southeast Asia, the gradual erosion of Defense Department military contracts seriously undercut vital segments of Connecticut's economic foundation. In sum, the cumulative effects of these tumultuous events and policies proved harmful to Connecticut's economic vitality.

In her Inaugural Address, delivered January 8, 1975, Ella emphasized at the outset how serious the economic problems were by stating, "the state of our state is in disarray. The financial condition of state government today is unsound. A balanced budget and an operating surplus do not exist." It was a bracing, somber, serious message that she delivered to the General Assembly and the state's citizens on that inaugural day. Estimating that a gap of $200 million existed between revenues and expenditures, she predicted that, "the discussion will be painful," and that, "restraints" to balance the current budget and "planning for the new fiscal year will require heroic efforts." All of this, she noted, "will be accomplished without recourse to a state personal income tax."[25]

Her reliance on George Conkling, a friend and fellow brain truster from the Ribicoff and Dempsey administrations, was critical because he was extremely knowledgeable about the state's finances. Whereas Conkling served as Acting Commissioner of Finance in the first months of Ella's tenure, he did not seek to become an agency head in her new administration. He preferred to undertake temporary assignments. Ella's search for a chief of finance led her to select native New Yorker Jay Tepper then living in Ohio. He was seeking a key position in state government after the defeat of Ohio Governor John Gilligan (D) for whom Tepper had worked in Ohio's budget office. Tepper, came highly recommended by Roger Dove an insurance company executive who had served in government under Governor Ribicoff. Tepper sent in his resume and was interviewed by the Governor-elect and John Bailey, and he was appointed Commissioner of Finance and would become the architect of Ella's long-term fiscal plan.

Tepper's deputy, Anthony Milano, of Bridgeport had been recommended for that post by State Comptroller J. Edward Caldwell. Milano, who would later succeed Tepper, had not known the new Governor prior to his appointment to the state position. His municipal experience as Comptroller for the City of Bridgeport, his work in banking, and his knowledge of Connecticut's political scene offset Tepper's lack of Connecticut experience. The plan, noted Milano, was to "get through the immediate fiscal crisis," and Ella "wanted to send a message that it was time for austerity."[26]

In her Inaugural Address, she called the financial condition of Connecticut "unsound and serious" and the "long range prospects . . . not encouraging," but she promised to "turn around the condition of our state" and give "new direction to policies that affect the lives of our people." Noting that the prospects of a gap between revenue and expenditures in the next fiscal year (beginning July 1, 1975) would require "expenditure cuts" she also promised to exercise "strict restraints" to insure a balanced budget "in this fiscal year." And she repeated her pledge of not instituting a state personal income tax.[27] Ella's dire warnings to the legislature and the public were made unmistakably clear on that cold January day.

It was not an auspicious way to launch her administration. In discussions with staff about the inaugural speech, she had hoped to lay out new programs and initiatives to address problems and unmet needs. However, to commence her new administration in such somber tones, largely dictated by the enormous fiscal challenges facing Connecticut, was a great disappointment to Ella Grasso.[28]

The Governor did propose creation of a Public Utility Control Authority, fulfilling a promise made during the campaign. Her proposal was to plan to "hold down ever-escalating utility bills and to bring back public confidence in utility regulation." And she followed through on another campaign promise of rewriting the "right to know" law which she announced "will be . . . strengthened to ensure that the processes of local and state government will be totally open to public view and constructive public criticism." The third campaign promise that Ella addressed in her initial speech as Governor focused on revitalizing the Commerce Department. Realizing that the main aim of the proposal was to "make our economy more stable," she spoke of the "top priority" being to find ways and means "to retain and strengthen Connecticut companies" while forging an "aggressive out of state campaign to attract new industry and seek . . . major growth industries" to solidify Connecticut's economic future.[29] Her comments would prove to be the opening salvo of a very aggressive, energetic program she enthusiastically and consistently pursued with the able assistance of Commissioner Edward Stockton of the Department of Commerce.

Ella understood the absolute necessity of broadcasting and diversifying Connecticut's economic base. The lesson she learned in the face of the economic distress of the 1970s was that Connecticut's reliance on a traditional economic base of defense-related industries, coupled with the Nutmeg State's long history of nurturing small machine tool manufacturers and businesses so dependent on defense orders, could not continue to drive and sustain adequate employment levels for Connecticut's skilled labor force. The Governor was determined to bring new businesses to Connecticut, which could utilize those skilled workers and take advantage of Connecticut's favorable geographic location, which was linked to vital transportation networks (interstate highways, railroads, and air links). She worked diligently to eventually attract biopharmaceutical companies such as Bayer Pharmaceuticals, Bristol-Myers, Boehringer-Ingleheim, Danish toy manufacturer Lego Toys, and

Union Carbide, which established its world headquarters in Danbury, Connecticut. Those companies, it was believed, would provide sustainable, long-term employment for the well-educated research and development personnel and the highly skilled labor force so vital to the state's economic future.

The Governor also promised an "open and cooperative relationship" a "close partnership" with the legislature, which on her inaugural day seemed a reasonable expectation.[30] After all, Ella Grasso had twenty-two years of experience in government as a State Representative, Secretary of the State, member of Congress, and now Governor, and her party was in top-heavy control of the General Assembly. The high hopes and a spirit of cooperation between both branches of government was very much in evidence that Inaugural Day in 1975. As Ella once reminded both Governor Ribicoff and John Bailey, "the test of responsibility comes in the translation of platform into programs into action. There was the challenge and the opportunity and we Democrats had to keep faith with all the things we had said. Now we had to do something."[31] And the legislature, controlled by the Governor's party, was the conduit through which her programs would be put into action.

At the outset, however, there was an underlying tone of tension between the new, politically ambitious legislative leadership in the House and Senate and the Executive branch. "I think at times, I could discover there was tension among the leadership and a challenge that they entertained against her," explained Senator Joseph Fauliso, a key Grasso advisor. "For what reason, I don't know, but after meetings I would stay on and talk to her, keep encouraging her . . . she felt that there was this challenge . . . not overtly . . . but it existed."[32] Some tension may have existed because the legislative leaders were not used to dealing with a female governor whom some barely knew, since they emerged in leadership positions during her years in Washington. Another observer noted that often some members of the legislative leadership team did not want to "carry the water" without receiving a quid pro quo in return.[33] "But in time, she won them over of course," added Fauliso, "because she became so popular . . . and she practiced austerity . . . we were in deep (financial) trouble."[34]

Likewise, while Ella knew the legislative leaders she had not worked closely with any of them except Senator Fauliso whom she had met years earlier when he was an attorney in John Bailey's law firm. It seems clear that the initial tension existed, in part, because the leaders had their own agendas. They entertained the notion that they had "a future in government" and they were trying "to assert themselves . . . ambitions always play a role in politics" emphasized the Senate leader. But gradually, over time, the tension diminished," he added, "as the legislature realized that her popularity was deep-seated among the electorate," and "they soon learned that it's better to cooperate than cause a breach . . . for the good of the party."[35]

Another observer, a former Grasso staff member, suggested that many of the newly elected freshmen legislators brought in by the Governor's overwhelming electoral victory "were not skilled politically" and "did not understand the game . . . the process." He remembers in particular one Democratic legislator, who had not been voting with the Governor on some of her key issues including condominium reform. He was not supportive, even after the Governor's legislative liaison went to him and asked for support. As a result, when a bonding request was put forward for the State Bond Commission's agenda, an item important to the legislator's district, the Governor had it stricken from the proposed agenda. When that legislator came to see the Governor regarding the matter, she told him that, "you have not supported me on any significant piece of legislation important to me."[36] Yet, that item did reappear on the Bond Commission agenda after the November 1976 election. The Commission eventually approved the item, but, ironically, the recalcitrant lawmaker lost his reelection bid.

A view offered by Lieutenant Governor Robert Killian provides another interesting perspective on her relationship with legislative leaders and the rank and file. He asserts that Ella did not want to "share state government with other people. She wanted to be the sole person in charge." He also believed that she "resented the intrusion of the legislature on legislation," and she "did not try to make adjustments" where compromise was often required. In his opinion, the Governor conducted the executive department as if it were not a co-equal branch of democratic government.[37]

That observation gives substance to a perspective offered by Senator Cornelius O'Leary (D-Windsor Locks). Ironically, the freshman legislator was asked to stop by the Governor's Office in the early days of the transition before Ella took the oath of office. He had the distinction of being the senator from the district that included Ella's hometown. She told the new Assistant Majority Leader that she wanted him to "submit" any of his proposed legislation to her "before he submitted it officially into the legislative hopper." O'Leary recalls Ella being quite authoritative and high-handed in her tone and manner. Feeling somewhat intimidated and obligated to respond to her demands, the Windsor Locks senator returned several days later with his list of legislative proposals. In a quick look at his list of bills, she told him it was quite an "impressive" list of legislative proposals. Her demeanor was dramatically different than her brusque manner in her initial meeting with him. It was as if she wanted to test him to see if this young legislator would follow her "orders" and her "demands."[38]

The nexus of tension between the Governor and the legislators revolved around the expectations of two traditional Democratic constituencies — state employees and municipal officials.[39] Both groups expected substantial increases in financial support, not spending restraints or reductions in state funding from a Democratic Governor and legislature.[40] After four years under Governor Meskill, a fiscal conservative, much more was expected from the new administration to make up for the four previous lean years. Yet it was obvious that, because of the "deep (financial) trouble,"[41] the Grasso administration "didn't deliver what we wanted to deliver" to those traditional Democratic Party groups, explained Aaron Ment, the Governor's legal counsel.[42]

Among those anticipating increases in state financial assistance were the urban city mayors and their liberal supporters like Hartford's Deputy Mayor Nick Carbone who recognized in Ella's "truly . . . austere budget" that less aid and financial support would be forthcoming for municipalities.[43] In addition, with her inability to expand or increase funding for many social service, welfare, and educational programs, Governor Grasso initially alienated core Democratic supporters such as Carbone and groups representing minorities, unions, poor, low income individuals, as well as human service advocacy organizations.

Another component of Ella's difficulty was her reliance, to a large extent, on a small core of staffers of whom not all were political insiders skilled at dealing with the demanding, independent-minded legislators. Many lawmakers had become increasingly contentious toward the executive branch during the Meskill gubernatorial years, and that environment would continue during Governor Grasso's tenure. The lack of harmony ensued despite the fact that a Democrat was the Chief Executive with large Democratic majorities in the legislature. And that discord made the relationship between the Governor and the legislature a struggle.[44]

Ella's selection of Aaron Ment as her legal counsel was widely applauded since he had been involved in Connecticut politics for many years and was a familiar figure to the legislative leadership. He had been counsel to the Speaker of the House of Representatives William Ratchford (D-Danbury), as well as a close associate and aide to John Bailey. Ment, who later became a Superior Court judge, acknowledges that mistakes were made early on in the Grasso administration particularly in developing positive relations with the legislative leaders, an area of responsibility he was expected to assume along with state party chairman John Bailey.[45] Precisely because he was a Bailey protégé may, in part, account for some of the difficulties Ment encountered. With Bailey's absence from the daily legislative scene, Ment's clout was diminished in the eyes of the legislative leadership and rank and file.

The Governor's appointment of Nancy Lewinsohn as Executive Aide (Chief of Staff) was an appointment that stirred controversy and skepticism at the outset. Lewinsohn had been Ella's chief administrative aide in her Washington office and involved in Ella's second Congressional campaign.[46] She also managed her gubernatorial campaign and had experience dealing with Connecticut politicians, particularly those from the Sixth Congressional District, as well as those from the First Congressional District, which included Hartford. While Lewinsohn was considered a very able, highly intelligent, and knowledgeable Washington, D.C., player (she had also worked for Senator Abraham Ribicoff), Ella's selection of a woman for such a key position irritated the ranks of male politicians in various quarters in the Land of Steady Habits.

The new governor reached into the ranks of the Fourth Estate for two other key staff appointments. Jeff Daniels, a former *Hartford Times* reporter, was selected as the Governor's special assistant for policies and programs. He had been her press spokesman during the gubernatorial campaign and was brought on staff to work on key policy issues, such as utility regulation and energy problems. But he admits he had no "political credentials."[47] Her appointment of Larrye DeBear as Press Secretary drew on Ella's long-time acquaintance with a veteran journalist and television reporter who covered the State Capitol scene for many years. While both appointees were well thought of, they were not seen as staffers possessing close connections to the legislative leadership, nor did they possess experience working in the hard-nose world of Connecticut politics.

Another appointee John Dempsey, Jr., son of the former governor, as Executive Assistant was seen as a political plus because of his family name recognition and his familiarity with legislators, particularly those from eastern Connecticut where the Dempsey name was revered. Despite those family ties, Dempsey's role was limited in terms of being a significant or consequential member of the governor's legislative team.

It was a lean staff with talent and ability, and much of the stroking and cajoling of the legislators fell on the shoulders of Aaron Ment. He worked closely with the young, ambitious legislative leaders in the General Assembly.

Among many long-time traditional Democratic Party leaders undercurrents of grumbling surfaced regarding the appointees.[48] The key staff appointments, except for Ment, were all outsiders, newcomers to the hardball politics played at the State Capitol. And, while no one would talk openly about it, ethnicity became a point of contention and caused discontent among the disgruntled (three were Jewish; the exceptions being Dempsey and DeBear). The traditional Irish-Italian control and dominance was clearly undermined by the Italian-Jewish alliance that Ella assembled with her initial staff appointees.

Responding to that undercurrent, Nancy Lewinsohn explains that she brought the issue up at meetings with the Governor. The appointments were not made without considerable thought, and "Ella gave it (the ethnic controversy) considerable thought and discussed it with John M. Bailey." The Governor told her inner circle "she intended to have the people she wanted in her office." Furthermore, the most important thing was to get "the best qualified people with whom she was comfortable."[49]

Most dispiriting to the new Governor in the early months of her tenure was the absence of John M. Bailey, who was confined to Hartford Hospital during the final weeks of his life. His influence with legislators and his steady hand on the rudder of the fractious, often contentious Democratic Party was coming to an end. On April 10, 1975, Bailey, "the great leveler" passed away.[50] Ella's political mentor, friend, and counselor was no longer there as the wise, steady, formidable presence he had been throughout her entire political career. In a hastily assembled news conference, minutes after learning of Bailey's death, Ella issued a somber statement saluting Bailey as a "noble warrior who . . . made every combat an exercise in excellence," emphasizing that he brought to the "political arena a rare combination of vision, judgment, and respect."

And she added that he had a "special sense of decency and civility that made the political process and all of us better than we were."[51] It was a monumental loss for Ella and the state Democratic Party.

Bailey's death also marked the end of an era in Connecticut's political history. His passing left a major void in the leadership of the Democratic Party and it ended a "powerful political alliance" between the venerable State Chairman and Connecticut's first woman Governor.[52] Ella Grasso was now both de facto party leader and governor, dual roles she had neither expected nor hoped would fall on her shoulders. The ensuing difficulties and struggles with the Democratic-led General Assembly, without Bailey running strong interference, proved to be a most significant challenge and principal reason why Connecticut's first woman Governor had a difficult and controversial first year in office. "Nothing will be the same any more," exclaimed an old Democratic party stalwart after hearing the news of Bailey's demise.[53]

Essentially, Ella's start as Connecticut's 83rd Governor was hardly a smooth beginning. And *Hartford Courant* reporter Jack Zaiman's observation, concerning a gubernatorial administration's rise and fall depending on its initial impact on the public, was never truer than in the case of the new Grasso administration.[54] The severity of the financial problems that the Governor faced upon assuming office, coupled with the ensuing political and Democratic Party troubles, served as the basis for the overall predicament she confronted in governing Connecticut. Also, her prescription for dealing with the financial woes was not initially well received by the legislative majority, adding to the fallout within the party of Jefferson and Jackson.

Her remedies for the bleak financial picture in 1975 were clearly tough medicine for the lawmakers and the public to swallow. Noting the deteriorating fiscal condition of the state, Ella uttered a phrase in her first Budget Message on February 13, 1975, that will be associated with her forever: "The cupboard, my friends, is very bare." Those candid and forthright words directly informed both the legislature and the public that the budget she inherited was not only projected to be $65 million dollars in deficit but the budget she proposed for the next fiscal year commencing July 1, 1975 was projected to contain a $150 million dollar shortfall.[55]

The specific solutions she laid out to the General Assembly were to increase taxes to meet the projected deficit. They included: raising the state sales tax from 6 percent to 7 percent, including rental and lease of personal property; increasing the corporate business tax from 8 percent to 9 percent; expanding the cigarette tax from 21 cents to 25 cents per pack; and enlarging the tax on capital gains from 6 percent to 7 percent, as well as reinstating the tax on dividends at a level of 7 percent. Admitting the fiscal "picture . . . is not a pretty one," the Governor pointedly mentioned that her proposal "will mean additional burden and sacrifice . . . It is a burden that comes with these troubled times."[56]

It would be a burden that would follow Ella Grasso for two years until the state's economic condition improved and the tough fiscal remedies she proposed turned deficits into modest surpluses. Furthermore, it would be a time of challenge and testing of Ella Grasso's resolve and tenacity as a political leader as she faced the ordeal of governing in a time of widening economic distress and increasing political tension within her own party.

As Governor, she was caught in the middle of tensions and difficulties between the desires of the Legislature to fund favored projects and support new programs that would be helpful to constituents and coincidentally to their own reelection bids, and her desire to give cities and towns financial help to offset rising costs and higher property taxes. Ella Grasso took the road less popular and more politically dangerous, which in retrospect was the proper course for Connecticut to follow. While raising taxes and fees is never popular, she had few other alternatives in order to put the state's fiscal house in order. By following that course and weathering the pressure from the Democratic legislative majority and the opposition from a vocal Republican minority, Ella's policies of fiscal austerity tapped into a well-spring of public support from citizens who understood that few new programs or projects could be undertaken while the fiscal situation was so dire. And while paying higher sales taxes and other increased fees (cigarette and motor vehicle fees) put extra burdens on the public, she believed the public understood the need for increased taxes to help put the state's financial condition back in balance.

Her view was that, "you know when you talk to people and explain . . . they understand and they know every effort is made to restrict spending, not have unnecessary spending, then people will bear those financial hardships."[57] In essence, this was her way of expressing her long held belief that patience was required in order to achieve what she hoped would be an economic and budgetary turnaround in the state's fiscal picture. Eventually, as she hoped, would come a modest surplus.

Her political troubles also expanded in another direction—her badly deteriorating relationship with Lieutenant Governor Robert Killian. A veteran Hartford politician, Killian was a long-time "buddy" of John Bailey.[58] It was Bailey who interceded to have Killian appointed Attorney General of Connecticut in 1967 to fill a vacancy in that office. In 1970, Killian won a full four-year term, managing to win by a very thin margin. Killian and Secretary of the State Gloria Schaffer (D-Woodbridge) were the only two Democratic statewide officers elected in the November 1970 Republican victory.

While bowing to John Bailey's entreaties to run for Lieutenant Governor in 1974 with Ella Grasso, Killian recalls he was "personally never close to Ella."[59] Moreover, it became clear as the administration moved forward in its early months that the "unique accommodation" that Ella Grasso and Bob Killian agreed to in July 1974, was "their affectionate" gift to John M. Bailey instead of representing "their own desires for their own careers." And it was unthinkable they would have linked up at all if it had not been for Bailey and the "sentimental opportunity" to give him one last political miracle.[60] Indeed, not long after Bailey's death,

Ella's uncomfortable relationship with her Lieutenant Governor became decidedly worse.

Besides presiding over the State Senate and casting any tie-breaking vote required under the State Constitution, the Lieutenant Governor's role in Connecticut is effectively limited to what the Governor assigns to the second in command. With this in mind, Ella announced in her first Inaugural Address that Killian would be the administration's point man with the federal government. She indicated that he would direct the office of federal–state relations "to secure the federal aid to which the state is entitled."[61]

It was agreed, noted Killian, that there would "have to be Washington contacts," and since the Governor would be less able to travel there with any regularity, the responsibility would be his.[62] And from the outset it was a task that Killian was eager and determined to perform well even though it was not a flashy or attention-getting role. For his part, being assigned that task provided the Lieutenant Governor some leeway to work on matters emanating from the nation's capitol without gaining much of a public profile in Connecticut to rival Grasso. And it was obviously important, in fact crucial, for Connecticut to facilitate access to federal monies and financial assistance due the state and its financially strapped municipalities and towns.

A Washington, D.C., office was created and it became the conduit for establishing a working liaison with the federal agencies for the state's Lieutenant Governor. Killian came to believe that one reason Ella Grasso felt comfortable with placing him in that role was to keep him at a distance. "She would not want to be close to anybody like me who might became competition," he emphasized. "She was always concerned and really jealous of anyone who could compete with her or rival her. Everything had to be her way — Ella's way." Many people would go along with her "out of some kind of concern" maybe it was out of "fear."[63]

It became obvious to Killian, who often discussed policy decisions with the Governor in the early months of her administration, that she was unable to "give and take, forgive and forget," and gradually over time their political and personal relationship deteriorated so that by 1977 there was little contact between them.[64] The following year, in fact, Bob Killian challenged Ella Grasso for the gubernatorial nomination in a bitter statewide primary.

The resentment between the Governor and her Lieutenant Governor was obvious to another constitutional officer, Secretary of the State Gloria Schaffer, who felt that as time passed, "Ella treated Bob badly." At that time, it was "unusual to have a woman bossing a man around . . . she was attempting to dominate Bob." According to the former Secretary of the State, "Being a macho type," Bob Killian's psyche "couldn't take it. He really could not. She could have been more tactful."[65] Clearly, the Governor's acrimonious personal relationships, which developed with the legislative leaders, as well as with Bob Killian, would be a major factor that led the Lieutenant Governor to lay a primary challenge on Ella Grasso in 1978.

Ella Grasso's initial difficulties as Governor were made more stressful because of her personal characteristics such as the lack of personal tact in her dealings with subordinates and other politicians. That observation, in part, reflects a similar character assessment John Bailey often quietly proffered to certain individuals. One of his primary concerns about Ella Grasso's candidacy for Governor in 1974 was whether she had the kind of temperament suitable to be the state's Chief Executive. Her domineering, often contentious, "strong-willed," authoritative way of interacting with party leaders and legislators, as well as staff members were not characteristics suitable or helpful for developing consensus and successful executive leadership.[66]

An additional factor that one cannot ignore contributed mightily to Ella Grasso's first term troubles. After all her years in the political fray, being a woman in a political world dominated by men placed her in a vulnerable position. The reality of not truly being a co-equal in the early inner circles of government power perhaps left its enduring mark on her psyche. She had been accepted into the "brain trust" of Governors Ribi-coff and Dempsey on the basis of her intellectual brilliance, her skillful talent as a writer, and as an articulate spokeswoman for the Connecticut Democratic party. While that access, provided her entry into privileged enclaves, as many women have discovered, "entering did not necessarily mean becoming a full member."[67]

Her access would not erase the arms-length, fundamentally male chauvinistic treatment she endured over the decades of her public life. Often excluded from the "power lunches" that Bailey, Ribicoff, or Dempsey would host, Ella Grasso was in truth a lonely political war-rior—successful, enormously popular with the electorate, but bereft of close, personal, social companionship and close friendships with her political peers. Ever the outsider, the immigrant's daughter found that even after her path-breaking success at the polls, she still had to *prove* to a new generation of young politicians, exemplified by the Young Turk legislative leaders in 1975, that she could successfully shoulder the bur-den of being governor in one of the most troubling and challenging eco-nomic periods since the Great Depression of the 1930s.

Moreover, some party leaders perceived her gender as being a weak-ness, and she became convinced that she would have to make up for that by demonstrating her firmness, toughness, and strong ability to deal forthrightly, albeit not tactfully, with the tension that emerged from her interactions with the legislative leaders.

Governor Ella Grasso struggled during the first year of her steward-ship of the state. It was for her a stress-filled and in some ways a dispirit-ing time, and it would be an uphill struggle to regain political goodwill and to firm up her political standing that was present on that wintry Inaugural Day in January 1975. While she drew strength from the pub-lic's support and affection, being governor in a time vastly different than the Ribicoff-Dempsey era of governing the state ("I will run the govern-ment," said Ribicoff) presented multiple challenges for the daughter of twentieth-century pilgrims.

❈ 9 ❈

I LOVE YOU . . . I LOVE YOU ALL

Ella Grasso's numerous problems as Governor were caused to a large extent by a confluence of controversies that were present throughout her tenure as Governor. The untimely death of John Bailey and the need to find an able party chairman to succeed him was a major challenge for the Governor. Her choice, Representative Bill O'Neill, became a political disappointment after she selected him as Bailey's successor. Serious disputes associated with the fiscal condition of the state budget coupled with the often-strained relationship between the Governor and the legislative leadership of the General Assembly added to the contentious and stressed-filled atmosphere during her tenure as governor. Ultimately the hostile feelings that underscored and characterized the relationship between the Governor and Lieutenant Governor Robert Killian led to a bitter primary for the Democratic gubernatorial nomination in 1978.

With John Bailey's death in April 1975, the chairmanship of the Democratic Party fell on the broad shoulders of Representative Bill O'Neill (D-East Hampton), Majority Leader of the House of Representatives. He was Ella Grasso's handpicked choice to assume the helm of the Connecticut Democratic party. The East Hampton legislator, who had been her campaign chairman, was a congenial, popular Irishman who possessed good political instincts, and the conservative Democrat was popular among the fractious Democratic majority in the lower chamber of the General Assembly. Unquestionably the Majority Leader possessed a genuine willingness to assist the Governor in her policy and program initiatives. Years later, he would say that he had made "few enemies" among his fellow legislators, and that factor was certainly one that resonated with the Governor.[1] He was also seen as the consensus choice of the regional leaders in the party organization. Former Governor John N. Dempsey, Hartford leader Peter Kelly, and New Haven County Sheriff Henry Healey among others supported the Governor's selection of O'Neill.[2]

Bill O'Neill's "personal and political friendship" with the Governor had grown decidedly since the 1974 campaign.[3] While that friendship was forged in the heat of an election campaign, Ella Grasso and Bill O'Neill established a respectful and cordial relationship, though it never reached the level of deep admiration and personal friendship she maintained with John Bailey. O'Neill was a reliable, moderate Democrat who was a bridge to the influential Irish legislative contingent in the General Assembly, as well as among the party rank and file so vital to Democratic unity in Connecticut.

The Governor told the assemblage of party leaders and members of the State Central Committee on the evening when he was named to succeed Bailey that Bill O'Neill "understands and appreciates the contributions and responsibilities of the State Central Committee and our various party organizations."[4] She expected the East Hampton legislator's leadership and support in his role as party chairman and Majority Leader in the House of Representatives, and expected also that he would be an effective and persuasive influence among his legislative colleagues in order to move her programs through both chambers of the General Assembly.

In her prepared remarks to the State Central Committee, the Governor noted that "our job now . . . is . . . to develop new leadership and renewed unity to meet the challenges ahead."[5] Emphasizing that Bill O'Neill "has been a diligent laborer in the vineyards, working in his town and district, serving in the General Assembly," she went on to remind party leaders the fact Bill O'Neill had also acted "as my campaign manager in a hard and long election year." And as if she had a premonition of the future, she then noted that, "If he's going to quarrel, he'll quarrel with me. And he will be loyal and true to his governor." In a plea for unity, Ella said, "as we meet to face soberly and realistically all of the challenges that are before us, we do have the strong high hopes that come when a party is united. When its members in office—in the General Assembly and in the Administration—are working in tandem to serve the best interests of the State of Connecticut."[6]

The following year, however, the Governor and O'Neill were at odds, and she maneuvered to have him removed as the Democratic Party chairman. By wearing two hats as party leader and as House Majority Leader, Bill O'Neill tried to be the consensus builder and Grasso stalwart in an increasingly fractious Democratic-controlled legislature. He had to deal with various legislative factions, including un-regenerated supporters of an income tax whose agenda derived from a liberal core of political leanings. Senator Audrey Beck (D-Mansfield), for example, Co-Chairman of the legislature's Finance Committee made no secret of her support for an income tax and consequently was not in favor with the Governor.[7] Another income tax advocate was Senator Joseph Lieberman (D-New Haven), whose undisguised support for the additional tax levy always raised concerns about his loyalty and willingness to shepherd gubernatorial legislative initiatives through the Assembly's upper house. Lieberman's Senate colleague Joseph Fauliso (D-Hartford), President Pro Tempore of the State Senate and an ally of the Governor, recalls that, "Lieberman would take a stand in the caucus, and then do the opposite on the floor when a piece of legislation came up for a vote."[8]

O'Neill not only had to deal with obvious divisions among Senate Democrats, he was expected to take the lead on moving the Governor's programs through the House Democratic caucus. One contentious issue brought forward in December 1975 at a special emergency legislative session was the Governor's call to tap into the Soldiers, Sailors, and

Marines Fund and shift some of the fund's money ($30 million) to the General Fund to help reduce the state's deficit. The fund, established in 1919, helped needy wartime veterans and their families with financial assistance for a limited time period to meet certain needs, such as rent, utilities, medical and funeral expenses.

The Majority Leader told the Governor that, "he could not support that initiative," and that "every American Legion post in the state would stand against it."[9] O'Neill found himself in a very difficult place because it put him in a position where he publicly opposed a major part of the Governor's fiscal plan to reduce the state's deficit. He understood that not only was her proposal controversial, it did not generate a great deal of support among the lower house rank and file. And although her initiative to tap into the fund would go a long way to help reduce the budget deficit, it evoked loud opposition among both political parties. Over time it became clear the Governor's proposal could not win support of the Democratic majority in either the House or Senate. That turn of events weakened the cordial relationship that was present in April 1975 when Ella Grasso nominated O'Neill for state party Chairman. The Governor, believing her attempt to use the Soldiers, Sailors, and Marines Fund was a practicable way to help reduce the huge deficit, turned a deaf ear to the loud outcry of opposition that arose from veterans and veterans groups throughout the state.

As a result, one year later when the party chairman's term was up in July 1976, Ella Grasso moved to oust Bill O'Neill from that position. She questioned his ability "to fulfill . . . his dual role as party chair and majority leader of the House of Representatives, which he refused to give up."[10]

When the December 1975 Special Session of the General Assembly was called by the Governor to address a projected $80 million dollar deficit, O'Neill was not able to deliver the Democratic-controlled General Assembly's support for her fiscal program, including the raid on the veteran's fund. A few months later, during the regular session of the legislature in 1976, the Democratic majority once again refused to "yield to Mrs. Grasso on essentially the same program." As a consequence of these legislative defeats, the long festering personal rift came to a head in mid-July 1976. At that time the Democratic State Central Committee met to select a Chairman for a full two-year term. The Governor added to the controversy by indicating she was going to "let the Committee make its own choice."[11]

By stepping aside and not designating the state party chairman the Governor abandoned a strong political tradition, which permitted the governor to designate an individual as party Chairman, who would then be rubber-stamped by the Democratic State Central Committee. "That's one tradition that had gone its way," she said. "The party is coming of age."[12]

When her announcement was made, a wave of speculation ensued, which brought to the surface underlying tensions that had developed between the Governor and Chairman O'Neill. First was the chairman's opposition to Ella Grasso's budget programs, votes, she noted, that were "of course" votes against her.[13] Ella, as was her wont, did not easily forgive or forget those who voted against her key legislative proposals. The lack of communication between the party leader and the Governor was another sign of discord.

It became public knowledge that O'Neill and Grasso went "separate ways" in their choice of a 1976 Democratic presidential nominee: O'Neill was uncommitted while the Governor supported Senator Henry "Scoop" Jackson from the State of Washington, "a move O'Neill tried to talk her out of." And a third indicator of tension developed when the two were working on separate plans "for the move by the Jackson supporters (Grasso) and uncommitted Connecticut delegates (O'Neill) to support former Georgia Governor Jimmy Carter. Neither told the other." The *Hartford Courant* reported that, "it is clear that relations between the two have not been particularly happy."[14]

Although Ella "abandoned O'Neill" in his drive to be elected State Chairman, she worked actively "behind the scenes for Peter Kelly's election." And Kelly, the Democratic Town Committee Chairman in Hartford, began "to talk with leaders about the job."[15] But it was too late for him to make significant inroads among party leaders from around Connecticut. Bill O'Neill was a popular politician among Connecticut's Democratic Party leaders, and his election as party Chairman for a full two-year term was a reflection of that strong sentiment.

Several days after O'Neill's election on July 19, 1976, Ella told a reporter "I don't feel it is a personal setback for me."[16] Despite her claim, it *was* a setback but not a politically fatal wound. And the speed with which she buried the hatchet with O'Neill was testimony to her political resiliency and flexibility to move forward despite the embarrassment of the rejection of her choice. She telephoned Bill O'Neill the next day to congratulate him. A few days later, she met with him and stated she expected their future relationship would be "amicable."[17] It was vintage Ella Grasso swallowing the bitter medicine but moving forward for the good of the Democratic Party, and putting a brave face on the obvious embarrassment to her political standing. Fortunately for both Grasso and O'Neill their working relationship improved in the years ahead and remained respectful though never close.

As 1977 unfolded, it became clear Ella Grasso had "turned full circle" and joined hands with Chairman O'Neill. Their working relationship provided substance to a reporter's observation that the Governor followed one of the oldest rules in John Bailey's legendary political rulebook: "If you can't lick 'em, join 'em."[18]

Another stressful and discordant controversy the Governor faced was the growing distance between herself and Lieutenant Governor Robert Killian. While an initial working relationship had been formed at the beginning of the Grasso administration in 1975, it was obvious over time that even that thin thread of partnership frayed as Ella's treatment of Killian became more hurtful, distant, and cold.

The icy Grasso-Killian relationship was characterized by an underlying suspicion that Bob Killian would likely challenge Ella Grasso for the

Democratic gubernatorial nomination in 1978. Killian, for his part, gave out mixed signals about his intentions. At first he told her that, "he was not interested in challenging her for her job in 1978." And acknowledging her understanding of his disinterest that dated back a few months, the Governor added she "heard nothing to alter it." In fact, she went on to say that, "she would welcome him as her running mate in 1978."[19]

Eventually, the Lieutenant Governor indicated that he would not seek reelection as Grasso's running mate. At the same time, he was urged by some Hartford area party leaders to challenge the Governor for the gubernatorial nomination. John Larson of East Hartford, later a leader in the State Senate and Congressman from the First Congressional District, and Barbara Gordon, a State Central Committeewoman from West Hartford, were two leading Killian supporters who encouraged him to challenge the Governor. Killian, for his part, indicated he believed Ella Grasso was "vulnerable" based on his assessment of the Governor's political struggles:[20] unhappiness among some party officials about the lack of patronage, especially voiced by Arthur Barbieri, Democratic leader in New Haven, whose wish to become State Liquor Commissioner did not materialize; the administration's unpopular fiscal policies; and several polls, which showed her popularity at a low point. One statewide poll, commissioned by State Senator Joseph I. Lieberman, placed the Governor's favorable ratings at well below 50 percent.[21]

In contrast, a poll commissioned by Fairfield County Democrats gave the Governor a "favorability rating of 61 percent and name recognition of 99 percent."[22] Many years later when questioned about his decision to challenge the incumbent Governor, Killian's provocative reply was he believed Ella Grasso did not have anything to show for her four years in office. In a sharp, blistering comment Killian charged that the Governor "did not do a damn thing about education. All she wanted to do was survive in office, hold the fort . . ."[23]

If the Killian barbs were not bad enough, the Democratic Party's liberal wing weighed in and expressed its reservations about supporting the Governor. The Caucus of Concerned Democrats (CCD), a statewide liberal group, passed a resolution saying it would vote next year (1978) to "support a 'progressive' for the Democratic nomination." The CCD, led by Mary Sullivan, a Democratic National Committeewoman from Greenwich, listed reasons why the group did not recognize Ella Grasso as a "progressive." "She refused to consider an income tax," noted Sullivan. "As a result we have not had the funds to pay for needed state programs." Sullivan also pointed out that Connecticut's "outmoded financial structure" (reliance on the sales tax to generate needed revenues) "forced poor residents" to help "balance her budget." The liberal spokeswoman then commented that the liberals might support the Governor "if she would sort of relent and express more of an open attitude on better ways of state financing, then it certainly would be considered."[24]

Bob Killian's public criticism and the clear liberal opposition served to fire up Ella Grasso, and she reaffirmed her intention to run for a second term. She announced in late November 1977 that she would be a "candidate for reelection,"[25] and that she did not "intend to be intimidated" by Lieutenant Governor's Killian's comments.[26] Her announcement, however, concealed months of indecision, anguish, and uncertainty in the Governor's mind about whether to seek a second term.

The Governor's Chief of Staff Chad McCollam, who succeeded Nancy Lewinsohn in that position, revealed in 1994 that Ella Grasso had serious reservations about running for a second term.[27] Taking note of the Governor's difficult first term, McCollam emphasized that her reluctance stemmed from several heartfelt concerns: the economic and budgetary problems of her first term; her often contentious relationship with the legislature and some of its leaders; and her ongoing distress and profound frustration about not being able to adequately fund support for various human service programs of state government and non-profit agencies. All of those concerns brought on serious soul-searching by the Governor as to whether she would run for a second term.

James Grasso, Ella's son, acknowledges his mother's hesitancy about seeking the party nomination for a second term. He remarked that his mother had expressed interest in being appointed Ambassador to Italy "to get her out of the difficulties of the governorship."[28] And Nancy Lewinsohn remembers seeing a letter from the White House received in the Governor's office, which also confirmed a possible inquiry about a federal appointment. The letter acknowledged receiving Ella Grasso's resume. Lewinsohn concluded that Ella had made discreet inquiries to officials in the Carter White House regarding the embassy appointment. Her recollection and James Grasso's comment confirm what had been speculated in the press: the Governor was seeking an embassy appointment.

Senator Abraham A. Ribicoff told a reporter he had "a conversation with her [Ella] in which she indicated an interest in the position of Ambassador to Rome."[29] Shortly after Ribicoff's statement appeared in the press, the Governor explained she had only a "casual interest in becoming U.S. Ambassador to Italy," and added she did not talk to "aides of President-elect Carter about the subject"; her interest, Ella noted "was only casual and expressed to Ribicoff alone . . ."[30] It is clear Grasso put out feelers regarding a possible job in the Carter administration, which did not come to fruition for Connecticut's 83rd Governor.

Chad McCollam's interview also revealed Mrs. Grasso's inclination not to pursue re-nomination. McCollam, in his capacity as the Governor's Chief of Staff, disclosed he had been told by the Governor to speak to the Lieutenant Governor and inform him that Ella might not run for another four-year term. As her emissary, McCollam said he urged Bob Killian to be patient. He noted Ella directed him to use the Italian word "pacienza" to stress to Killian he should wait and his turn would come.[31]

McCollam mentioned he met Killian twice to urge "pacienza," which the Lieutenant Governor chose to ignore. Despite Killian's public stance of not showing interest in running for the gubernatorial nomination, behind the scenes he was strategizing and maneuvering in 1977 and early 1978, laying the groundwork to challenge Ella Grasso for the Democratic nomination.

In December 1977, Killian indicated that he had "been touring the state . . . and received an awful lot of encouragement to run for Governor. I have felt intense pressure to run."[32] The Lieutenant Governor told the Governor in 1977 he was going to run against her. But adding to the confusion, Ella indicated that, "He also told me he was not going to run."[33] However, when Killian began to openly criticize the Governor in late 1977, it became clear he would challenge her for the party's gubernatorial nomination. After his public criticism, including laying the state's fiscal woes squarely on her shoulders, she reacted with fury and "all bets were off and she was going for it."[34] Any expectation that Bob Killian and Ella Grasso would reconcile their differences and be running mates in 1978 completely dissolved in the face of the acrimonious political and personal relationship that had developed.

The prospect of a looming party battle for the nomination and a possible primary contest was not something an incumbent welcomes and Ella Grasso was no exception. However, her political reputation and her long commitment and dedication to serving the people of Connecticut were on the line, and she was not about to shy away from the coming political battle. It would be the first intraparty challenge for the gubernatorial nomination in the history of the Connecticut Democratic Party, and it would be a bitter personal and political battle between Governor Grasso and Lieutenant Governor Killian.

In retrospect, the spiteful and hostile relationship between the state's two highest elected political figures can be harkened back to the day John M. Bailey decided to put the two party stalwarts together as running mates in 1974. It was an unusual political marriage between two people who truly did not know each other well, nor had they worked together in any capacity within the Democratic Party. Rather it could be said this was a team of rivals, each of who over time grew wary of the other, suspicious of the other's intentions and ambitions, and who did not trust each other as colleagues or political partners.

One quite revealing aspect of the party divide that developed was that the state's two former Democratic Governors, Abraham Ribicoff and John Dempsey, withheld their endorsement of Ella Grasso. Perhaps they were hedging their bets that the Lieutenant Governor might defeat the Governor, might get the party nod for Governor and defeat her in a primary battle. Despite knowing Ella Grasso for many years, Ribicoff announced that he would remain "neutral in this year's fight over the Democratic gubernatorial nomination."[35] Likewise, former Governor John Dempsey disclosed that he intended to stay neutral in the Grasso-Killian contest. And one explanation offered was that he "may be able, later in the campaign to act as party peacemaker."[36] Yet Dempsey's son John Jr., a member of Grasso's gubernatorial staff, was named chairman of Grasso's reelection campaign committee. But the former Governor had a less cordial relationship with Ella Grasso than in the days when she was his right hand—a part of his kitchen cabinet, in the 1960s. Ella's not so subtle private sniping at what she perceived to be Dempsey's limited intellectual skills and political judgment and diminished political stature when he left office in 1971, had taken its toll on their political alliance. Another factor that affected their relationship was Ella's attempt to oust Bill O'Neill as party chairman. Dempsey and O'Neill were both from eastern Connecticut, both Irish, and politically close. In effect, while Dempsey's decision had limited impact within the statewide Democratic party, it demonstrated how Ella Grasso's personal reputation of being difficult to get along with especially among politicians and party leaders came back to haunt her.

In the final analysis, Bob Killian knew that continuing as Lieutenant Governor for a second term was not for him. Recalling his time as Ella Grasso's Lieutenant Governor, Killian explained, "I had no contact with her and she wanted no contact with me." And "I have not been an integral part of her administration. The Governor has chosen to get her advice elsewhere." He added, "I resented her attitude toward the party and the State of Connecticut," which he explained, was as if "she were the proprietor of both." According to Killian, "No one, should ever hold or possess that attitude or feeling" toward both institutions.[37]

As a result, Ella Grasso and Bob Killian headed into a fierce political battle for the 1978 Connecticut Democratic Party gubernatorial nomination. Killian's official announcement in mid-January 1978 signaled his intention to challenge the Governor for the party nomination. He took on a very difficult mission: to defeat Ella Grasso in a hardball game, which she could play with the best male politicians. Killian's quip that, "I thought I'd raise a little hell" by taking on a seasoned "consummate political pro" places him in a position which seriously questions his judgment and decision about undertaking a primary campaign. The Lieutenant Governor admitted he had differences with the Governor while at the same time he believed he "could not beat her."[38] His admission raises the obvious question: Why did he challenge Ella Grasso for the nomination in the first place?

Personal dislike, ego, and individual animosity have often been motives in political party-battles and certainly were obvious in this dispute. Killian's attitude and decision to challenge the governor reflects an arrogance, anger, and frustration that goes beyond simple personal dislike. It verges on true hostility to a woman whom he judged possessed an "attitude and arrogance" that "intimidated people," which left them "fearful" of speaking out or acting in spirited opposition to her.[39] The contentious fight between the two Democrats would continue through September 1978 when registered Democrats would go to the polls in the party's first gubernatorial primary.

Compounding these political difficulties and challenges, Ella Grasso also confronted ongoing controversies and disputes with the legislature focused primarily on the state's fiscal crisis. It began, notes one *Hartford Courant* analyst, over the state's "celebrated 1976 'fiscal crisis'" during which Ella Grasso's relations with the Democratic legislature "soured."[40]

As Ella Grasso's first term moved forward, her first budget message to the Legislature and people of Connecticut called for a budget request of $1.658 billion dollars for the fiscal year 1975–76. The Governor's budget proposal was increased by the Legislature to $1.678 billion. A sales tax increase from 6 percent to 7 percent, which she proposed was made retroactive by the legislature to April 1975. That decision contrasted sharply with the Governor's proposal to make the tax hikes effective July 1.[41] A significant part of her budget called for reductions or hold-the-line appropriations for social service programs. State employees were also informed that the pay raises they were expecting would not go forward. The Governor upset Democratic constituencies, such as state employee labor unions and advocates and providers of human service programs, with her proposed budget cuts and lack of increases in appropriations for several government agencies.

With heavy Democratic majorities in both houses, it became clear as the legislative session progressed that the majority party legislators were not inclined to pass her budget as it had been presented to them. After July 1, 1975, with the new budget in place, sales tax revenues showed a precipitous decline as a result of a serious downturn in the national and state economy. As a result, painful reductions on the spending side of the budget became necessary for programs and services that aimed to help those deemed most in need.

The General Assembly's legislators were "scrambling for additional revenue and deeper budget cuts."[42] The legislature cut $35 million dollars from Grasso's original budget, which was the result of some "very painful decisions."[43] Their unwillingness to support the Governor's budget proposal was a clear sign the Democrat's legislative leaders lacked the ability to forge a unified force among the party's rank and file behind the Governor's budget. The lack of discipline "angered Ella a product of the school of strict Democratic discipline."[44] The recalcitrance of the Democratic representatives to support the Chief Executive's budget resulted in a budget that allocated more money than she had proposed—

about $20 million in excess of what she had proposed. By their action, the legislators demonstrated to some observers, including the Governor, that the legislative Democrats lacked firm commitment and support for her policies and failed to demonstrate discipline and loyalty to the Democratic Party and the Governor's agenda on fiscal matters.

As the weeks and months moved toward the close of the 1975 calendar year, the state budget management office reported that the state was facing another budget deficit projected to be close to $80 million dollars.[45] In order to address that growing fiscal predicament, Ella called the legislature back into special session in December 1975 in order to address the revenue decline. This time, however, the anticipated shortfall had Grasso's fingerprints on it, as well as those of the Democratic legislative majority in the General Assembly. Despite the adopted tax increase, a budget crisis loomed on the horizon, in part because of lower than anticipated tax revenues in the state's coffers, coupled with the slowdown in the national economy. The Governor came forward with proposals to address the impending fiscal crisis, which in turn "soured" relations with members of the General Assembly.

Her proposals included tapping into the Soldiers, Sailors, and Marines Fund, alluded to previously. She also called for a forty-hour workweek for state employees with no increase in pay. The Governor warned that if her proposals were not approved, she would be forced to lay off five hundred employees in an effort to curtail spending and eliminate the impending deficit.

Laying off five hundred state employees with the Christmas holiday season approaching was a decision that was sure to roil the temper of state employee union members, particularly those workers directly affected by her decision. Jay Tepper, Grasso's Commissioner of Finance, remarked that she asked him to present her with alternative proposals to help cut state expenditures.[46] One of the suggestions forthcoming from Tepper's staff was to lay off state employees. Yet Ella had developed close relations with the state employee unions over many decades and to undertake an across the board employee reduction of that magnitude seems out of character.

There is credence to some people's belief that she was prompted to take drastic action to demonstrate her seriousness about getting the deficit under control and to dispel any doubts that she lacked intestinal fortitude to order such a move with huge political consequences. Some critics did not believe she would stand up to the unions or that she would follow through on her threats. The Governor, however, lived up to her word and five hundred men and women received lay-off notices with an effective date put off until post-Christmas.[47] It was the "toughest decision she . . . made as governor."[48]

It seems fair to say that by taking the action she did Ella Grasso counteracted skeptics who questioned whether she had the inner strength and determination to exhibit leadership qualities during a time of crisis. Moreover it became clear she was serious about her resolve to make bold moves in the face of a mounting state fiscal crisis.

What led her to take drastic action was the reluctance of the Democratic-led General Assembly to act favorably on the Governor's proposals. Despite large Democratic majorities in both legislative chambers, the Governor's initiatives to tap the Soldiers, Sailors, and Marine Fund, and to require state workers to work a forty-hour week "could not get out of" legislative committees.[49] State Representative John Groppo (D-Winsted), Chairman of the Appropriations Committee, noted that veterans groups "jammed the hearing room" and gave "strong and very convincing" arguments for maintaining the fund. "It couldn't get four votes out of twenty," noted the Winsted representative.[50]

Ella Grasso's two major proposals were defeated in committee 17–11 against the raid on the veterans' fund, and 7–5 against extending the state employees work week. The Governor, who was described as being in a "quiet burn," harshly criticized the defeats. Another two of the Governor's proposals did survive legislative scrutiny: the use of instant lottery proceeds to help offset the looming deficit; and requiring state sales tax collections every month instead of quarterly. However, even with those initiatives, Connecticut's projected revenues would be "$38 million dollars short of filling the $80 million dollar deficit estimated by her administration." The Governor noted that it was of "no satisfaction for me to witness the failure of the legislative process." And she went on to say, "when push comes to shove, someone has to act and then the responsibility rests with the administration." In addition to the layoffs, the Governor went further and promised "a shakedown of state government operations . . . so we can live within our resources."[51]

Her timely announcement in November 1975 creating the Filer Commission to re-structure state government (Committee on the Structure of State Government), and later in 1977 the appointment of the Gengras Commission (Committee on Government Productivity and Efficiency) were two major gubernatorial efforts to suggest ways to consolidate government agencies and recommend measures to make government more efficient, responsive, and fiscally prudent in the face of the shortfall the administration anticipated.

In retrospect, the fiscal crisis and legislative rejection of the Governor's proposals in December 1975 forced the Governor's hand to follow through with the employee layoff notices in the post-Christmas period. Her actions alienated unions, state employees and their families, union supporters and liberal Democrats, and they also deepened resentment, anger, frustration, and outright hostility toward the embattled Chief Executive.

Resentment about Ella's decisions lingered not only among the affected workers and their families, it also continued among union leaders and the rank and file. Her bold actions, however, won support for the Governor's political standing among independent voters and the business community, whose objectives had been to reduce government spending and decrease the numbers of state employees on the government payroll.

This was a low-point of Mrs. Grasso's first term. It became clear with the rejection of her proposals she decided to turn her back on legislative leaders. When the General Assembly returned in February for its regular legislative session, she proposed essentially the same initiatives for the 1976–77 budget that she had put forward in the December Special Session. The legislature again rejected the Governor's budget proposals.

It was this crisis that "cost her the allegiance of state employee unions and opened a schism in her party."[52] In some respects the absence of John Bailey and his masterly ability to influence and persuade legislators to not embarrass a Democratic governor was sorely missing.

This struggle between Governor Grasso and the party's legislative majorities was described as a "revolt against gubernatorial programs," reminiscent of the 1970 tug-of-war between Governor Dempsey and the ambitious legislative leaders Ed Marcus and Bill Ratchford. Their challenges to the then Democratic Governor precipitated Dempsey's decision not to seek reelection. In Ella Grasso's case, while she certainly gave serious thought to not seeking reelection she sent clear signals to the public demonstrating her determination to personally help reduce the state's looming deficit. Showing a "flair for popular symbolism," she sold the state's airplane, stopped using the limousine assigned to her, and turned down a $7,000 pay raise, which she legally had to accept. (The salary went from $35,000 to $42,000, and she donated the difference to the state treasury).[53]

In a further effort to show her commitment to helping the state's fiscal plight, Ella Grasso embarked on a speaking tour around the country and turned over the honorariums she received to the state General Fund. She went so far as to "even venture" the suggestion of possibly selling the silver at the governor's residence in order to generate more revenue for Connecticut.[54] While these efforts would not have filled the state coffers to cover the deficit, they were initiatives that were bound to win the public's favor.

The governor acknowledged that savings from layoffs would save between $500,000 and $1,000,000,[55] however, the 1975–76 fiscal year ended with a $34 million dollar surplus leading the Republican legislators to cry "foul" and Democrats "quietly grumbled."[56] While the surplus was a modest one, it showed that the revenue gained for the state from the increase in the sales and gas taxes, alongside significant proceeds from the state Instant Lottery and an overall improved state and national economy, all helped to bring about the surplus. The projected deficit had been turned around and Ella Grasso received credit as the architect of the budget surplus.

What also became clear is that while she lost some political friends in these budget battles, particularly in her own party, she gained immense good will among Connecticut's independent voters. She "rebounded slowly from the low point of her gubernatorial career" and positioned herself as a fiscal conservative showing strength, determination, and fortitude cutting spending to help resolve the fiscal crisis while at the same time displaying warm "mothering the state during troubled times."[57]

Political columnist Jack Zaiman wrote, "Mrs. Grasso appears to have general support in the state." Earlier cries that she "wasn't showing leadership suddenly stopped." "Now," he emphasized, "she is out there all by herself abandoned by her own people . . . doing what she thinks is right for the state as a whole."[58]

Budgetary worries continued to concern the Governor, and that concern affected her relationship with the legislative leaders. Ella Grasso's strong intellectual belief in the positions she articulated left her averse to extending her hand to achieve political accommodation or compromise. She "cut off communication with Democratic Party leaders" in the early gubernatorial years and "withdrew into the quiet recesses of her office."[59] Her behavior led one writer to observe that "Mrs. Grasso has ricocheted from one political disaster to another . . . turning friends into enemies."[60] The prescient observation attributed to John Bailey that he had concerns about Ella's temperament and ability to work successfully with political colleagues was never more on display than in this and subsequent budget battles with the General Assembly.

In the aftermath of the initial budget struggles the Governor enjoyed the luxury of three straight state budget surpluses in subsequent years. Austere budgeting plus an upswing in the national economy were factors helping the state's fiscal picture brighten.

The Governor "did not sign and did not veto the state budget for the year beginning July 1, 1977."[61] Her opposition was primarily because it called for an 11 percent increase in state spending. By refusing to sign the budget "she is trying to shuck off all the blame for any deficit the increase may later create." It is a "transparent attempt to hang any of the blame for the document on the General Assembly. It is a cop out, abdication of her responsibilities, an affront to legislators."[62] The 1977–78 budget, however, later generated a $93 million dollar surplus in large measure due to the revenues from a 7 percent sales tax, which "spiraled upward" with a 13 percent increase in revenues.[63]

While the surplus was welcome news for Ella Grasso, it provided the political opposition reason to accuse the Governor of playing "an old-fashioned political trick—buying votes with taxpayers dollars," according to Republican Senator Lewis Rome (R-Bloomfield).[64] His pointed criticism, unfortunately for him, fell on deaf ears because the surplus was so large and unexpected. The year 1978 was an election year, and Ella Grasso was seeking reelection and could point to the good news of a budget being in the black.

Although she had been critical of that budget because of the large 11 percent increase in General Fund expenditures, representing a 14 percent increase in the overall budget, the significant increase expanded funds for social services, something previous budgets had been unable to do. The 1977–78 budget appropriated additional funds for more daycare centers, expanded programs for seniors, increased welfare benefits, and so forth. Fortunately for the Governor fiscal prudence in offering austere budgets in her first years in office reaped some rewards as the dynamics of the state and national economies showed signs of improvement in 1978. However, she chose not to have her fingerprints on the budget document fearing she would be labeled a big-time spender.

Another aspect of Connecticut's economic policy during the Grasso years was a vigorous, strong, ongoing, concerted effort to broaden the diversity of the state's manufacturing and industrial base. A large portion of the state's economy was composed of industries and manufacturers, which produced material for national defense needs. It became obvious in the mid-to late 1970s that the federal government's Guns and Butter policy, which included significant expenditures to meet the needs of the military, would be greatly reduced as the Vietnam War ended. As the American military involvement in Southeast Asia diminished, Connecticut's military-industrial complex led by Pratt and Whitney Aircraft (jet engines), Sikorsky (helicopters), and other weapons manufacturers heavily reliant on Defense Department procurements saw contracts cancelled because of America's pullout from Vietnam. For a state traditionally and historically called the Arsenal of Democracy, development of a new path was needed to provide alternative opportunities in the industrial and manufacturing work place "for a labor force consisting of over 400,000 men and women."[65]

The Governor announced on NBC's *Meet the Press* that, "we are hoping that we will be able to revitalize our Department of Commerce [later called the Department of Economic Development] and . . . we are going to find those areas where there are rapid growth industries, persuade them . . . to come and live and work in our state."[66]

The Governor and her well-respected Commissioner of Economic Development Edward Stockton implemented a multi-faceted policy to provide economic development grants and financing (bonding programs, including utility revenue bonds) to communities to encourage and enable those entities to acquire land to build industrial parks and to provide funding for appropriate infrastructure (roads, sewers, etc.) to attract new businesses to Connecticut.

In March 1975 Stockton addressed the New England Council Board of

Directors comprised of executives from banks, utilities, and corporations. He outlined the policy the Grasso administration would follow. First, there would be close coordination of Connecticut's development grants and financial programs with the federal Economic Development Administration and the Small Business Administration. Second, the state would encourage and foster close partnerships between the state and regional groups and agencies associated with business, industry, and manufacturing. Third, Connecticut's Departments of Labor, Economic Development, and Transportation would direct their efforts to match manpower needs in geographic areas with idle manpower in other geographic areas linked by a transportation system, which will make it all possible.[67]

The strategy included making available economic development grants and bonding allocation programs for Connecticut towns and cities, which continued throughout the Grasso administration and remained the heart of the administration's effort. The grants and bonding availability provided a special stimulus a shot in the arm for economic development, creating industrial parks, as well as opportunities to attract businesses and industries for many towns and cities throughout Connecticut. Largely targeting areas of the state that had persistent high rates of unemployment (eastern Connecticut) or suffered significant loss of manufacturing and industrial capacity resulting in significant joblessness (Naugatuck Valley), Ella's administration moved forward to provide money for planning grants, monetary support for land acquisition, as well as negotiated agreements with companies who agreed to come to the state and construct facilities or purchase existing facilities for their industrial or manufacturing enterprises.

Underlying these constructive efforts was the long-range goal of providing employment opportunities for the state's large population of skilled labor, craftsmen, machinists, and toolmakers — the unemployed and underemployed individuals. Another objective was to encourage and stimulate economic recovery and sustainability of the general Connecticut economy over time.

Following is a partial list of towns and municipalities that received economic grants, and an additional brief list of foreign companies attracted to the state, reflecting some of the results of the Economic Development Department's vigorous and aggressive efforts. In 1975 over a period of five months, the towns of Thompson ($74,793), Killingly ($49,941), Mansfield ($52,080), and Naugatuck ($1,003,284) received planning grant money to develop industrial parks.[68] Those communities (with the exception of Naugatuck) are located in eastern Connecticut and had high rates of unemployed workers. In 1978, economic development efforts produced agreements with several foreign manufacturers and industries, revealing successful efforts made to recruit manufacturers from across the Atlantic. SPM Instrument AB (Sweden) announced it would construct a manufacturing plant in Marlborough; Kistler Instruments AG (Switzerland) agreed to bring manufacturing jobs to a facility in the town of Hamden; Plenty Group (England) signed on to establish their headquarters and plant in Brookfield.[69] Those companies were expected to provide hundreds of employment opportunities for Connecticut's workforce.

On January 3, 1979, Hallmark Cards announced its decision to construct a large distribution center in Enfield, adding between 450–550 jobs to the Connecticut labor market.[70] Commissioner Stockton recalls that, when initial discussions ensued between Hallmark and the Department of Economic Development, he called the Governor to ask if he might bring the Hallmark officials to her office.[71] She happened to be in Boston attending a conference but assured him that she would welcome the group at the Governor's Residence late in the afternoon upon her return from the Bay State.[72] He recalls that the group was charmed by the Governor and as a result of that informal get-together the deal went forward. One of the nation's largest privately held corporations established its presence in Connecticut.

Following that announcement a major German manufacturer Jagenberg-Werke AG of Dusseldorf indicated that it had selected Enfield, Connecticut, as the location for its first American manufacturing plant.[73] The 50,000-square-foot facility provided a major boost to the economy of the greater Hartford region.

In retrospect, the energetic, aggressive economic development program with the active, hands-on, personal participation and encouragement of the Governor went a long way to enable Connecticut to expand its industrial and manufacturing base and in so doing made Connecticut a more attractive and appealing place to do business. On NBC's *Meet the Press* Ella Grasso emphasized factors she believed would bring new business to the state: a "tremendous resource of labor; a good community in which to live; we have the interest and the ingenuity of our industrial process and we are going to go out . . . to do the hardest sell possible."[74] Part of the sell was the presence of a large skilled labor force including machinists, toolmakers, and talented craftsmen, accessible land, and financial incentives. Connecticut offered many advantages for attracting potential businesses and industry, but one special advantage was the Governor herself. A vital component of Commissioner Stockton's strategy was to introduce officials of the prospective business to the Governor. The unique position Ella Grasso held as Connecticut's Governor, the first woman elected in her own right as Chief Executive of one of the U.S. States, often helped persuade businesses to come to the Land of Steady Habits.

Similarly the endeavor to attract large pharmaceutical enterprises to locate research facilities in Connecticut became another major component of the Grasso-Stockton economic development strategy. The decisions by Miles Laboratories (later Bayer Corp.) to build in West Haven, by Bristol-Myers, which constructed a large research facility in Wallingford, and by the Boerhinger-Ingleheim pharmaceutical firm, which developed a facility in Ridgefield and later Danbury, provide clear evidence that those well-known companies recognized the important links their businesses could make with Yale University and the University of Connecticut. Both institutions of higher education were nationally recognized for their outstanding work in the fields of medical and scientific research. Easy proximity to the two well-respected research centers added an important dimension to the corporate decisions to locate facilities in Connecticut.

Clearly the strategy of the Grasso administration to pursue an energetic, vigorous, and purposeful policy to broaden and expand Connecticut's industrial and manufacturing base was the right path to follow in the 1970s. The long-range vision to create a viable, sustainable, diverse economic base not so closely dependent on military and defense contracts remains a beneficial legacy of the Grasso administration.

As the election year 1978 unfolded, the Governor received an unexpected boost from Mother Nature, which improved her political standing as Governor. In early February 1978, a monster northeaster storm descended on New England and blanketed the region with nearly two feet of snow. Connecticut's winter season, like that of other New England states, can be treacherous and dangerous, and this storm proved to be particularly devastating. The heavy snow accompanied by unusually high winds caused blizzard-like conditions throughout the state.

Storm Larry, as it was called, began in the morning of February 6, and by noon schools throughout the state had closed, businesses sent employees home, and the state prepared for a storm emergency. Connecticut's emergency storm center, located in the State Armory in Hartford, was adjacent to the State Capitol. The Governor, who had been making public appearances that day, arrived at the storm center after she "walked several blocks" through the snow-covered streets because the state police car she was traveling in became stuck in the snow.[75]

She immediately took charge of emergency operations, and later that evening issued a state of "civil preparedness emergency" and banned all traffic on Connecticut roads and highways.[76] The ban was effective from Monday February 6 at 10 P.M. through Wednesday February 8 at noon when it would expire. This decision was made not only in the interest of safety for drivers—preventing serious accidents, injuries and possible fatalities—but also to enable the state's Department of Transportation to "get out and clear the roads without having to worry about traffic snarls."[77]

The Governor's actions that day and over the next several days give testimony to Ella Grasso's passionate commitment to the well-being of the state and its citizens. Closing the state in the face of a challenging natural disaster was rare, but it demonstrated her genuine compassion and concern for Connecticut. Taking full charge of the emergency operations, she stayed on top of matters for three days, spending one "night, catching a few hours of sleep on an office sofa" in the Emergency Center.[78]

Her constant availability to the press and media, along with almost hourly appearances on statewide television stations, afforded her multiple opportunities to reassure the people of Connecticut that their Governor was working in their best interests and for their safety during the state's worst blizzard in decades.

One of her actions was to call the White House and ask President Carter to declare Connecticut a disaster area. The President issued a declaration (Massachusetts and Rhode Island also received that designation) and authorized dispatch of federal troops from Ft. Hood, Texas, to assist Connecticut's National Guard in cleanup efforts. The federal government response also included much-needed vehicles and equipment to aid in the snow removal effort.

Ella Grasso's sincere and genuine concern for the safety and welfare of Connecticut and its citizens was never more apparent than in this crisis. When the storm cleared she flew in a Connecticut National Guard helicopter, enabling her to survey damage around the state.

A memorable message ELLA HELP was spelled out in the snow by two young men from Norwich who "used their skis to trace" that plea in the deep snow. In a letter that the Governor sent to the young men she noted that she "saw your work as I was flying from Norwich to Montville . . . the day after the blizzard during my tour of eastern Connecticut."

She added that "your appeal was very timely and our state was able to offer direct assistance to many of our towns and cities . . . and to secure additional federal help." In a particularly thoughtful but characteristic plea, she urged the young men to "retain an interest in matters of public concern throughout your lives" and expressed the hope that "the initiative and bravery you exhibited . . . will be translated . . . during the years ahead into community service."[79]

The overwhelmingly positive reaction from Connecticut citizens to the Governor's proactive leadership during Storm Larry reveals a wellspring of deep admiration and enormous respect people held for her. The Governor received an avalanche of letters and messages from local officials and ordinary citizens. Comments included such praise as "masterful performance," "superb leadership," "outstanding direction," "wise and compassionate leadership."[80] A letter from First Selectman Dan Vece (D) of Clinton lauded her and said, "Where there is dedication there is no procrastination, no hesitation, and no vacillation."[81] A Naugatuck Valley newspaper editorial exclaimed, "Mrs. Grasso has been soundly blasted for inaction in a number of economic areas . . . Today she richly deserves the thanks of all."[82]

In the storm's wake Connecticut reported four deaths and damage estimated at $25 million dollars. Citing Connecticut's early cancellation of work and the traffic ban, a national publication praised Connecticut for its quick action, which the journal emphasized, "prevented drivers from being stranded on the road and probably alleviated this source of mortality." The brief article pointed out that in Massachusetts twenty-seven people lost their lives. "Some of the deaths [in Mass.] which occurred immediately after the blizzard might have been prevented if traffic had been banned earlier."[83]

Some critics accused the Governor of overplaying her role by her constant presence on the television screen and her domination of the airwaves. Democratic Lieutenant Governor Robert Killian was especially critical of the Governor's handling of the emergency. "She did not do anything that anyone else would not have done," he said. Storm Larry "saved her," Killian added sarcastically.[84] These comments offered many years later came from the man who in 1978 was an announced candidate challenging Ella Grasso for the Democratic gubernatorial nomination. His conclusion, however, reflects the reality of that moment in 1978: Ella Grasso received significant political advantage from her handling of the storm emergency.

Killian's statements, aided by the luxury of hindsight, reflect a wounded and bruised ego harking back to the moment in time when Ella effectively kept him out of the spotlight and virtually froze him out of the media's attention during the emergency operations. Her forceful take-charge attitude, clever manipulation of the press and media, and her warm, motherly display of concern and compassion for the State of Connecticut certainly outwitted the Lieutenant Governor. Ella Grasso's firm and savvy management of the crisis, calling on her best political instincts and skills, enabled the Governor to out maneuver, out shine, and snub her potential rival who stood helplessly on the sideline.

Ella's leadership during this crisis in 1978, an election year, gained her a huge outpouring of public support and confidence. By firmly leading the state through difficult days, reassuring her fellow citizens that her concern was their safety, and by her constant motherly presence in their living rooms via TV she put to rest any remaining doubts about her leadership capabilities, skills, and personal dedication to guiding the state through a crisis. There is no doubt, however, that she clearly understood the political stakes in this emergency and saw it as an opportunity to gain the upper hand in what would be the opening round of the political storms that lay ahead.

The acrimonious and acerbic political battle between Ella Grasso and Bob Killian took center stage in the weeks and months after Storm Larry. The political fight between the two rivals developed into a contentious and hostile environment, the likes of which Connecticut had never seen.

It was the first time in Connecticut history that a Lieutenant Governor challenged an incumbent Governor of the same party. It would be a nine-month-long struggle between two officeholders, whose personal and political relationship had deteriorated over three years to an icy and distant separation.

Bob Killian, in early December 1977, issued a strongly worded statement indicating he was leaning toward making a run for Governor. He summarized his problem with Ella Grasso and her administration as: "it all adds up to a lack of decisiveness, a lack of direction and a lack of accessibility." Killian pointed out that he did not have a part in the administration, and as a result, "I have felt that I have been wasted in some sense." And he added, "I can't think of anything . . . that will keep me from running for governor."[85]

In mid-January 1978, the Lieutenant Governor formally announced plans to seek the Democratic nomination for Governor. His statement included a "slashing," blistering verbal attack on Ella Grasso, accusing her of "playing political games, using fiscal gimmickry, and bowing to political expediency" during her three years in office. He went on to say the Governor abdicated the responsibilities of leadership by "failing to face the problems of urban areas, of the unemployed, and the underemployed, and the deterioration of the quality of our humane and compassionate institutions." The "paramount issue," he emphasized, "is leadership," and "what we lack is an executive willing to grasp the reins of leadership."[86] Bob Killian's opening volley is an example of the subsequent war of words that became a hallmark of the spirited contest between the two political rivals.

Connecticut's electoral nominating procedures for state office did not include a direct primary, rather it included several steps that candidates were required to follow under party regulations and state law. The first stage was to secure party delegates, who were selected at the local levels, and who would attend and vote for a full slate of constitutional officers at the state convention in July. If a candidate received 20 percent of first-ballot delegate votes on the convention floor, the minimum thresh-old was met to wage a primary against the convention nominee. If the threshold number was not attained, that individual would not be able to proceed to pursue a primary for the nomination.

Securing 20 percent meant a primary campaign could be waged statewide, culminating in a September vote. Once a primary winner was chosen, by enrolled party members, the last step would be the general election campaign, concluding on Election Day, the first Tuesday after the first Monday in November.

Ella Grasso's strategy was to reach out to Democratic political leaders, elected officials, as well as to meet with Democrats at the local level to gain delegate support at the grass-roots level. Her efforts were also di-rected at precluding Bob Killian from attaining the minimum 20 percent delegate support at the July 21–22, 1978, state convention in Hartford.

Bob Killian's plan from the outset was to use the media and press to verbally assail the Governor in harsh, aggressive, and hard-hitting ways. He continually criticized her lack of leadership ability, believing that charge would irritate the Governor and get under her "thin skin" despite the tough image she projected in public.[87] Therefore he set out to amass a minimum of 272 delegates committed to his candidacy, hoping this approach would muster the necessary support to launch a primary against Ella Grasso.

As the hunt for delegates moved forward, Killian ramped up the rhet-oric, using a tone far more "vivid than any yet from the Republicans."[88] The Lieutenant Governor aimed his criticism at Governor Grasso in areas where he thought she was politically vulnerable. He repeatedly ac-cused her of abdicating responsibility of leadership, and in the "most acrimonious language" blasted the governor for "building a surplus on the suffering of kids, and those who are mentally ill or mentally retarded."[89] His words signaled "a rough fight to come" noted one re-porter.[90] By questioning the Governor's commitment to state programs for people most in need, Killian's credibility was put into question. The public's awareness of Ella Grasso's recent display of leadership during Storm Larry combined with her well-known, lengthy public involvement with organizations and groups associated with children, mental health, and mental retardation issues undermined any political traction Killian hoped to gain from that accusation.

Her defense against Killian's attacks was to constantly remind voters of her cautious efforts to control spending, her opposition to an income tax (which Killian said he would not rule out),[91] and three budget surpluses resulting from judicious use of taxpayer dollars. Further she extolled some of her "first term accomplishments — solvent state finances, 200,000 new jobs," and aggressive efforts to bring new businesses to Connecticut.[92]

One early test of Killian's strategy occurred in New Britain where Democratic voters selected a forty-four-member delegation to the state convention. The slate that pledged to support the Governor decisively defeated Killian's delegate hopefuls 6,656 to 3,708. Celebrating her victory, Ella expressed "delight . . . results were much better than I had expected." In what was expected to be a "close battle" the turnout was 42 percent, an impressive vote for a local delegate primary. "Many people . . . have been watching these results," she noted. "This has been a testing ground."[93]

As the mid-summer convention neared, the rhetoric and charges continued to heat up between the two opponents. Killian's campaign charged that Ella Grasso's team was working to secure delegates by threatening them. Exhibiting growing anger at her opponent's tactics, she replied, "I would not threaten them. I have too much respect for myself. I have too much respect for the political system to do anything like that."[94]

The Democratic convention opened the evening of July 21, 1978, with the keynote address delivered by Senator Abraham A. Ribicoff. His long career in state and national politics served as a reminder to the convention audience of a time when party unity under John M. Bailey's strong leadership brought a long cycle of victories to the party of Jefferson and

Jackson. With Bailey gone and party unity unraveling, Ribicoff's presence as a unifying figure offered hope to the Democratic faithful that the party might avoid a serious political rift, weakening Democratic chances for victory in the fall election.

That hope never materialized, as both candidates' supporters worked with determination and commitment for their respective candidate. The Grasso convention forces led by party chairman Bill O'Neill and Senator Joseph Fauliso worked earnestly and diligently to preclude the Lieutenant Governor from reaching the 272 votes he needed to mount a primary challenge. Killian's supporters led by former Norwalk Mayor Frank Zullo and Hartford State Senator Sanford Cloud as Co-Chairmen, along with Nicholas Carbone a former Grasso supporter in her first run for Governor, worked aggressively to secure support for their candidate.

On Saturday July 22, 1978, the convention delegates endorsed Ella Grasso with 1,079 votes for a second term as the Democratic Party standard bearer. Killian received 278 votes, achieving a six-vote margin above the minimum needed, which "sanctioned a statewide gubernatorial primary between Ella Grasso and Robert Killian."[95]

The convention also endorsed Bill O'Neill (D-East Hampton) to be the party's candidate for Lieutenant Governor. Ella Grasso had not handpicked a running mate but let the convention delegates decide. While a number of individuals threw their hats in the ring, including State Senator Joseph I. Lieberman, O'Neill captured the nomination due in large part to strong backing from legislative colleagues working the convention floor on his behalf. He had also built up strong loyalty among local and regional party leaders in his capacity as State Chairman of the Democratic Party.

Months later, the Governor revealed that Bill O'Neill wanted "very badly" to be her running mate in 1974, and that "I would have accepted him" for the second spot.[96] Instead she bowed to the entreaties of John M. Bailey to put Bob Killian on the ticket as the candidate for Lieutenant Governor.

After the convention, the gubernatorial rivals quickly engaged in non-stop, eighteen-hour days on the primary trail, with their paths crossing one summer day. The story unfolded when the two campaigners unexpectedly came head to head at a Democratic Party event in Madison, Connecticut. Killian extended his hand; Ella ignored him but was reportedly heard muttering the unladylike phrase *son of a b*—— at her opponent. Her penchant for using salty language was well known, although it was usually reserved for conversations out of the public arena. This verbal altercation hardly resonated with most people, though it made newspaper headlines. It was not that politicians—male or female—did not use colorful language on occasion. It was more that people were surprised the Governor would be overheard using such a phrase within earshot of reporters and the public.

Killian's camp also leveled charges against Mrs. Grasso because her name appeared on campaign literature endorsing the candidacy of the Democratic candidate for Probate Judge in New Britain. Such advertising was not permitted in probate judge elections. While she was eventually cleared by the court of authorizing the use of her name in the New Britain campaign, it was an embarrassment for a sitting Governor to be brought into a courtroom in the middle of a political campaign.

In early September a public debate was held, and the two contenders "parried gingerly" and displayed "little emotion" during an hour-long face-off. One topic that was discussed was abortion. Bob Killian opposed abortion but was in favor of "using state funds for such procedures when pregnancy resulted from rape or incest or when a doctor certified an abortion was needed to preserve a woman's physical or mental well-being." Ella Grasso, on the other hand, had been subjected to pointed criticism for her refusal to allow state funds to be used to pay for abortions on demand. Despite holding that opinion, the Governor reminded the audience that, "there are state funds available for abortions to end pregnancies resulting from rape and incest.[97]

The candidates' positions on issues were often low-keyed in the press

as the media focused on the personal acrimony between the two contenders. One topic the two Democrats did not agree on did find its way
into the media's spotlight. Bob Killian announced a proposal for the
state takeover of welfare costs. He called his proposal a "key piece" of
his "urban strategy," but the Governor opposed his suggestion calling it
"too costly, too difficult," and saying it would "offend" people living outside urban centers.[98] Killian, in response, noted that 90 percent of welfare costs were paid for by the state, and the remaining cost would not
be overly burdensome for the state to manage. His proposal, while well
intentioned, lost him support among voters not sympathetic to urban-
centered problems.

The contentious and often bitter primary concluded on September
12, 1978. The result was a lopsided triumph for Ella Grasso: 137,466 for
Grasso, 66,038 for Killian.[99] The vote tally signaled overwhelming support for Ella Grasso as the Democratic Party candidate for Governor.
Bob Killian privately acknowledged, "I knew I could not beat her."[100]

In the remaining weeks of the general election campaign, the Governor campaigned tirelessly against three-term Republican Fifth District
Congressman Ronald Sarasin. Sarasin, considered a potentially strong
candidate by the GOP establishment, was persuaded to give up a safe
seat in Congress to return and run for Governor.

Republican Party State Chairman Frederick Biebel indicated early in
1978 that the GOP was prepared to spend $1 million dollars on the gu-
bernatorial campaign.[101] Ella Grasso was seen as beatable because of her
perceived vulnerability on several issues: questions about her leadership
on budgets, fiscal issues, taxes, and spending. Many in the Republican
Party were convinced the bruising Killian-Grasso primary decisively diminished her chances for reelection.

For the balance of the summer of 1978, the Democratic state primary
monopolized the attention and daily headlines in the state's newspapers
and media outlets. Meanwhile Sarasin and his running mate State Senator Lewis Rome (R-Bloomfield) were on the sidelines, virtually ignored,

receiving scant public attention. It left the GOP candidates little time to gain statewide familiarity, to discuss their platform and positions on issues, resulting in their inability to engage voters or generate enthusiasm among the voting citizenry.

A September 25, 1978, poll disclosed that four of ten voters said, "they don't know much about him [Sarasin]," and of those voters, two-thirds support Mrs. Grasso. In a talk to students at Connecticut College in New London, Congressman Sarasin declared he was "frustrated" that his message "doesn't seem to be getting across" to the media. He asserted that in his view the public had been misled by "the myth of Ella Grasso," that she had reduced spending and taxes when, "he charged, the opposite is true."[102]

Sarasin also pointed to another problem his campaign was facing. He expressed concern that raising money to conduct his campaign was a big challenge. The campaign, he explained, would "probably end up spending $800,000" and would be "lucky if it could raise that much."[103] In effect the expectation discussed early in 1978 by the GOP State Chairman of raising one million dollars was not happening with just a few weeks remaining before the election.

The Fifth District Congressman, a former state legislator before his election to Congress, had been in Washington for nearly six years, and the impression he conveyed on the campaign trail was that his knowledge and understanding of state issues was not easily articulated. Responding to a reporter's question Ella Grasso observed that her opponent was "not as well-informed nor as articulate as Bob Steele" the GOP candidate in 1974.[104] She added that a head-to-head match between herself and Senator Rome (candidate for Lt. Governor) would have "been a lively event indeed," a not so subtle jab at the Republican gubernatorial nominee.[105]

Sarasin raised two important issues: one was a proposal to put a limit on state spending by passing a constitutional amendment, which the Governor opposed. The GOP candidate also suggested passing legislation barring the imposition of an income tax. However, in a poll released in September 1978, the results showed more people knew of Ella Grasso's opposition to imposing an income tax than knew of Sarasin's stand on the same issue.[106]

Sarasin continually repeated his charge that Ella Grasso had "abdicated" her gubernatorial leadership responsibilities. It was a charge leveled at her in similar fashion by Bob Killian, and it gained him little traction in their primary battle. Sarasin discovered, not surprisingly, in the same September poll that more voters saw Mrs. Grasso as a strong leader, undercutting the Congressman's oft-stated accusation.[107]

Ella Grasso's campaign statements continually reminded voters of her determination to continue to develop the state's economy, to support additional opportunities for job training, and to increase state assistance for Connecticut's urban centers.[108] She repeated frequently her opposition to an income tax, despite a statement many years later by her husband that, "intellectually," she believed it to be a fairer levy on individuals.[109]

Election Day November 7, 1978, resulted in an impressive reelection victory for Ella Grasso and her running mate, Representative Bill O'Neill (D-East Hampton). Ella Grasso's vote total was 613,109 to Ronald Sarasin's 422,316, a margin of 190,793 votes. The victory was a resounding win and a significant personal triumph for her.

She received election results at her home in Windsor Locks surrounded by her husband, children, beloved Uncle Nat, friends, and a small group of staff. Fielding phone calls from a number of well-wishers including President Carter and ABC's Barbara Walters, Ella expressed cautious optimism about the election returns as they were phoned into her home that evening. "I'll worry until the last vote is counted," she explained.[110] Eventually the congratulatory phone call came from Congressman Sarasin and her victory was complete. The Governor finally leaned over and kissed her husband and said, "Tom, we've won."[111]

Ella Grasso's reelection brought personal satisfaction—some might say vindication—to the Windsor Locks native, though it had been a very stressful, difficult, and trying first term and a tough primary campaign. With her usual energetic, enthusiastic resolve to move forward, Ella Rosa Giovanna Tambussi Grasso would unknowingly come face to face with unexpected personal challenges in the months ahead.

On January 4, 1979, Ella Grasso took the oath of office commencing her second term as Governor of the State of Connecticut. Amid the joyful atmosphere of that first day she addressed the newly sworn members of the General Assembly in what one editorial described as a "short speech of generalities, devoid of solutions, more pious than promising."[112] The Governor's Inaugural addressed reprised some of the same ideas and themes discussed in the campaign. She emphasized her belief that government has a responsibility to "develop an economic climate to attract new business . . . and to help Connecticut firms grow." Her statement also noted that Connecticut had an obligation to "develop training programs for the job skills that are needed by expanding business and industry."[113]

The Governor also gave recognition to the reorganization of the executive branch, a major reform in her first term, which she supported and which passed the General Assembly in 1977. The restructuring occurred as a result of recommendations the Filer Commission proposed to the Governor and legislature, not only as a potential cost-saving measure in the midst of the state's fiscal crisis, but as proposals that promised to bring Connecticut's government into a modern mode of governance. The "executive reorganization now in place," she explained, "provides new techniques for accountability and service by administrators and state employees."[114]

The Executive Branch reorganization reduced the number of executive departments and consolidated the functions of twenty-six government departments to twenty.[115] The logic of reducing or eliminating and consolidating state agencies, boards, and commissions was primarily directed to make government more productive, efficient and responsive to the needs of the people of Connecticut.

The Filer Commission also recommended the "creation of two major staff agencies, the Office of Policy and Management and the Department of Administrative Services."[116] Arguably, the Office of Policy and Management, created October 1, 1977, as an agency of the Governor's Office has been a "mainstay of the executive branch and a source of gubernatorial power and expertise."[117] OPM functions as the agency that "prepares the governor's budget, coordinates interagency policies and intergovernmental relations.[118]

Weeks later in February 1979, the Governor presented her budget message to the General Assembly. She requested an increase in spending of $116.3 million dollars for a total budget request of $2.398 billion dollars. Anthony Milano, Secretary of the Office of Policy and Management, conceded that the budget is an "extremely austere budget."[119] But he realized the initial "glum" reaction of the legislators was due in large part to the absence of additional appropriations for programs that could assist them in their communities in the next elections.[120] Milano, who was Ella's chief adviser on the budget, was the administration's key point man on questions related to state finances.

Economic issues became more challenging in 1979 and 1980, sparked by rising costs due to inflation, skyrocketing oil prices, and OPEC placing strict controls on oil production, resulting in cutbacks and curtailing oil supplies reaching American refineries, gas stations, and homes. That situation resulted in the implementation by the Grasso administration of a distribution system of odd-even availability of gasoline for vehicles, based on the last digit on license plates. The objective was to avoid "hoarding and long lines at gas stations.[121]

Ella's second term commenced with serious fiscal problems and challenges. In 1980, faced with another revenue shortfall, projected to be over $128 million dollars, she resorted to calling for an increase in the sales tax to 7.5 percent and over $63.3 million in new taxes.[122] The General Assembly responded by approving a 0.5 percent raise in the sales tax and a 2 percent tax on gross earnings of the state's major oil companies.[123] The Governor, "a fiscal conservative," continued to resist any consideration of imposing an income tax.[124] She believed that despite significant revenue decline the traditional mix of taxes would enable the state to meet its obligation "to live within our means" without resorting to another new tax on Connecticut's taxpayers.[125] The state's economic problems persisted, along with a continued downward slide in the nation's economy. Ella Grasso's careful and cautious guidance of the Ship of State, especially in troubled times, was suddenly thrown off course as a more personal problem emerged in her second term.

In the spring of 1980, Ella experienced health problems brought on by severe bleeding and entered Hartford Hospital to undergo a dilation and curettage procedure. After her discharge from the hospital, upon examination of tissue, malignant cancer cells were found. Weeks later she underwent exploratory surgery, which revealed an ovarian tumor resulting in a complete hysterectomy. While the extent of the tumor could not be determined, her doctor Dr. Joseph Russo recommended a regimen of chemotherapy. Ella started treatments in May after the General Assembly adjourned.

While trying to cope with the reactions to the treatments, the Governor continued her limited public schedule and attending to state government matters. In a handwritten note to President Carter, she first thanked him for his decision to return the U.S. navy submarine Nautilus to Connecticut. Then she added that, "I am feeling better and have almost finished week 1 of the treatments — 5 to go!"[126] She attended the state Democratic Party Convention in Hartford in July, husbanding her strength in order to attend the opening session and to hear the keynote speech delivered by Governor Bill Clinton (D-Ark.). In August, she traveled to New York City to attend the Democratic National Convention, attending only night sessions and frequently resting in her hotel room during the day. In the following weeks she did campaign for state legislative candidates, and she hosted both President and Mrs. Carter and Vice President Walter Mondale when they visited Connecticut during the fall campaign. These appearances took a great deal of energy and physical strength, but she felt a special obligation to undertake campaigning for the Carter-Mondale ticket.

It became apparent to those around her that the Governor continued to display uncommon efforts to carry on her public duties, though often in great discomfort. On the Friday before Thanksgiving 1980, the Governor left her State Capitol office for what turned out to be the last time. She was driven to her home at the shore in Old Lyme where she planned to rest before resuming her schedule the following week. "I hope you have kept my schedule light for next week because I need all my strength to prepare for the Holiday and the dinner which I intend to have at my home."[127] Reassured her schedule was purposely limited, she exited the Executive Office of the State Capitol where she had been a familiar figure for more than twenty-five years.

Ella Grasso was readmitted to the hospital that weekend. Further tests disclosed cancer had spread to her liver. It was a grim and tragic diagnosis with an "approximate 90-day-to-life sentence" for the 61-year-old governor.[128]

On December 5, 1980, Ella Grasso announced that she would resign the Office of Governor effective December 31, 1980. Her final communication to the people of Connecticut was succinct, sincere, and heartfelt:

> Regretfully, it is my belief that I do not have the stamina or the endurance
> for the rigors of the new legislative session and the myriad of problems
> that face the administration of a vital and vibrant state. All of my life has
> been one of dedication to working for people. I ask God's help that I may
> continue to do so. I thank again the many who have sent me prayers and
> good wishes. I love you. I love you all.[129]

Doctors offer many theories about how people contract cancer, however, no one can offer definitive answers in every individual case. There is evidence suggesting stress may play a role in the onset of cancer. Perhaps that was true in Ella Grasso's case. Her selfless commitment to serving others always centered on Connecticut and its citizens, first, and her own personal well-being, second.

The Governor did not seek a second opinion after her initial hospitalization. She often refused medication to ease the pain she endured, fearful she would not be able to make reasoned decisions and judgments as Governor. Her determination not to leave the state to seek medical advice or additional treatment can be attributed to her deep and abiding affection for the state, refusing to be seen leaving Connecticut lest something happen in her absence that she could not control.

Looking back, Ella Grasso's life should be seen not only in the shadows of her last days but in the full brilliance of the harvest, an admirable life and career of service to others. Her political achievement as the Mother of the Freedom of Information legislation, a revamped, stronger, more accountable Public Utilities Control Authority, an enthusiastic supporter of government reorganization and modernization, caring governor in emergency crises, and cautious overseer of Connecticut's fiscal policies are among her lasting legacies.

Ella Grasso was unquestionably a woman of achievement whose life exceeded the hopes and dreams of many young girls from tiny Windsor Locks, Connecticut. Perhaps one can envision what Ella's dreams were like when she shared them with her Mount Holyoke roommate many years ago. In a touching, affecting letter, Anne Wonders Passel remembered "lying in our beds in the dark talking about all the things we meant to do in the world . . . well, she did them all, but even before she became great and full of grand achievements I never forgot that strong, clear spoken, straight standing girl in her blouse and long wool skirt who seemed to set the air around her vibrating with purpose and life"[130]

Her larger legacy is quite remarkable. Being the first in any walk of life is never easy, and being the first woman presents an even greater burden. She handled it with grace, humor, pleasure, and worry. Her worry, expressed on many occasions, was that she must do well so others may have a chance. Always dutiful, hard working, and dedicated to her public duties and responsibilities Ella Grasso State Representative, Secretary of the State, Congresswoman, and the first woman Governor of the State of Connecticut, understood that if she achieved a measure of success in elective public office then her success would pave the way for other women. Many have taken the path to elective office and often point to Ella Grasso's path-breaking career as providing them with the inspiration and incentive to seek political success. Former Vice President Walter Mondale, a good friend and colleague from Ella's Congressional days, was asked, if Ella Grasso had lived would he have considered her as his running mate when he sought the Presidency in 1984? His reply was "yes."[131]

Ella Grasso was beloved by the citizens of Connecticut. That was demonstrated by the outpouring of grief that accompanied her death on February 5, 1981. Thousands of citizens paid their respects at the State Capitol where Ella lay in state.

There were many sides to her being—she was tough, aggressive, hard working, and impatient. She could also be difficult to work with, strong-willed, vindictive, and blunt, but also charming, kind, and thoughtful. She was admired both by friends and political foes for her brilliant intellect and political skills, dedication to Connecticut and its people, and her honesty and integrity as a public servant.

Ella Grasso was an uncommon woman—a pioneer—who went where no one else had been, to do what no one else had done. Ella Rosa Giovanna Tambussi Grasso lived up to the gentle advice offered by her beloved teacher Sister DeChantal. The nun told Ella and her classmates in the eighth grade that each of them "had a *very special gift* and they had a *special opportunity*. There was one thing they could do better than anybody, and they had an *obligation* to develop that quality, because that's why they had been born."[132]

EPILOGUE

Octizing, luminous splendor of the glimmering crystal chandeliers in
the White House East Room. There before an intimate assemblage of
honorees, their families, and friends, President Ronald Reagan posthumously presented the nation's highest civilian medal, the Medal of Freedom to the late Ella Grasso.[1]

Citing her "long, hard ascent to distinction as an elected public servant," the Republican President seemed to relish the opportunity to
honor Connecticut's most distinguished woman Governor. His hoarse
sounding voice echoed the thoughts of her family and friends as he
noted that Connecticut's late Governor had been "tireless in the pursuit
of duty and courageous in the face of illness," and "has earned the admiration of all Americans as a legislator and Governor and a woman of
outstanding character and achievement."[2]

Those gracious sentiments had special meaning for me as I sat among
the guests in the historic East Room of the White House. The warmth of
the President's words recalled similar tributes sent to the late Governor
and her family during her final illness and death. Thousands of cards, letters, telegrams, and notes were received, and they reflected people's deep
affection and fond memories of Connecticut's first woman Governor.

One letter from a former Mount Holyoke classmate was especially
poignant as she reminisced about her memories of Ella Tambussi Grasso.
"I remember walking with Ella through the snow on Mr. Skinner's place

next to the sycamores and on cold New England Saturday nights walking out to Ella's church." And "I remember our room in Rocky [Rockefeller Hall] and lying in our beds in the dark talking about all the things we meant to do in the world. Well she did them all," concluded Anne Wonders Passel, '40.[3]

The governor's notable achievements were also obvious measures of success to many American women. Several leading public figures wrote of their admiration for her. One note, from television personality Barbara Walters, stated that Ella Grasso "had shown such courage and dignity" and was "an inspiration to us all . . . an inspiration to me for a very long time."[4]

California Supreme Court Chief Justice Rose Bird wrote an affectionate letter. "What an inspiration you were and are to women," she penned. "In many ways you personify what all women seek — equality and acceptance as an individual of merit."[5]

Dr. Martin Luther King's widow, Coretta Scott King, sent a telegram to the Grasso family expressing her sentiment that Mrs. Grasso was an "exemplary woman who combined an illustrious public career with marriage and a family. She immortalized herself in state and national annals."[6]

Clare Booth Luce, herself a woman of inspiration to many, noted in her message that "Ella Grasso was an extraordinary women who will be much missed by her country."[7]

It was the ordinary citizens who wrote, who would have impressed Ella Grasso by the depth and sincere affection they expressed. One telegram from a Massachusetts mother of eight daughters noted, "I am grateful for her integrity as a Governor and her example as a woman."[8]

Even in the far reaches of distant Africa, Ella Grasso's prominence was noted. A touching letter from a Peace Corps doctor whose hometown was Meriden, Connecticut, recalled that, "every time there is mention made among my African friends that I'm from Connecticut, ministers, judges, counselors, and officials of all levels in Cameroon and in Gabon all want to know about my Lady Governor—how she got there, how she is doing, and how the people support her."⁹

As I left the White House that afternoon, exiting through the North Portico to Pennsylvania Avenue, the beautiful fall foliage of a sparkling October day brightened my way from the Executive Mansion. At that moment, I rejoiced that a grateful nation had not forgotten this remarkable child of twentieth-century pilgrims.

NOTES

Introduction *(pages xiii–xvii)*

1. Elizabeth Flynn Van Uum, Commissioner of St. Louis County, Missouri, in conversation with the author April 17, 1982.

2. Governor Ella Grasso, interview with author, Hartford, Connecticut, March 1979.

3. "Observe the Pagentry . . . A Personal Remembrance," *New Haven Register*, May 10, 1981.

4. Barbara Tuchman, "Biography as a Prism of History," in *Telling Lives*, ed. Marc Pachter, 144 (Philadelphia: University of Pennsylvania Press, 1981).

5. Richard Brookheiser, "Who Counted," *New York Times* Book Review, January 23, 2000.

6. Arnold Toynbee, "What the Book Is For," in *Chronicle of Higher Education*, November 3, 1975.

7. *Ella*, Connecticut Public Television documentary, February 1981.

1. Child of Twentieth-Century Pilgrims *(pages 1–16)*

1. Vera Brittain, *Testament of Youth: An Autobiographical Study of the Years 1900–1925* (New York: Penguin Books, 1994), 654.

2. Herbert F. Janick, Jr., "Senator Frank Brandegee and the Election of 1920," *The Historian*, 35, no. 3 (May 1973): 441.

3. United States Information Agency, miscellaneous information on Ella Grasso (hereafter cited as USIA information).

4. Jon E. Purmont, "Ella Grasso and Her Preparation for Leadership," *Connecticut History*, 36, no.1 (spring 1995): 68.

5. Mark Williams, "Immigrants to Connecticut by Decade," *Connecticut Case Studies: Newcomers to the Land of Steady Habits* (Connecticut Humanities Council, n.d.). (Hereafter, Williams, in *Land of Steady Habits*.)

6. *Christian Science Monitor*, July 1974 (n.d.).

7. *Ella*, Connecticut Public Television, documentary, February 9, 1981.

8. *Hartford Courant*, May 23, 1954, p. 3.

9. Bernard Asbell, "In Power and Down and Out," *New York Times Magazine*, July 27, 1975, p. 15.

10. Questionnaire (survey taken of all female members of Congress), *Family Circle* magazine (February 1972), Ella Grasso Papers, Mount Holyoke College Archives, Series 5, Box 14, p. 9.

11. Ibid., p. 2.

12. Ibid., p. 10.

13. Ella Grasso, "When I Think of Him It's in a Golden Glow," *Good Housekeeping* (July 1975): 154.

14. *Hartford Courant*, May 23, 1954.

15. *Hartford Times*, October 19, 1965.

16. Questionnaire, p. 6.

17. Ibid., pp. 3, 4.

18. James A. Grasso, interview with the author, West Hartford, Conn., January 18, 2000.

19. *Good Housekeeping*, July 1975, p. 154.

20. Ibid.

21. Questionnaire, p. 3.

22. Ibid., pp. 10, 11.

23. James A. Grasso interview 1/18/00.

24. Questionnaire, p. 6.

25. Ibid., p. 2.

26. Katherine Lebow, "Education and the Immigrant Experience: An Oral History of Working Women and Men of New Haven," *New Haven Colony Historical Society Journal*, 40 (fall 1993): 19.

27. *Fairpress* (Westport, Conn.), March 7, 1979.

28. Barbara Bailey, interview with the author, West Hartford, Connecticut, April 8, 2006.

29. Questionnaire, p. 2.

30. *Boston Sunday Herald-Advertiser*, November 10, 1974.

31. Questionnaire, pp. 1, 2.

32. Ella Grasso, letter to Professor Melvin Williams, June 18, 1974, Ella Grasso Papers, Mount Holyoke Archives, Series 5, Box 13.

33. Questionnaire, p. 4.

34. Ibid.

35. Questionnaire, p. 10.

36. Ibid., p. 2.

37. Thomas A. Grasso, interview with author, Old Lyme, Connecticut, February 15, 1997.

38. Letter from Rabbi Levine, May 18, 1978, Texarkana, Texas, includes a column "Ask" from *Family Circle Magazine*, Connecticut State Library (hereafter CSL), Ella Grasso Papers, Box 162.

39. Questionnaire, p. 7.

40. Ibid., p. 9.

41. Ella Grasso, letter to Professor Williams 6/18/74.

42. Questionnaire, p. 7.

43. Ibid., p. 11.

44. Ibid., p. 1.

45. *New Haven Register*, December 29, 1974.

46. *Ella*, Connecticut Public Television, documentary, February 9, 1981.

47. Blanche Wiesen Cook, *Eleanor Roosevelt, 1884–1933*, (New York: Penguin Books, 1992), 299.

48. Questionnaire, p. 3.

49. Questionnaire, p. 2.

50. Ibid., 9.

51. *Hartford Courant*, December 31, 1981.

52. Ibid.

53. USIA information.

54. "Six Women Who Could Be President," *Redbook* (November 1975): 134.

55. Questionnaire, p. 2.

56. Ibid., pp. 1, 2.

57. Herbert F. Janick, Jr., *A Diverse People: Connecticut 1914 to the Present*, (Chester, Connecticut: Pequot Press, 1975), 1.

58. Williams, "Immigrants to Connecticut by Decade."

59. Carroll S. Rosenberg, "The Female World of Love and Ritual," in *Women's America*, ed. Linda K. Kerber and Jane S. DeHart, 176 (New York: Oxford University Press, 1995).

60. Questionnaire, p. 1.

61. Susan Bysiewicz, *Ella: A Biography of Ella Grasso* (Old Saybrook, Conn.: Peregrine Press, 1984), 5.

62. Asbell, p. 15.

63. *New York Times*, May 4, 1975.

64. USIA information, p. 4.

65. *New York Times*, May 4, 1975.

66. Ibid.

67. Questionnaire, p. 3.

68. Harriet Fish, *The News Mill*, Carlsborg, Washington, March 31, 1976, CSL, Ella Grasso Papers, Box 162.

69. *Hartford Courant*, December 31, 1978, p. 5.

70. Thomas A. Grasso, interview, July 10, 1997.

71. Ibid.

72. Ibid.

2. *One of the Country's Most Wonderful Women (pages 17–29)*

1. John Mack Faragher and Florence Howe, eds., *Women and Higher Education in American History* (New York: W.W. Norton, 1988), 4.

2. Ibid., xiv.

3. Linda Malconian, interview with the author, Agawam, Mass., March 15, 1996.

4. Arthur C. Cole, *A Hundred Years of Mount Holyoke College: The Evolution of an Educational Ideal* (New Haven: Yale University Press, 1940), 332.

5. Ibid.

6. Lucille Ritvo, interview with the author, Woodbridge, Conn., July 17, 1995.

7. Barbara M. Solomon, *In The Company of Educated Women: A History of Women and Higher Education in America* (New Haven: Yale University Press, 1985), 144.

8. Ritvo interview 7/17/95.

9. Elaine Kendall, *Peculiar Institutions: An Informal History of the Seven Sisters Colleges* (New York: G.P. Putnam's Sons, 1976), 174.

10. Anna Macy Wells, *Miss Marks and Miss Wooley* (Boston: Houghton Mifflin, 1978), 211.

11. Ibid., 213.

12. Ibid., 40.

13. Ibid., 55.

14. Kendall, *Peculiar Institutions*, 174.

15. Ibid., 35.

16. Ella Grasso, Commencement speech, Mount Holyoke College, June 1, 1975, Mount Holyoke College Archives, Box 204: folder 5.

17. Walter Metzger, *Academic Freedom in the Age of the University* (New York, Columbia University Press, 1955), 134.

18. Carol S. Pearson, Donna Shavlik, and Judith G. Touchton, *Educating the Majority: Women Challenge Tradition in Higher Education* (New York: American Council on Education/MacMillan, 1989), 164.

19. Jon E. Purmont, "Ella Grasso and Her Preparation for Leadership," *Connecticut History*, 36, no. 1: 70.

20. *Springfield Union*, August 13, 1956.

21. Madeleine P. Grant, "In Memoriam — Amy Hewes," *Mount Holyoke Alumnae Quarterly*, 54, no. 1 (spring 1970): 32.

22. Judith Fisher Kidney, interview with the author, Simsbury, Connecticut, May 30, 1995.

23. Judith Fisher Kidney, in remarks for the presentation of the Award of Merit from the United States Department of Labor to Amy Hewes, March 16, 1962.

24. Ibid., 3.

25. Grant, "In Memoriam — Amy Hewes," p. 32.

26. Catherine Roraback, interview with author, Winsted, Connecticut, December 13, 1999.

27. *New York Times*, January 5, 1916.

28. Ibid.

29. Ibid.

30. Economics and Sociology Department Report to the President of Mount Holyoke, 1935–1936, Mount Holyoke College Archives.

31. Economic and Sociology Department Report to the President of Mount Holyoke, 1939–1940, 8, Mount Holyoke College Archives.

32. Ibid., 9.

33. Ibid., 10.

34. Amy Hewes, letter to Margaret Wiesmann, June 12, 1940, Economics and Sociology Department Records, Box 23, Mount Holyoke College Archives.

35. Ella Tambussi, "Workmen's Compensation in the United States," unpublished senior thesis, 1940, Mount Holyoke College, Ella Grasso Papers, 75.

36. Ibid.

37. Susan Ware, *Beyond Suffrage: Women in the New Deal* (Cambridge, Mass.: Harvard University Press, 1981), 186.

38. Richard Altenbaugh, *Education for Struggle: The Labor Colleges of the 1920s and 1930s* (Philadelphia: Temple University Press, 1990), 47.

39. Ibid.

40. Nancy Cott, *The Grounding of Modern Feminism* (New Haven: Yale University Press, 1987), 89.

41. "Open The Windows of Your Mind at the Hudson Shore Labor School," Hudson Shore Labor School Brochure, 1940, Franklin D. Roosevelt Library, Hyde Park, New York.

42. Judith Fisher Kidney interview 5/30/95.

43. Ibid.

44. Placement Papers for Ella Tambussi, Appointment Bureau Form in Ella Grasso Papers, Mount Holyoke College Archives.

45. Ella Tambussi, "Building a Background for a Practical Life" *Mount Holyoke College Alumnae Quarterly*, 24, no. 4 (February 1941): 165.

46. James A. Grasso remarks to author's Connecticut History class, May 9, 1995, Southern Connecticut State University, New Haven, Connecticut.

47. Blanche Wiesen Cook, *Eleanor Roosevelt, 1933–1938*, vol. 2 (New York: Viking, 1999), 357.

48. Ibid., 356.

49. Judith Fisher Kidney interview 5/30/95.

50. Catherine Roraback interview 12/13/99.

51. Doris Kearns Goodwin, *No Ordinary Time: Franklin and Eleanor Roosevelt: The Home Front in World War II* (New York: Simon & Schuster, 1994), 135.

52. Thomas A. Grasso, interview with author, Old Lyme, Conn., February 15, 1997.

53. Judith Fisher Kidney interview 5/30/95.

54. Thomas A. Grasso interview 2/15/97.

55. Judith Fisher Kidney interview 5/30/95.

56. Thomas A. Grasso interview 2/15/97.

3. *The Whole Day . . . a Rosy Glow (pages 30–50)*

1. James A. Grasso, interview with author, West Hartford, January 18, 2000.

2. Ibid.

3. Ibid.

4. Ibid.

5. Anne Wonders Passel, letter to Thomas A. Grasso, February 9, 1981 (copy in author's possession).

6. Juliet Fisher Kidney, interview with the author, Simsbury, Connecticut, May 30, 1995.

7. *Llamarada*, Class of 1940 yearbook, Mount Holyoke College Archives.

8. Ibid.

9. Seymour M. Lipset, *Rebellion in the University* (Boston: Little, Brown and Company, 1971), 179.

10. Ibid., 179.

11. Ibid., 180.

12. Ella Grasso, Commencement Speech, Mount Holyoke College, June 1, 1975, Ella Grasso Papers, Mount Holyoke College Archives, Box 204: Folder 5.

13. *Mount Holyoke News* (various issues, 1936–1940).

14. *Mount Holyoke News* (April 29, 1938): 1.

15. Ibid.

16. Lipset, *Rebellion in the University*, 179.

17. Grasso, Commencement Speech 6/1/75.

18. Caroline Ware, *Holding Their Own: American Women in the 1930s* (New York: Twayne Publishers, 1982), 60.

19. *Mount Holyoke News*, October 20, 1939.

20. Professor John Lobb, miscellaneous material in Ella Grasso Papers, Mount Holyoke College Archives.

21. Ibid.

22. *Mount Holyoke College Alumnae Quarterly*, 24 no. 4 (February 1941).

23. Ibid.

24. Ibid.

25. Catherine Roraback interview 12/13/99.

26. *Mount Holyoke College Alumnae Quarterly*, Feb. 1941.

27. Ibid.

28. Grasso, Commencement Speech 1975.

29. Ibid.

30. *Mount Holyoke News* (various issues, 1936–1940), Mount Holyoke College Archives.

31. Economics and Sociology Department Annual Report to the President, 1938–39, Mount Holyoke College Archives, pp. 11, 12.

32. Economics and Sociology Department Annual Report to President, 1939–1940, Mount Holyoke College Archives, pp. 7, 8.

33. Centennial Bulletin, Economics and Sociology Department, May 1937, Mount Holyoke College Archives, p. 9.

34. Economics and Sociology Department Annual Report to the President, 1938–1939, p. 7.

35. Economics and Sociology Department Annual Report to the President, 1939–1940, p. 7.

36. Grasso, Commencement Speech 1975.

37. *Mount Holyoke News*, June 10, 1940, p. 2.

38. Ibid.

39. Grasso, Commencement Speech 1975.

40. Elizabeth Tidball, "Women's Colleges: Exceptional Conditions, Not Exceptional Talent, Produce High Achievers," in *Educating the Majority*, ed. Carol S. Pearson, Donna Shavlik, Judith G. Tonchton, and the American Council on Education, p. 158 (New York: Macmillan, 1989).

41. Eleanor Tidball, *Mount Holyoke Alumnae Quarterly*, 54 (fall 1970): 176.

42. Blanche Weisen Cook, *Eleanor Roosevelt, 1933–1938*, vol. 2 (New York: Viking, 1999), 299.

43. Questionnaire (survey taken of all female members of Congress), *Family Circle* magazine (February 1972), Ella Grasso Papers, Mount Holyoke College Archives, Series 5, Box 14, p.1.

44. Ella Grasso, letter to Cara Cook, March 10, 1971, Mount Holyoke College Archives, Ella Grasso Papers, Series 5, Box 13.

45. Questionnaire, p. 7.

46. John Lobb, Ella Grasso papers.

47. Amy Hewes, letter of recommendation, Ella Grasso Papers, Mount Holyoke College Archives.

48. Ella Tambussi, "The Knights of Labor," (unpublished Master Thesis, Mount Holyoke College), Ella Grasso Papers, 1.

49. *New York Times*, May 4, 1975.

50. *West Hartford News*, October 18, 1974.

51. Marilyn M. Kushick, letter to Ella Grasso, Ella Grasso Papers, Connecticut State Library (hereafter CSL), Box 676. (Ms. Kushick wrote to Ella Grasso, indicating Mount Holyoke would use Ella's quote in a development brochure and sought her approval to print it.)

52. Grasso, Commencement Speech 1975.

53. *Hartford Times*, August 31, 1942.

54. Questionnaire, p. 12.

55. Ella Grasso, speech to Connecticut AFL-CIO, September 8, 1974, Ella Grasso Papers, CSL Box 783.

56. Questionnaire, p. 13.

57. Herbert F. Janick, Jr., *A Diverse People: Connecticut 1914 to the Present*, (Chester, Connecticut: Pequot Press), 14.

58. Ibid., 38.

59. Ibid., 40.

60. Carol Wallace, "Ella Grasso: A Governor with the Human Touch," *Dynamic Years* (November-December 1980).

61. *Hartford Courant*, March 21, 1979.

62. *Hartford Courant*, December 31, 1978.

63. *Ella* (privately printed by the Ella Grasso Foundation, 1981), 4.

64. *Hartford Courant*, December 31, 1978.

65. Barbara M. Solomon, *In The Company of Educated Women: A History of Women and Higher Education in America* (New Haven: Yale University Press, 1986), 167.

66. *Fairpress* (Westport, Conn.), December 10, 1980.

67. *Fairpress*, March 7, 1979.

68. *Ella*, 1981, 4.

69. Wilbur Cross, speech, September 3, 1932, Wilbur Cross Papers, Yale University.

70. Ibid.

71. Janick, *A Diverse People*, 52.

72. Ibid.

73. Wilbur Cross, speech, April 1932, Wilbur Cross Papers, Yale University Archives. 12.

74. Ibid., 13.

75. Ibid., 17.

76. Ibid.

77. *Ella*, 1981, 4.

78. "My Name is Ella," radio broadcast, WPOP, February 9, 1981.

79. Susan Ware, "American Women in the 1950s: Nonpartisan Politics and Women's Politicization," in *Women, Politics and Change*, ed. Louise Tilly and Patricia Gurtin, 297 (New York: Russell Sage Foundation, 1990).

80. Carole Nichols, *Votes and More for Women's Suffrage and After in Connecticut* (New York: Haworth Press, 1983), 3.

81. Ibid., 5.

82. Ibid., 32.

83. *Connecticut Register and Manual* 1922.

84. Nichols, *Votes and More for Women's Suffrage*, 50.

85. Ibid., 4.

86. Ruth Barnes Moynihan, "Coming of Age: Four Centuries of Connecticut Women and Their Choices," (originally published in *The Connecticut Historical Society Bulletin*, 53, no. 1: 1990) reprinted by Aetna Life and Casualty (1991): 35.

87. Speech to League of Women Voters, "Day at the Capitol," Ella Grasso Papers, CSL, Box 755, March 29, 1978.

88. Moynihan, "Coming of Age," 35.

89. Susan Hartman, *From Margin to Mainstream: American Women and Politics Since 1960* (Philadelphia: Temple University Press, 1989), 17.

90. *Washington Star-News*, June 7, 1974.

91. Nancy Lewinsohn, interview with the author, Washington, D.C., January 15, 1995.

92. Jeane J. Kirkpatrick, *Political Woman* (New York: Basic Books, 1974), 43.

93. Hartman, *From Margin to Mainstream*, 17.

94. Ibid.

95. *Christian Science Monitor*, July 1974 (n.d.).

96. *Fairpress*, December 10, 1980.

4. Involved in the Making of a Government (pages 51–68)

1. *Register-Star* (Hudson, New York), April 27, 1976, c-10.

2. Ella Grasso, letter to the *Hartford Courant*, July 21, 1977.

3. Bernard Asbell, "In Power and Down and Out," *New York Times Magazine* (July 27, 1975): 16.

4. Susan Tolchin and Martin Tolchin, *Clout: Woman Power and Politics* (New York: Coward, McCann and Geoghegan, 1974), 99.

5. *Hartford Courant*, October 20, 1974.

6. Ella Grasso, letter to Jack Joy, December 14, 1976, Ella Grasso Papers Connecticut State Library (hereafter CSL), Box 162.

7. James A. Grasso, interview with author, West Hartford, Conn., April 30, 2000.

8. Questionnaire (survey taken of all female members of Congress), *Family Circle* magazine (February 1972), 9.

9. USIA information, 6.

10. Susane Grasso, interview with author, Branford, Conn., July 25, 2000.

11. James A. Grasso interview 4/30/00.

12. *Hartford Courant*, February 20, 1955.

13. Questionnaire, 13.

14. *Hartford Courant*, February 20, 1955.

15. Chester Bowles, *Promises to Keep—My Years in Public Life* (New York: Harper & Row, 1971), 241.

16. Asbell, "In Power and Down and Out," *New York Times Magazine* (July 27, 1975): 16.

17. Bowles, *Promises*, 190–191.

18. Ibid., 198.

19. Albert E. Van Dusen, *Connecticut: A Fully Illustrated History of the State from the Seventeenth Century to Present* (New York: Random House, 1961), 384.

20. Bowles, *Promises*, 202.

21. Van Dusen, *Connecticut*, 384.

22. *Hartford Courant*, February 20, 1955.

23. Thomas A. Grasso, interview with author, Old Lyme, Conn., January 27, 1997.

24. *Hartford Courant*, February 20, 1955.

25. *Detroit News*, January 28, 1975.

26. Ella Grasso, speech to the Intercollegiate Student Legislature, State Capitol House Chamber, Hartford, Conn., March 7, 1975.

27. Asbell, *New York Times Magazine*, 7/27/75, 16.

28. *Hartford Courant*, December 27, 1953.

29. *Northern Connecticut News*, April 17, 1958, 1.

30. Asbell, *New York Times Magazine*, 7/27/75, 16.

31. Thomas A. Grasso interview 7/10/97.

32. David Broder, interview with author, Washington, D.C., November 15, 1999.

33. Thomas A. Grasso interview 7/10/97.

34. Barbara Bailey, interview with the author, West Hartford, Conn., April 8, 2000.

35. *New York Times*, February 6, 1981, p. 1.

36. Abraham Ribicoff Papers, Columbia University Archives, vol. 2, p. 362.

37. Joseph I. Lieberman, *The Power Broker: A Biography of John M. Baily, Modern Political Boss* (Boston: Houghton Mifflin, 1966), 246.

38. Mary Louise Dunn, interview with author, Hartford, February 8, 1981.

39. Joseph I. Lieberman, *The Legacy: Connecticut Politics 1930–1980* (Hartford: Spoonwood Press, 1981), 197.

40. James A. Grasso, interview with the author, West Hartford, May 19, 1995.

41. Peggy Lamson, *Few Are Chosen* (Boston: Houghton Mifflin, 1968), 217.

42. Lieberman, *Power Broker*, 170.

43. *Hartford Courant*, June 6, 1954.

44. Ibid.

45. Ibid.

46. Asbell, *New York Times Magazine*, 7/27/75, 16.

47. Thomas A. Grasso, interview with author, Old Lyme, Conn., January 27, 1997.

48. Ribicoff Papers, vol. 2, p. 362.

49. *Hartford Courant*, May 6, 1979, p. 39.

50. Ibid.

51. *Hartford Courant*, February 6, 1981.

52. Joan Hoff Wilson and Marjorie Lightman, *Without Precedent* (Bloomington: Indiana University Press, 1984), 36.

53. Blanche Wiesen Cook, *Eleanor Roosevelt: The Defining Years, 1933–1938* (New York: Viking Penguin, 1999), 66.

54. Asbell, *New York Times Magazine*, 7/27/75, 16.

55. Ibid.

56. Van Dusen, *Connecticut*, 389.

57. Thomas A. DeLong, *John Davis Lodge: A Life in Three Acts* (Fairfield, Conn.: Sacred Heart University Press, 1999), 199.

58. Van Dusen, *Connecticut*, 390.

59. *Hartford Courant*, June 26, 1954.

60. Ibid.

61. Ibid.

62. Ibid.

63. *Boston Globe*, November 11, 1974.

64. Lieberman, *Power Broker*, 170.

65. *Hartford Advocate*, March 4, 1981.

66. *Hartford Courant*, November 3, 1954.

67. *Hartford Courant*, November 6, 1974.

68. Theodore White, *The Making of the President 1960* (New York: Atheneum, 1961), 12.

69. Ribicoff Papers, vol. 2, p. 364.

70. Ibid.

71. Lieberman, *Power Broker*, 230.

72. Ribicoff Papers, vol. 2, p. 363.

73. Ibid.

74. Ibid.

75. *Connecticut Register and Manual*, 1959.

76. Lieberman, *The Legacy*, ix.

77. *Hartford Courant*, November 6, 1974.

78. *Hartford Courant*, February 20, 1955.

79. Duane Lockard, *New England State Politics* (Princeton: Princeton University Press, 1959), 263.

80. Ibid.

81. Asbell, *New York Times Magazine*, 7/27/75, 18.

82. *Transcript-Telegram* (Holyoke, Mass.), August 15, 1956.

83. Lieberman, *Legacy*, 214.

84. Lamson, *Few Are Chosen*, 218.

85. Asbell, *New York Times Magazine*, 7/27/75, 18.

86. Ibid.

87. Lamson, *Few Are Chosen*, 219.

88. Ibid.

89. Ella Grasso, "Ours Is the Obligation," *Mount Holyoke Alumnae Quarterly*, XL, no. 2 (summer 1956): 49.

90. Ibid.

91. Lamson, *Few Are Chosen*, 219.

92. Ella Grasso, speech to Connecticut Association of Conservation Officers, June 15, 1974, Ella Grasso Papers, CSL Series Box 733.

93. Asbell, *New York Times Magazine*, 7/27/75, 16.

5. *Working in the Vineyards (pages 69–92)*

1. David Broder, interview with the author, Washington, D.C., November 5, 1999.

Notes

2. Asbell, "In Power and Down and Out," *New York Times Magazine* (July 27, 1975): 18.

3. *Bridgeport Post*, April 19, 1977.

4. *Hartford Courant*, February 19, 1962.

5. Joseph I. Lieberman, *The Power Broker: A Biography of John M. Bailey, Modern Political Boss* (Boston: Houghton Mifflin, 1966), 243.

6. Peggy Lamson, *Few Are Chosen*, (Boston: Houghton Mifflin, 1968), 220–221.

7. Joseph I. Lieberman, *The Legacy: Connecticut Politics 1930–1980* (Hartford: Spoonwood Press, 1981), 81.

8. Ibid., 81.

9. Duane Lockard, *New England State Politics* (Princeton: Princeton University Press, 1959), 28.

10. Susan Bysiewicz, *Ella: A Biography of Ella Grasso* (Old Saybrook, Conn.: Peregrine Press, 1984), 41.

11. Amalia Toro, interview with the author, Hartford, Conn., January 29, 2001.

12. *Hartford Courant*, August 30, 1961.

13. Toro interview 1/29/01.

14. Ibid.

15. William A. O'Neill, interview with the author, East Hampton, September 29, 1999.

16. Nancy Lewinsohn, interview with the author, Washington, D.C., August 16, 2001.

17. *Bridgeport Post*, July 21, 1974.

18. *Hartford Courant*, September 28, 1959.

19. *Hartford Courant*, October 8, 1959.

20. *Hartford Courant*, February 5, 1964.

21. *Hartford Courant*, October 3, 1959.

22. Joseph Treaster, "Ella Grasso of Connecticut: Running and Winning," *Ms.* magazine, 3, no. 4 (October 1974): 81.

23. Robert Killian, interview with the author, Hartford, Conn., August 9, 2001.

24. *Hartford Courant*, December 23, 1959.

25. *Hartford Courant*, June 18, 1974.

26. *New London Day*, August 19, 1974.

27. *Hartford Courant*, March 3, 1962.

28. Toro interview 1/29/01.

29. Bysiewicz, *Ella*, 40.

30. *Hartford Courant*, July 26, 1959.

31. Ibid.

32. Lamson, *Few Are Chosen*, 221.

33. Lieberman, *Legacy*, 88.

34. *New London Day*, August 19, 1974.

35. Nancy Lewinsohn, interview with the author, Washington, D.C., June 10, 2001.

36. Bysiewicz, *Ella*, 44.

37. *Fairpress*, December 10, 1980, A2.

38. Lieberman, *Legacy*, 89.

39. Lieberman, *The Power Broker: A Biography of John M. Bailey Modern, Political Boss* (Boston: Houghton Mifflin, 1966), 265.

40. Lieberman, *Legacy*, 91.

41. Ibid.,100.

42. Ibid., 121–22.

43. *Hartford Courant*, June 18, 1974.

44. Ella Grasso, speech to Connecticut Daily Newspaper Association, October 19, 1974, Ella Grasso Papers, CSL Box 733.

45. *Hartford Courant*, May 5, 1966.

46. Press release, June 24, 1974, Ella Grasso Papers, CSL Box 732.

47. *Hartford Courant*, May 8, 1966.

48. Ibid.

49. Toro interview 1/29/01.

50. Press release, May 6, 1974, Ella Grasso Papers, CSL Box 732.

51. Lieberman, *Power Broker*, 332.

52. *Connecticut Constitutional Convention 1965*, video documentary, WHNB-TV (New Britain, Conn.), Film and Video Collection, CSL.

53. Constitutional Convention Planning Committee, minutes, June 30, 1965, 46.

54. Chad McCollam, interview with the author, Bethel, Conn., June 6, 2000.

55. Connecticut Constitutional Convention Minutes, Session, Book 2, vol. 3.

56. McCollam interview 6/6/00.

57. *Connecticut Register and Manual*, 1966.

58. Larrye DeBear, interview with the author, Old Saybrook, October 16, 1999.

59. Ibid.

60. McCollam interview 6/6/00.

61. Remarks by Meade Alcorn, Constitutional Convention Minutes, October 28, 1965.

62. *New Haven Register*, September 4, 1965.

63. McCollam interview 6/6/00.

64. Alcorn remarks 10/28/65.

65. James A. Grasso, interview with the author, West Hartford, Conn., January 18, 2000.

66. *Hartford Courant*, March 1, 1959.

67. Lieberman, *Legacy*, 53.

68. *Hartford Courant*, September 27, 1964.

69. Ibid.

70. Theodore H. White, *The Making of the President 1964* (New York: Atheneum, 1965), 281.

71. Ibid.

72. *Hartford Courant*, August 22, 1964.

73. Lewis House, Ira Leonard, and Jon E. Purmont, *A Concise History of the United States with Documents* (New Haven: TLI Press, 1994), 77.

74. *Hartford Courant*, August 28, 1968.

75. *Hartford Courant*, August 30, 1968.

76. Theodore H. White, *The Making of the President 1968* (New York: Atheneum, 1969), 323.

77. *Hartford Courant*, February 6, 1981.

78. Ibid.

79. White, *Making of the President 1968*, 343.

80. Lewinsohn interview 8/17/00.

81. Ribicoff Papers, vol. 2.

82. *Connecticut Register and Manual*, 1969.

6. I Can Be a Gadfly Here (pages 93–129)

1. Linda Malconian, interview with the author, Agawam, Mass., March 15, 1996.

2. John Farrell, *Tip O'Neill and the Democratic Century* (New York: Little, Brown Company, 2001), 140.

3. Rudolph Englebarts, *Women in the United States Congress 1917–1972* (Littleton, Colorado: Libraries Unlimited, 1974), 137–139.

4. Women in the Congress—Fact Sheet, Center for American Women and Politics, Eagleton Institute of Politics, Rutgers University, New Brunswick, New Jersey, 1.

5. Linda Witt, Karen M. Paget, and Glenna Matthews, *Running As a Woman: Gender and Power in American Politics* (Simon & Schuster: New York, 1995), xi.

6. Ibid., 252.

7. Hope Chamberlin, *A Minority of Members* (New York: Henry Holt, 1973), 188–189.

8. Englebarts, *Women in the United States Congress*, 134.

9. Malconian interview 3/15/96.

10. James A. Grasso, interview with the author, West Hartford, Conn., April 30, 2000.

11. *West Hartford News*, October 18, 1974, p. 8.

12. Thomas A. Grasso, interview with the author, Old Lyme, February 2, 1997.

13. *Hartford Courant*, April 24, 1964.

14. Peggy Lamson, *Few Are Chosen* (Boston: Houghton Mifflin, 1968), 226.

15. *West Hartford News*, October 18, 1974, p. 8.

16. Chad McCollam, interview with the author, Bethel, Conn., June 6, 2000.

17. Jay Jackson, interview with the author, Hartford, Conn., June 9, 2000.

18. Joseph I. Lieberman, *The Legacy: Connecticut Politics 1930–1980* (Hartford: Spoonwood Press, 1981), 164.

19. William A. O'Neill, interview with the author, East Hampton, Conn., September 29, 1999.

20. Aaron Ment, interview with the author, Hartford, Conn., December 6, 1999.

21. *New Britain Herald*, February 16, 1970.

22. Lieberman, *Legacy*, 172.

23. James A. Grasso, interview with the author, New Haven, Conn., May 9, 1995.

24. *Hartford Courant*, March 9, 1970.

25. Ibid.

26. *Hartford Courant*, March 11, 1970.

27. *New Britain Herald*, March 17, 1970.

28. *New Britain Herald*, March 18, 1970, editorial.

29. *New Britain Herald*, March 17, 1970.

30. *Hartford Courant*, June 21, 1970.

31. James A. Grasso interview 5/9/95.

32. *Hartford Courant*, November 20, 1972.

33. Herman Wolf, interview with the author, Shelton, Conn., December 7, 1999.

34. Zena Temkin, interview with the author, Torrington, Conn., February 20, 2000.

35. *Hartford Courant*, November 4, 1970.

36. *Enfield Press* (Enfield, Conn.), May 12, 1981.

37. *Hartford Courant*, November 4, 1970.

38. Biesiewicz, 54.

39. Englebarts, *Women in the United States Congress*, 115.

40. "The Psychology of Unemployment," *First Tuesday*, NBC News television show, September 7, 1971..

41. Ibid.

42. *Hartford Courant*, January 21, 1971.

43. Ella Grasso, letter to Congressman James A. Burke, November 30, 1970, Ella Grasso Papers, CSL.

44. Ibid.

45. Ella Grasso, letter to Congressman Olin Teague, December 3, 1970, Ella Grasso Papers, CSL.

46. *Hartford Courant*, January 31, 1971.

47. *Hartford Courant*, January 21, 1971.

48. Ibid.

49. Joseph B. Treaster, "Ella Grasso of Connecticut: Running and Winning," *Ms.* magazine, 3, no. 4 (October 1974): 81.

50. *Hartford Courant*, January 21, 1971.

51. Ibid.

52. Treaster *Ms.* magazine, 122.

53. *Hartford Courant*, January 21, 1971.

54. Malconian interview 3/15/96.

55. Ibid.

56. Ibid.

57. *Washington Star-News*, June 7, 1974.

58. Malconian interview 3/15/96.

59. *Torrington Register*, July 10, 1973.

60. Ella Grasso, letter to Congressman Michael Harrington, June 24, 1971, Ella Grasso Papers, Mount Holyoke College Archives, Series III, Box 37.

61. Susan Tolchin and Martin Tolchin, *Clout: Woman Power and Politics* (New York: Coward, McCann and Geoghegan, 1974), 90.

62. Ibid.

63. Fair Packaging and Labeling Act, Ella Grasso Papers, Mount Holyoke College Archives, Series 2, Box 11.

64. Ella Grasso, letter to Joseph Gontarz, March 15, 1972, Ella Grasso Papers, Mount Holyoke College Archives, Series 2, Box 11.

65. Virginia Knauer, letter to Ella Grasso, October 2, 1974, Ella Grasso Papers, Mount Holyoke College Archives, Series 4, Box 2.

66. *Hartford Courant*, April 4, 1971.

67. Esther Peterson, letter to Ella Grasso (n.d.), Ella Grasso Papers, Mount Holyoke College Archives, Series 5, Box 13.

68. Summary of the Congressional Record of United States Representative Ella Grasso, January 1971–mid-July 1974, Ella Grasso for Governor Committee, p. 3.

69. *Hartford Courant*, January 16, 1971.

70. *Hartford Courant*, March 4, 1971.

71. Summary of the Congressional Record, Grasso, p. 3.

72. Ibid.

73. *Bridgeport Post*, September 8, 1974.

74. "The Psychology of Unemployment," *First Tuesday*, NBC News television show, September 7, 1971.

75. Ibid.

76. Ibid.

77. Ibid.

78. *Hartford Courant*, November 4, 1971.

79. *Hartford Courant*, April 25, 1971.

80. Nancy Lewinsohn, interview with the author, Washington, D. C., August 1, 2004.

81. Ibid.

82. Kathleen Bowman, *New Women in Politics* (Mankato, Minnesota: Creative Education Society, 1976), 44.

83. Lewinsohn interview 8/1/04.

84. *Springfield Republican*, August 18, 1974.

85. Letter from Anne C. Edmonds, January 17, 1975, Ella Grasso Papers, Box 1, Mount Holyoke College Archives.

86. Jane S. DeHart, "The New Feminism and the Dynamics of Social Change," in *Women's America*, ed. Linda Kerber and Jane S. DeHart, 545 (New York: Oxford University Press, 2000).

87. Ibid.

88. Ibid.

89. Ella Grasso, letter to Mary Knihnicky, December 5, 1970, Ella Grasso Papers, Mount Holyoke College Archives, Series I, Box 12.

90. Joseph Treaster, *Ms.* magazine, 82.

91. Janann Sherman, *No Place for a Woman* (New Brunswick, New Jersey: Rutgers University Press, 1999), 56.

92. Jay Jackson, interview with the author, Hartford, Conn., June 9, 2000.

93. Sherman, *No Place for a Woman*, 56.

94. Congressional Record, October 12, 1971, Ella Grasso Papers, Mount Holyoke College Archives, Series IV, Box 31.

95. Kathleen C. Berkeley, *The Women's Liberation Movement in America* (Westport, Connecticut: Greenwood Press, 1999), 76.

96. Tolchin and Tolchin, *Clout*, 115.

97. Ibid.

98. Nancy Lewinsohn, interview with the author, Washington, D. C., January 15, 1995.

99. *New Britain Herald*, June 2, 1970.

100. *Hartford Courant*, February 14, 1973.

101. Congressional Record, Grasso, 1971–1974, p. 8.

102. Ibid.

103. *Hartford Courant*, October 3, 1971.

104. Congressional Record, Grasso, 1971–1974, p. 12.

105. John Farrell, *Tip O'Neill and the Democratic Century*, 316.

106. Ibid.

107. Ibid.

108. Ibid., 317.

109. Ella Grasso, letter to Representative Carl Albert, December 31, 1972, Ella Grasso Papers, Mount Holyoke College Archives, Series 5, Box 16.

110. *New Britain Herald*, June 2, 1970.

111. Lewinsohn interview 8/1/04.

112. *Hartford Courant*, October 23, 1972.

113. Lewinsohn interview 8/1/04.

114. *Hartford Courant*, October 23, 1972.

115. Wilma Scott Heide, letter to Ella Grasso, January 3, 1972, Ella Grasso Papers, Mount Holyoke College Archives, Series 5, Box 15.

116. Malcolm Baldrige, letter to Ella Grasso, November 8, 1972, Ella Grasso Papers, Mount Holyoke College Archives, Series 5 Box 15.

117. Susan Bysiwicz, *Ella: A Biography of Ella Grasso* (Old Saybrook, Conn.: Peregrine Press, 1984), 62.

118. Ella Grasso, letter to Joseph Wilson, May 15, 1974, Ella Grasso Papers, Mount Holyoke College Archives.

119. *Hartford Courant*, October 22, 1973.

120. Ibid.

121. Press release, Ella Grasso for Governor, letterhead (n.d.).

122. *Hartford Courant*, August 8, 1974.

123. *Fairpress* December 10, 1980.

124. Lieberman, *Legacy*, 191.

125. Lewinsohn, interview with the author, Washington, D.C., August 17, 2000.

126. Ibid.

127. Ibid.

128. Thomas A. Grasso, interview with the author, Old Lyme, Conn., July 10, 1997.

129. *Detroit News*, January 26, 1975.

130. Treaster, *Ms.* magazine, 122.

131. Lewinsohn interview 8/17/00.

132. Susane Grasso, interview with the author, Branford, Conn., July 25, 2000.

7. I Believe Working for People Is the Noblest Profession (pages 130–157)

1. *Washington Post*, July 7, 1974.

2. Amalia Toro, interview with the author, Hartford, Conn., January 29, 2001.

3. Susanne Grasso, interview with the author, Branford, Conn., July 25, 2000.

4. Ella Grasso, Announcement Speech, January 19, 1974.

5. Ibid.

6. Ibid.

7. *Hartford Times*, November 11, 1973.

8. William A. O'Neill, interview with the author, East Hampton, September 29, 1999.

9. Ibid.

10. *New Haven Register*, July 7, 1974.

11. Ibid.

12. *Hartford Courant*, September 3, 1978.

13. William A. O'Neill interview 9/29/99.

14. Herman Wolf, interview with the author, Shelton, Conn., December 7, 1999.

15. Ibid.

16. Nancy Lewinsohn, interview with the author, Washington, D.C., August 4, 2004.

17. *Connecticut Register and Manual*, 1971.

18. Lieberman, *Legacy*, 190.

19. *Hartford Courant*, March 23, 1974.

20. Lieberman, *Legacy*, 191.

21. *Hartford Courant*, July 3, 1973.

22. Jay Jackson, interview with the author, Hartford, Conn., June 9, 2000.

23. Thomas A. Grasso, interview with the author, Old Lyme, Conn., February 15, 1997.

24. Jay Jackson interview 6/9/00.

25. *Hartford Courant*, February 13, 1974.

26. *Washington Post*, July 7, 1974.

27. Grasso, campaign press release, March 23, 1974, CSL, Box 754.

28. Joseph I. Lieberman, *Legacy*, 193.

29. William A. O'Neill interview 9/29/99.

30. Joseph I. Lieberman, *Legacy*, 190.

31. *Washington Post*, July 7, 1974.

32. William A. O'Neill interview 9/29/99.

33. *Hartford Times*, May 6, 1974.

34. *Bridgeport Post*, April 29, 1974.

35. *Hartford Times*, September 5, 1974.

36. Joseph I. Lieberman, *Legacy*, 194.

37. *New Haven Register*, May 24, 1974.

38. *Hartford Courant*, July 4, 1974.

39. Robert Killian, interview with the author, Hartford, Conn., August 9, 2001.

40. Bob Conrad, interview with the author, Hartford, Conn., June 28, 2000.

41. Larrye DeBear, interview with the author, Old Saybrook, Conn., October 16, 1999.

42. *Hartford Courant*, July 4, 1974.

43. Ibid.

44. *Hartford Courant*, January 9, 1975.

45. *New York Times*, July 22, 1974, Ella Grasso Papers, CSL Box 734.

46. Ella Grasso, Acceptance Speech, July 20, 1974.

47. Ibid., 2.

48. Newsletter, Zullo for Governor Committee, *Connecticut Democrat*, 1, no. 6 (May 1974): 4.

49. Joseph Treaster, "Ella Grasso of Connecticut: Running and Winning," *Ms.* magazine (October 1974): 81.

50. *Washington Post*, July 7, 1974.

51. Treaster, *Ms.* magazine, Oct. 1974, 81.

52. *Washington Post*, October 7, 1974.

53. Robert Steele Jr., Acceptance Speech, July 27, 1974, 3, 4.

54. Joseph I. Lieberman, *The Legacy*, 196.

55. Nancy Lewinsohn, interview with the author, Washington, D.C., January 15, 1995.

56. Grasso Campaign, press release, May 12, 1974, CSL Box 754.

57. Grasso Campaign, press release, September 20, 1974, CSL Box 754.

58. Edward Stockton, interview with the author, Hartford, Conn., October 7, 2005.

59. Grasso Campaign, press release, September 20, 1974, CSL Box 792.

60. Grasso Campaign, press release, September 25, 1974, Grasso Papers, CSL Box 754.

61. Bysiewicz, *Ella*, 76.

62. Steele, acceptance speech, July 27, 1974, 3.

63. Joseph Treaster, *Ms.* magazine, 82.

64. Grasso Campaign, press release, August 12, 1974, Grasso Papers, CSL Box 754.

65. *Bridgeport Post*, September 8, 1974.

66. Ibid.

67. Ella Grasso, speech, September 5, 1974, Grasso Papers, CSL Box 733.

68. Ella Grasso, speech, September 13, 1974, Grasso Papers, CSL Box 733.

69. *Hartford Courant*, September 11, 1974, Grasso Papers, CSL Box 734.

70. *Bridgeport Post*, September 8, 1974.

71. Grasso Campaign, press release, October 1, 1974, Grasso Papers, CSL Box 792.

72. Grasso Campaign, press release, October 2, 1974, Ella Grasso Papers, CSL Box 792.

73. *Washington Post*, October 7, 1974.

74. Press release, October 3, 1974, Ella Grasso Papers, CSL Box 733.

75. Ibid.

76. Grasso Campaign, press release, October 7, 1974, Ella Grasso Papers, CSL Box 733.

77. Grasso Campaign, press release, October 16, 1974, Ella Grasso Papers, CSL Box 733.

78. Grasso Campaign, press release, October 18, 1974, Ella Grasso Papers, CSL Box 733.

79. *Washington Post*, October 7, 1974.

80. Ibid.

81. Proposed Bill, Legislative Commissioners Office, Ella Grasso Papers, CSL Box 734.

82. United States Information Agency, information sheet, 2, 3.

83. Grasso Campaign, press release, October 2, 1974, Ella Grasso Papers, CSL Box 732.

84. Ibid.

85. Grasso Campaign, press release, July 29, 1974, Ella Grasso Papers, CSL Box 30.

86. Nancy Lewinsohn, interview with the author, Washington, D.C., August 17, 2000.

87. *West Hartford News*, October 18, 1974.

88. Betty Hudson, interview with the author Simsbury, Conn., August 24, 2000.

89. *Washington Post*, October 7, 1974.

90. Ibid.

91. Ibid.

92. Grasso Campaign, press release, September 30, 1974, Ella Grasso Papers, CSL Box 792.

93. *Washington Post*, October 7, 1974.

94. Ibid.

95. *New Britain Herald*, September 16, 1974, Ella Grasso Papers, CSL Box 734.

96. *Hartford Times*, September 5, 1974, Ella Grasso Papers, CSL Box 734.

97. Michael Barone, August 25, 2000, www.mclaughlin.com.

98. *Bridgeport Post*, August 11, 1974, Ella Grasso Papers, CSL Box 734.

99. Lewinsohn interview 8/17/00.

100. *Washington Post*, October 7, 1974.

101. *Bridgeport Post*, August 11, 1974.

102. *Waterbury Republican*, July 2, 1974, Ella Grasso Papers, CSL Box 279.

103. *Newsweek*, November 4, 1974, 21.

104. David Broder, interview with the author, Washington, D.C., November 5, 1999.

105. *Washington Post*, July 7, 1974.

106. *Connecticut Register and Manual*, 1975.

107. *Hartford Courant*, January 1, 1976.

108. *Connecticut Register and Manual*, 2000.

109. *Hartford Courant*, November 10, 1974.

8. *The Daughter of a Tortonese Governs Connecticut (pages 158–180)*

1. *Hartford Courant*, November 8, 1974.

2. *Hartford Courant*, April 25, 1975.

3. *Hartford Courant*, November 6, 1974.

4. *Wall Street Journal*, June 19, 1974.

5. *Hartford Courant*, November 10, 1974.

6. *New York Times*, November 9, 1974.

7. Ella Grasso, speech at the Gridiron Club Dinner, March 21, 1975 (copy in author's possession).

8. Ella Grasso, letter to Isabelle Shelton, Ella Grasso Papers, CSL Box 279.

9. *Connecticut Register and Manual*, 1975.

10. Wilda Hamerman, interview with the author, West Haven, Conn., February 28, 2000.

11. *New York Times*, November 7, 1974.

12. *Hartford Courant*, November 21, 1974.

13. Edward Stockton, interview with author, Wallingford, Conn., August 9, 2011.

14. Ibid.

15. Jay Tepper, interview with author, New Canaan, Conn., June 24, 2002.

16. *Hartford Courant*, December 31, 1978.

17. *Hartford Courant*, April 10, 1975.

18. *Hartford Courant*, January 9, 1975.

19. Nancy Lewinsohn, interview with author, Washington, D.C., August 8, 2004.

20. Robert Killiian, interview with the author, Hartford, Conn., August 9, 2001.

21. Ribicoff Papers, Columbia University Archives, vol. 2, p. 364.

22. Joseph I. Lieberman, *In Praise of Public Life* (New York: Simon & Schuster, 2000), 56.

23. Ella Grasso, letter to Governor Thomas Meskill, November 20, 1974, Ella Grasso Papers, CSL Box 74.

24. *New London Day*, August 19, 1974.

25. Ella Grasso, Inaugural Address, January 8, 1975.

26. Anthony Milano, interview with author, Hartford, Conn., August 2, 2000.

27. Grasso inaugural address 1/8/75.

28. Lewinsohn interview 8/8/04.

29. Grasso inaugural address 1/8/75.

30. Ibid.

31. Peggy Lamson, *Few Are Chosen*, (Boston: Houghton Mifflin, 1968), 219.

32. Fauliso interview 9/6/00.

33. Lewinsohn interview 8/8/04.

34. Fauliso interview 9/6/00.

35. Ibid.

36. Jeff Daniels, interview with the author, Hartford, Conn., October 5, 2001.

37. Robert Killian interview 8/9/01.

38. Cornelius O'Leary, interview with the author, Hartford, Conn., July 6, 2006.

39. Lieberman, *In Praise of Public Life*, 56.

40. Ibid., 56, 57.

41. Fauliso interview 9/6/00.

42. Aaron Ment, interview with the author, Hartford, Conn., December 6, 1999.

43. Nicholas Carbone, interview with the author, Hartford, Connecticut, November 7, 2002.

44. Ment interview 12/6/99.

45. Ibid.

46. Susan Bysiewicz, *Ella: A Biography of Ella Grasso* (Old Saybrook, Conn.: Peregrine Press, 1984), 83.

47. Daniels interview 10/5/01.

48. *New York Times*, February 22, 1976.

49. Lewinsohn interview 8/8/04.

50. Killian interview 8/9/01.

51. *Hartford Courant*, April 10, 1975.

52. *Washington Post*, July 7, 1974.

53. *Hartford Courant*, April 12, 1975.

54. *Hartford Courant*, November 21, 1974.

55. Ella Grasso, budget message, February 13, 1975.

56. Ibid.

57. *Portrait of a Governor*, CPTV documentary, 1980.

58. Gloria W. Schaffer, interview with the author, Woodbridge, Conn., November 13, 2000.

59. Killian interview 8/9/01.

60. *Waterbury Republican*, September 11, 1974.

61. Ella Grasso, Inaugural Address, January 8, 1975.

62. Killian interview 8/9/01.

63. Ibid.

64. Ibid.

65. Schaffer interview 11/13/00.

66. Lewinsohn interview 8/8/04.

67. Jill Kerr Conway, "One Woman's Education," *Chronicle of Higher Education*, (November 2, 2001): B8.

9. I Love You . . . I Love You All (pages 181–221)

1. William A. O'Neill, interview with author, East Hampton, Conn., September 29, 1999.

2. *Hartford Courant*, April 22, 1975.

3. Ibid.

4. Ella Grasso, speech to Democratic State Central Committee, April 28, 1975.

5. Ibid.

6. Ibid.

7. Jay Tepper, interview with the author, New Canaan, Conn., June 24, 2002.

8. Joseph Fauliso, interview with the author, Hartford, Conn., September 6, 2000.

9. O'Neill interview 9/29/99.

10. *Hartford Courant*, July 22, 1976.

11. *Hartford Courant*, June 20, 1976.

12. *Hartford Courant*, July 2, 1976.

13. Ibid.

14. *Hartford Courant*, June 20, 1976.

15. *Hartford Courant*, June 22, 1976.

16. *Hartford Courant*, July 22, 1976.

17. Ibid.

18. *Hartford Courant*, January 9, 1977.

19. *Hartford Courant*, December 1, 1977.

20. Robert Killian, interview with the author, Hartford, Conn., August 9, 2001.

21. *Hartford Courant*, December 3, 1977.

22. *Hartford Courant*, October 27, 1977.

23. Killian interview 8/9/01.

24. *Hartford Courant*, July 4, 1977.

25. *Hartford Courant*, November 29, 1977.

26. *Hartford Courant*, December 8, 1977.

27. *Ella Grasso*, Connecticut Public Television (hereafter CPTV), documentary, February 25, 1994.

28. James A. Grasso, interview with the author, West Hartford, Conn., April 30, 2000.

29. *Hartford Courant*, January 11, 1977.

30. *Hartford Courant*, January 12, 1977.

31. *Ella Grasso*, documentary 2/25/94.

32. *Hartford Courant*, December 8, 1977.

33. *Hartford Courant*, Dec. 5, 1978.

34. *Ella Grasso*, documentary 2/25/94.

35. *Hartford Courant*, January 20, 1978.

36. *Hartford Courant*, December 18, 1977.

37. Killian interview 8/9/01.

38. Ibid.

39. Ibid.

40. *Hartford Courant*, December 5, 1980.

41. *Hartford Courant*, May 3, 1975.

42. Ibid.

43. Ibid.

44. Susan Bysiewicz, *Ella: A Biography of Ella Grasso* (Old Saybrook, Conn.: Peregrine Press, 1984), 89.

45. *Hartford Courant*, December 5, 1980.

46. Tepper interview 6/24/02.

47. *Hartford Courant*, December 6, 1980.

48. *Hartford Courant*, December 31, 1978.

49. *Hartford Courant*, December 3, 1975.

50. Ibid.

51. *Hartford Courant*, December 4, 1975.

52. *Hartford Courant*, December 5, 1980.

53. *Hartford Courant*, March 29, 1976.

54. *Hartford Courant*, December 5, 1980.

55. *Hartford Courant*, December 18, 1975.

56. *Hartford Courant*, December 5, 1980.

57. Ibid.

58. *Hartford Courant*, December 21, 1975.

59. Bysiewicz, *Ella*, 98.

60. *New York Times*, November 21, 1975.

61. *Hartford Courant*, October 8, 1978.

62. *Hartford Courant*, May 26, 1977, editorial.

63. *Hartford Courant*, October 8, 1978.

64. Ibid.

65. Edward Stockton, telephone interview with the author, January 12, 2012.

66. *Meet the Press*, transcript of Ella Grasso interview, NBC, January 12, 1975.

67. Edward Stockton, speech to New England Council Board of Directors, March 21, 1975, Ella Grasso Papers, CSL Box 51.

68. Press release, Department of Commerce, January 9–May 14, 1975, Ella Grasso Papers, 1975, CSL Box 51.

69. Press release, Department of Commerce, November 2, 1978, Ella Grasso Papers, CSL Box 748.

70. Press release, Department of Commerce, January 3, 1979, Ella Grasso Papers, CSL Box 748.

71. Stockton telephone interview 1/12/12.

72. Ibid.

73. Press Release, Department of Commerce, February 22, 1979, Ella Grasso Papers, CSL Box 748.

74. *Meet the Press*, transcript of Ella Grasso interview, NBC, January 12, 1975.

75. *Hartford Courant*, February 5, 1988.

76. Governor Grasso Proclamation (blizzard of 1978), February 6, 1978, Ella Grasso Papers, CSL Box 434.

77. *Hartford Courant*, February 5, 1978.

78. Bysiewicz, *Ella*, 110.

79. Ella Grasso, letter to David Barrett and Dean Allard (blizzard of 1978), February 23, 1978, Ella Grasso Papers, CSL Box 434.

80. Miscellaneous letters (blizzard of 1978), Ella Grasso Papers, CSL Box 434, 435.

81. First Selectman Dan Vece (Clinton, Conn.), letter to Ella Grasso (blizzard of 1978), February 10, 1978, Ella Grasso Papers, CSL Box 435.

82. *Ansonia Evening Sentinel*, editorial February 8, 1978, Ella Grasso Papers, CSL Box 435.

83. "Public Health Briefs," *American Journal of Public Health*, (October 1979), Ella Grasso Papers, CSL Box 434.

84. Killian interview 8/9/01.

85. *Hartford Courant*, December 8, 1977.

86. *Hartford Courant*, January 10, 1978.

87. Killian interview 8/9/01.

88. *Hartford Courant*, February 17, 1978.

89. *Hartford Courant*, January 20, 1978.

90. *Hartford Courant*, February 1, 1978.

91. *Hartford Courant*, August 24, 1978.

92. Bysiewicz, *Ella*, 111.

93. *Hartford Courant*, May 3, 1978.

94. *Hartford Courant*, September 21, 1978.

95. *Hartford Courant*, July 23, 1978.

96. *Hartford Courant*, September 3, 1978.

97. *Hartford Courant*, September 7, 1978.

98. *Hartford Courant*, August 18, 1978.

99. Bysiewicz, *Ella*, 117.

100. Killian interview 8/9/01.

101. *New London Day*, October 10, 1978.

102. Ibid.

103. Ibid.

104. *Hartford Courant*, October 29, 1978.

105. Ibid.

106. *Hartford Courant*, September 25, 1978.

107. Ibid.

108. Ella Grasso, letter to Jim Boyic, January 3, 1978, Ella Grasso Papers, CSL Box 496. *Hartford Courant*, November 8, 1978.

109. Thomas A. Grasso, interview with author, Old Lyme, Conn., January 27, 1997.

110. *Hartford Courant*, November 8, 1978.

111. Ibid.

112. Editorial, *Hartford Courant*, January 4, 1978.

113. Ella Grasso, Inaugural Address, January 4, 1979.

114. Ibid.

115. Lesley DeNardis, "The Politics of Reorganizing Connecticut State Government: Altering Administrative Structures in the Land of Steady Habits," *Journal of Public Administration and Governance*, Macrothink Institute, vol. 1 (August 2011): 329.

116. Ibid.

117. Ibid., 330.

118. Ibid.

119. *Hartford Courant*, February 8, 1979.

120. Ibid.

121. Bysiewicz, *Ella*, 123.

122. Ibid., 126.

123. Ibid.

124. Senator Joseph I. Lieberman, interview with the author, Hartford, Conn., November 12, 1997.

125. Ella Grasso, Inaugural Address, 1975.

126. Ella Grasso, letter to President Carter, May 15, 1980 (copy in author's possession).

127. Jon E. Purmont, entry in the author's diary, November 20, 1980.

128. James Battaglio, "Fondly EG," *Hartford Magazine* (November 2003): 61.

129. Bysiewicz, 129–130.

130. Anne Wonders Passel, letter to Thomas A. Grasso, February 9, 1981 (copy in author's possession).

131. Vice President Walter A. Mondale, telephone interview with the author, August 22, 2000.

132. United States Information Agency, miscellaneous material.

Epilogue (pages 222–224)

1. Medal of Freedom Citation, given at the White House, October 9, 1981 (copy in author's possession).

2. Ibid.

3. Anne Wonders Passel, letter to Thomas A. Grasso, February 9, 1981 (copy in author's possession).

4. Barbara Walters, letter to Ella T. Grasso, January 5, 1981 (copy in author's possession).

5. Chief Justice Rose Bird (Calif.), letter to Ella Grasso, (n.d., copy in author's possession).

6. Corretta Scott King, telegram to the Grasso Family, February 12, 1981 (copy in author's possession).

7. Clare Booth Luce, telegram to the Grasso Family, February 6, 1981 (copy in author's possession).

8. Madelyn Carney, Dorchester, Mass., telegram to the Grasso Family, February 5, 1981 (copy in author's possession).

9. Dr. Eugene Silliman, letter to Ella T. Grasso, December 15, 1980 (copy in author's possession).

INDEX

Index

McKinney, Stewart, 127

McLean, George, 1

Meat Inspection Act, 112

Meet the Press (NBC), 200, 203

Ment, Aaron, 172–73, 174

Meskill, Thomas J.: economy left by, 164–65; as governor, 97, 101, 102, 104, 106; Grasso's gubernatorial campaign and, 133–34, 135, 137, 141, 151, 152, 155

Milano, Anthony, 167, 217

Miles Laboratories, 203

milk, pasteurization dates on, 56

Minor, William, 5, 11

Monagan, John, 66

Mondale, Walter, 218–19, 221

Mount Holyoke College (South Hadley, Massachusetts), 15–16; Economics and Sociology Department, 34, 35–37, 39; ethnic/religious composition of student body, 18–19; goals for graduates of, 37–38; Grasso's commencement speech (1975), 37; Grasso's graduation from, xv, 30; *Llamarada*, 31; *Mount Holyoke Alumnae Quarterly*, 34; *Mount Holyoke News*, 33–34, 37; student activism, 31–33, 34–35; traditions of, xvii, 109; "two unit plan" of, 17–18

NAACP, 155

Nader, Ralph, 146

National Guard (Connecticut), 205

National Municipal League, 82

National Organization for Women (NOW), 125

National Women's Political Caucus, 159

NBC, 113–15, 200, 203

New Britain (Connecticut) probate judge controversy, 212

New Britain Herald, 103

New Deal: criticism of, 27; Cross and, 44–45; Grasso on, 33; Perkins and, 21

New England Council Board of Directors, 200–201

Newman, Jon, 70, 71

news reporters' rights, 124

Newsweek, 155

New York Times, 24, 139, 159, 161

Nineteenth Amendment, 1–2, 47–48

Nixon, Richard: pardon of, 156; presidential campaign (1960), 87; presidential election (1968), 92; presidential election (1972), 124; unemployment and, 114–15; Vietnam War and, 90–92, 93–94, 122–23, 166; Watergate and, 121, 126–27, 140, 156

Office of Consumer Advocate (Connecticut), 146

Office of Legislative Management (Connecticut), 99

Office of Mental Retardation, Department of Health (Connecticut), 74–77, 210

Office of Policy and Management (Connecticut), 217

Ohio National Guard, 94

oil: fuel cost adjustment charge, 144–48; gas tax, 198; prices (1970s), 111, 217; tax on, 217–18

O'Leary, Cornelius, 171

Olmstead, Alan, 140, 154

O'Neill, Tip, 108, 116, 123

O'Neill, William A. ("Bill"): on Connecticut legislative management, 100; as Democratic Party (Connecticut) chairman, 181–86, 191, 211; as governor, 100, 117; as Grasso's campaign chairman, 131–32; as House Majority Leader, 164; as lieutenant governor, 211

Orr, Kay, 159

Parker, Henry, 138

Passel, Anne Wonders, 220, 223

Garnet Books

About the Author

Jon E. Purmont is a professor emeritus of history at Southern Connecticut State University. His articles have appeared in *Connecticut Review* and *Connecticut Explored*, and he is coauthor of *A Concise History of the United States*.

About the Driftless Connecticut Series

The Driftless Connecticut Series is a publication award program established in 2010 to recognize excellent books with a Connecticut focus or written by a Connecticut author. To be eligible, the book must have a Connecticut topic or setting or an author must have been born in Connecticut or have been a legal resident of Connecticut for at least three years.

The Driftless Connecticut Series is funded by the Beatrice Fox Auerbach Foundation Fund at the Hartford Foundation for Public Giving. For more information and a complete list of books in the Driftless Connecticut Series, please visit us online at http://www.wesleyan.edu/wespress/driftless.